French Post-Modern Masculinities
From Neuromatrices to Seropositivity

Contemporary French and Francophone Cultures 12

LAWRENCE R. SCHEHR

French
Post-Modern Masculinities

From Neuromatrices to Seropositivity

LIVERPOOL UNIVERSITY PRESS

First published 2009 by
Liverpool University Press
4 Cambridge Street
Liverpool
L69 7ZU

British Library Cataloguing-in-Publication data
A British Library CIP record is available

ISBN 978-1-84631-215-1

Typeset by Carnegie Book Production, Lancaster
Printed in Great Britain by the MPG Books Group,
Bodmin and King's Lynn

For Keith
with all my love

Contents

Acknowledgments

Books are never written in a vacuum and are always written with the help, support, and advice of friends and colleagues. I should like to thank my colleagues in the Department of French at the University of Illinois, whose support has been inestimable. I should also like to thank, in particular, the following, for their encouragement, support, and guidance over the years: David F. Bell, Patrick M. Bray, James Day, William Edmiston, Maggie Flinn, Bertrand Gervais, Andrea Goulet, Florian Grandena, Laurence Grove, Greg Hainge, Robert Harvey, Michael A. Johnson, James Mandrell, Armine K. Mortimer, Murray Pratt, Denis M. Provencher, Érik Rémès, and Alistair Rolls.

Some of the material contained in this book has appeared elsewhere in a different form. Some of the work on Dustan appeared as "Writing Bareback: Guillaume Dustan," *Sites* 6:1 (2002). Work on Rémès appeared as "Reading Serial Sex: The Case of Erik Rémès," *L'Esprit Créateur* 44:3 (2004). Work on Dantec appeared as "Dantec's Inferno," in *Novels of the Contemporary Extreme*, ed. Alain-Philippe Durand and Naomi Mandel (Continuum, 2006). Work on the gay popular novel appeared in *Queer Sexualities*, in the French Literature Series published by Rodopi. I should like to thank the publishers, editors, and presses for their permission to reuse this material.

Special thanks and all my love to Keith Henry.

Introduction

For the first time in ages, we are witnessing a changing hegemony in which heteronormativity and phallogocentrism have themselves perhaps finally come face-to-face with notions of their own mortality, given changing discourses and mores. This book focuses on changes in the representations and depictions of masculinity and masculine sexualities evolving in the contemporary era in France, the causes for which I shall turn to shortly. These changes have had far-reaching effects not only in the standard fora in which we might have expected them, but in other areas that would once have seemed fairly safe strongholds of heteronormative masculinity. Thus do the cultural artefacts analyzed in this volume cross generic lines in a variety of ways. Two quick examples will suffice here. First, essays and fiction by two writers on the political right, Marc-Edouard Nabe and Michel Houellebecq, illustrate a crisis in masculinity/sexuality that relates to the ones depicted in gay popular fiction and film, though both rail, at times interminably, about gays. The work of Maurice Dantec and Fabrice Neaud, both on the right as well, though authors of different sexual inclinations, is strangely interrelated with larger contexts of networks and nodes, something we also see in the book on heterosexual pedophilia by Nicolas Jones-Gorlin, a book thought so dangerous that it was almost banned by the French government for those under eighteen.

This then is the subject of the book and its primary thesis: as traditional notions of masculinity and male sexualities have recently been put into question in France, there have been representational reactions to, and incarnations of, changing masculinities in the post-modern world, and this, in a variety of genres. Certain contemporary French cultural productions are illustrative of these changing masculinities and it will be the focus of this book to examine the manifestation of post-modern masculinity and male sexuality in the French context, and to do so across generic lines.

The book will be an analysis of constructions of masculinities in both mainstream fiction and more popular works, as well as considering the construction of the same in some mainstream films and the work of one graphic artist. But I shall look at that artist, Fabrice Neaud, as his work symptomatically relates to constructions of subjectivity in two seemingly unrelated works: the apocalyptic novels of Maurice Dantec and Nicolas Jones-Gorlin's novel engaging the forbidden sexuality of pedophilia, *Rose Bonbon*, in which simple oppositional notions of "homo" and "hetero" seem to have been discarded. I shall also look at the symptomology of the breakdown of the structural centrality of the heterosexual, male subject, himself the synecdoche or metonym of Western civilization and its cultural tradition, as the latter are figured in the non-fictional writings of Houellebecq and Nabe. Reacting to this crisis, Nabe, for example, introduces an entire apocalyptic vocabulary and imagery of sodomy in his writing about the events of September 11 2001, which he perceives as an act of anal penetration of New York City performed by al-Qaeda.

In order to understand these changes, we have to develop a context that is both cultural and theoretical. While I shall frame the cultural context below and throughout, it is meet to start with a theoretical framework, and for that, I turn immediately to Michel Foucault. In his epoch-making book, *Les Mots et les choses*, published in 1966, Michel Foucault examined what he termed epistemes, sets of discourses that form the basis of knowledge in a specific chrono-logical era in a given geographic and political space. And while the complexities of geopolitics have changed radically in the post-modern era, the concept of an episteme still obtains. For Foucault, these discourses are at once specifically localized (often in scientific documents) and also given a general weight. As Foucault points out, in commenting on his own work, the "verbal masses" he analyzes "were not scanned [*scandés*] by the regular units of book, collected works [*œuvre*], and author" (*Dits* 791). The discourses imply the existence of an epistemological network and, indeed, they serve to create and enable it. This network, while not free of contradictions, also orients the way in which a given individual is subjected to grids of power and discursivity, and determines as well the way in which he or she conceives of his or her subjectivity. While Foucault certainly does not imply a one-to-one correspondence between a word (signifier and signified) and the thing it is used to represent

– the title ensures a plural for both words and things – language's function, for Foucault, is primarily epistemological.

In 1969, Foucault published an article entitled "Qu'est-ce qu'un auteur?," in which he pushes further in one direction by examining the construction of the agency of the author. While he mentions some literary authors, including Kafka, Balzac, Rimbaud, Flaubert, and Beckett, among others, literature is not primarily the focus of this article. Rather, as was his wont, Foucault chooses writers in the ancient world whose focus in their writing was to interpret the truth of the world: historians, philosophers, scientists, economists, and the like. Foucault distinguishes as well between an older concept of the literary (*Dits* 799), which could remain happily in the realm of the anonymous, and a more recent sense of the literary, associated implicitly with humanism, the Renaissance and, a fortiori, the Enlightenment, and the modern era of the last two centuries. In more recent times, as Foucault points out (800), the author function is individuated: people want to know which individual wrote a literary work in order to situate it within a context and make it belong, as relates, or not, to figures of canonicity. This situation obviously corresponds to two different, though interrelated, phenomena. First, there is the rise of the modern subject as an individual. As Foucault argues throughout his writing, the post-Enlightenment, Western subject's sense of self is primarily related to an individuality, not to a collectivity or to a relational system. Readers thus ascribe the literary work to an author: we strive to do so precisely because we believe in the value and validity of the individual as subject and vice versa. Second, we also individuate and name the author precisely because literature, concomitant with the rise of the bourgeois subject as an individual in the post-Renaissance world, is seen as a pre-eminent means of communicating cultural value (Guillory). If a certain kind of post-classical, lay literature, as Bakhtin and Kristeva point out, starts in an ambiguous relation to the *doxa*, by the time the modern novel is invented in the eighteenth century (Watt), the genre, for all its possible seditiousness and non-disjunction in a work like *Moll Flanders*, is also a primary locus for the reinscription of value, as is the case for the same author's *Robinson Crusoe*. And if no real tragedies were written after the English Renaissance, French classicism, and German *Sturm und Drang*, poetry in the Romantic era became the literary praxis in which the vatic impulse was localized and focused. So in the nineteenth century, the lyric remains the inspired moment, one that, again, without excluding oppositional practice, enshrines a set of cultural values.

When Foucault ends his article with a series of rhetorical questions, we must nuance them somewhat, for literature in general since the Enlightenment, for literature during a period in which it was considered a dominant vehicle for the transmission of culture, and – and I shall discuss this below – for literature during a period in which rival vehicles for culture may actually have moved ahead. Foucault's questions include "How can [this discourse] circulate, and who can appropriate it for himself or herself?" and "What does it matter who is speaking?" (812). For literature, it does matter: for the appropriation of another's literary discourse is considered to be plagiarism. In that, it is distinguished from a concept or figure that has entered into general knowledge or culture. Hamlet as a figure or as a play is something anyone can mention or quote, but appropriating "To be or not to be" as one's own, were it even possible to do so, would be considered an act of plagiarism, as well as possibly being considered a sign of dementia. Foucault's questions must be nuanced as well for literature, in that literature is not solely concerned with providing epistemological information or content. Rather, it has a measure of self-consciousness in it relative to the use of language. Again, it is not the appropriation of discourse for the point of power or contents, but some sense of expression. I am stating the obvious here, but this is merely to finish the focus on Foucault; this blatantly obvious fact will be of importance below.

As all readers know, certain critics have seen a direct relation between social structures and literary form: Benjamin on the *Trauerspiel*, Lukács on various manifestations of the novel in the nineteenth century, including the historical novel, the realist work, and what he terms the novel of disillusionment, Goldmann on Racinian tragedy, Certeau and the phenomena of May 1968, and so forth. For example, in *Le Discours antillais*, Edouard Glissant has developed a genealogy for Antillean literature in which he shows the dominant literary forms during various colonial and post-colonial periods, from the missionary writing of the earliest period up to the present post-colonial moment in which there is "sterilization or creative explosion" (319). Thus Glissant shows how forms and genres change relative to a historical, social, and cultural context that itself is changing. And Michel de Certeau shows admirably how the events of May 1968 related to changing discourses about what was "believable."

My argument here is that while Foucault continues to be correct on cultural production in the post-modern era, the absence of the universal narrative to which all others were subjugated has allowed for both a liberation from the idea of the *grand récit* and a flexibility among the various forms of cultural production, so that we might see similar situations in literary novels, artefacts from popular culture, and didactic or philosophical treatises. Jean-François Lyotard's concept of the post-modern, with the breakdown of the grand narrative, allows us to see the flexibility of genres in the post-modern, one far greater than anything seen heretofore; though it must be said that Lyotard's own analyses of the modern in *Discours, figure* already hint at what is to come. Here, then, it is meet to turn from the generic constraints of the modern to the fluidity of the post-modern. Doing so requires a Foucauldian notion, that of social constructivism, which – despite its limitations, as we shall see – better establishes the discursive grid for the contemporary.

It is a safe assumption that anyone reading this book will be familiar with the theory of social constructivism of sexualities developed out of arguments put forth by Michel Foucault in the first volume of *Histoire de la sexualité*, originally published in 1976. Simply put, the theory of social constructivism that develops from Foucault's volume says that some time around 1870, the notion of sexuality in general, and homosexuality in particular, was born and that "(homo)sexuality" did not exist before that time, before it was named as such by Karl-Maria Kertbeny in 1869.[1] There have been as many critiques of this notion of social constructivism as there have been supporters thereof, and David Halperin's extremely influential volume *One Hundred Years of Homosexuality* became a lightning rod (or a straw-man argument) for those who wanted a more supple and subtle approach to the chronology. One could argue, for example, that, even while accepting the notion, there is a genealogy and pre-history, so that Honoré de Balzac's depiction of Vautrin in *Le Père Goriot* in 1834 was already a clear figure of the modern homosexual belonging to some representational categories that would come to be called "homosexuality."

One could argue as well that Foucault himself – and this is also

---

[1] In her excellent volume, *Mad for Foucault*, Lynne Huffer reminds readers to rethink Foucault's ideas about sexuality not only in relation to *Histoire de la sexualité* and *Les Mots et les choses*, but also in relation to *Histoire de la folie*.

clear in the work of Leo Bersani – as he came to know the work of John Boswell, revised his thinking enormously and allowed that Boswell's arguments held water. That is to say, quite simply: something like homosexuality existed much earlier in history. What would this mean? Simply put, even if the various legal systems defined the act of sodomy, legal language isolated the act from the agent because that is how legal systems often proceeded: one is guilty of an act, whatever one's essence may be. And already, just to take the most famous example, it is clear that when Dante condemned Bruno Latini and others to hell, it was not simply for their acts of sodomy, but because they were sodomites. In so doing, he allows for a different set of representational models to be used, one that may very well lead to a notion, whether named or unnamed, like that of inversion, to use an old-fashioned term, or what we called "homosexuality" back in the twentieth century.

So some queer theory, which develops out of notions of social constructivism, might have matters wrong in assuming that there are or were "one hundred years of homosexuality." Yet this is not the place to make that argument, mostly because my goal is to displace it into a productive understanding of some recent changes in notions of masculinity in general, and not just manifestations of queerness in particular, and while masculinity and male sexualities are not absolute equivalents for a whole host of reasons, there is a constant interplay between the two categories, and arguably, each stands, quite often, as a metonym for the other. Indeed, a separation of the two, through the imposition of some aspects of queer theory, can be useful for a radical reunderstanding of French masculinity as it is depicted in cultural artefacts from the late twentieth and early twenty-first centuries. The crux of the argument would be the following: let us assume that there is an important point made through theories of social constructivism and that that point is that sexualities, as we understand them today, are a relatively recent invention, a product of nineteenth-century thought. In particular, this thought comes, to use Foucauldian keywords, from a confluence of powers and discourses, specifically those from nineteenth-century codes from the medical, psychiatric, and juridical systems. Thus the invention of modern sexualities and, indeed, concurrent notions of masculinity and femininity that are in part based on medical, juridical, and/or psychiatric discourses, would depend on the double legitimation, through science and the law, of certain behaviors in particular, but generalized to a class of individuals who would perhaps share affective situations in which those specific sexual behaviors were coded. At the same time, certain behaviors would be stigmatized, doubly so, even if, to use the most famous example, the act of sodomy had been decriminalized after the French Revolution. So while not carrying a legal penalty, it could still be conceived of as illegitimate behavior through combined juridical, psychiatric, and medical discourses that created modern notions of sexuality.[2]

Taken in that light, modern sexualities could be understood as an Enlightenment or post-Enlightenment concept in which certain modalities and particular nodal points figured largely to assign loci and foci of desire and subjectivity, to (de)legitimate behavior, or to encode modes of acting and being, including notions of masculinity and femininity, and this in ways different from, though not unrelated to, earlier notions of sexualities. It would be argued that this is not a total paradigm shift or Kuhnian scientific revolution, but rather a category that changes over time and that continues to change. If that hypothesis is correct, it stands to reason that the components of these evolving sexualities themselves change. Simply put, in much of the West today, one would be hard put to assign medical, psychiatric, or juridical discourses to homosexuality as lived by an adult, while all forces would go at full tilt into assigning both discourses to an act of heterosexual pedophilia, and a combination of discourses (albeit a different set) would weigh in if it were a question of unprotected sex, be it heterosexual or homosexual.[3]

As I have already indicated, it is a relatively easy rhetorical move to say that a given starting date for something is erroneous; there is always a previous instance or a historical genealogy to look at. One classic example would be the argument about realism in fiction. If the theoretical book on the subject of realism appeared in 1856 and *Madame Bovary* a year later, one could say that *Le Rouge et le noir* and *Le Père Goriot* are not as different from the Flaubertian

---

[2] For historical background on notions of French masculinity, see Nye, whose work covers the period from the *Ancien Régime* through the early decades of the twentieth century, and Corbin, whose work goes from the Enlightenment to the invention of sexology at the end of the nineteenth century.

[3] These discourses change over time, as one can easily chart changes, especially within the gay community, of discourses relating to safe and unsafe sex, discourses that changed in part, in some circles, with the discovery and widespread use of combination therapy.

model as one might once have believed. But even that would not be enough, for the more persuasive argument about the "invention" of realism would depend on a different way of seeing that is associated with the invention of the daguerreotype. And yet that would have to relate back to a history of optics, to the telescope and microscope, and, as a result, the initial moment would keep retreating into the past, for it becomes not so much the practice of realism but the set of circumstances that allow a (Foucauldian) space for the eventual discourses of realism.

If we return to the contemporary and an analysis of the crisis in masculinity in the post-modern subject, any temporal beginning would be somewhat arbitrary, though in a historical perspective, the events of March 1968 at Nanterre, and May 1968 throughout France, as well as their aftermath and international echoes, would be convenient moments in which challenges to the system exploded and "les enfants de Marx et de Coca-Cola [the children of Marx and Coca-Cola]," as Jean-Luc Godard presciently put it in his 1966 film *Masculin féminin*, took to the streets. And the fact that Godard saw that change happening two years before the events of 1968 is indicative of the somewhat arbitrary nature of the beginning I am claiming for the spring of 1968; we could say then that this beginning is the first major visible beginning of the change.[4] In and of themselves, these initial acts at Nanterre, then two months later those at the Sorbonne and the Renault factory, Sartre's ironic and knowing grin that made the front pages of newspapers everywhere after he had been arrested for civil disobedience, and the like, had consequences that were borne out in public spheres, in industry, and in the educational system. Of course, this was retrospectively perceived by some, such as Ferry and Renaut, as the sign of anti-humanism. Here, I would argue that the events of 1968, along with the free speech movement, protests against the Vietnam War, the civil rights movement in the United States, and the movements of women's and gay liberation that saw the light of day a few years later, were not the signs of an anti-humanism, but the initial signs of the post-human and the post-modern.

Arguably, the most enduring and far-reaching effects were seen in the movements of liberation, particularly the women's movement

---

[4] And again, a retrospective glance would include rock music as it made its way through the US and British markets onto the world stage.

and gay liberation, which were both repositionings of the sexual and the political: Kate Millett's title, *Sexual Politics*, is perhaps even more than appropriate now than then. At the same time that the political was forging a path with sexualities, medical, psychiatric, and juridical discourses were retreating from their domination of the discussion of sex, sexualities, and concomitant notions of masculinity and femininity. The events of May 1968, along with various parallel phenomena that were attacks on the status quo, such as the free speech movement and the protests against the war in Vietnam, laid the groundwork for the establishment of liberatory discourses in the West, turned inward on themselves, as well as toward the exercise of civil liberties and, indeed, the redefinition thereof in certain cases. And that liberation takes the form of movements for minority rights: racial and ethnic minorities in multi-ethnic societies and sexual minorities, or rather those given second-class status within the dominant ideology, throughout the West. Specifically, this means women and gays.

It is perhaps more than symptomatic that the word "gay" seems to come on the scene in the same era, both to replace nasty words – and here I am talking about the West in general, though the focus in the following chapters will be on France in particular – and to replace the medical, juridical, and psychiatric term "homosexual," whose connotative echoes were invariably clinical and/or judgmental. This change in vocabulary, this move from a scientific and legal discourse that focused on nomination, with words such as "homosexual" and "homosexuality," to a positive adjective such as "gay" (and eventually "queer") that did not limit, was, to my mind, the beginning of a liberatory discourse in which both language and "lifestyle" evolved more or less in tandem. Yet it would be foolish, even with the perspectives offered by hindsight, to say that this liberation should not have happened, given the fact that AIDS (Acquired Immune Deficiency Syndrome), especially in its initial phases, spread in a way that depended in part on the relatively liberalized lifestyle associated with the 1970s. And by that, I mean that reaffirming a myopic, unexamined discourse of abstinence, chastity, or monogamy at this point, even given what we now know medically, would be and would have been foolish because it is a discourse tied to concepts of the subject that precisely were forged within the realm of the heteronormative and the phallogocentric notions that are being shed during the time period in question and that continue to change.

Hence, I think, the reactions in the writing of authors such as Maurice G. Dantec, Marc-Edouard Nabe, and Michel Houellebecq, who recognize, at least rhetorically, as the unconscious of the text speaks, that no matter how much they reaffirm the individuality, the humanity, the independence, and the heterocentrism of the subject, things have changed. Put another way, perhaps again in retrospect, Foucault will have been right: it is not the sex act itself that bothers others, but the lifestyle associated with that act, the being-there of homosexuality. So some will have reacted in thinking that we have all become queer, regardless of our individual sexuality. And that perhaps will have frightened others.

As it unfolded from 1968 to the early 1980s, sexual liberation was not alone in producing these changing notions of masculinity, though I should add that readers will discover that the changing visions and ideas of masculinity inevitably seem to be produced from within the masculine itself. Quite often, the discourses hardly engage the feminine, if at all, and often treat it is if it were something completely outside, external to, and unrelated to the evolution of the male species, something invisible or secondary at best. Arguably, this is and remains a blind spot in many of these cultural products. Some authors, such as Houellebecq, to use only the best-known example, use both an articulated and a silent misogyny to weave a plaint about the changing fortunes of the masculine. Others, especially the authors writing what I would term the gay *romans de gare* discussed in the chapter on cartography, generally do not include women or female characters as protagonists or even secondary figures.

If we were to put names on a turning point for this voyage toward new forms of masculinity, there would be two: AIDS and the Internet. I choose these two because they share a certain virological vocabulary, but other names would do as well – mobile phones, globalization, and GPS, just to name three. Arguably, all of these are signs of what we could conveniently call the post-human. By that, I mean that they are all signs of the end of the independent subject in the nineteenth-century sense of the anonymous or invisible Baudelairean *flâneur*, passing through the city. These new figures are signs of the fact that the individual is never fully alone and never fully himself. And I use the masculine here precisely because this seems symptomatically to be played out in all of these works with male protagonists or male rhetorical narrators. In its own way, each of these phenomena indicates the perpetuation of a network in which the individual is situated at a nodal point but a network that far surpasses the locus of the individual node. In a sense, each of these is the sign of the accomplishment or fulfillment of the Deleuzean idea of rhizomatics, a death-knell to arborescent thinking and being, and the sign of the impossibility of maintaining the illusion of independence that was the mark of the human or the sign of the ideology of phallogocentrism.

All of these phenomena are symptomatic of the predicted "death of the author," which we might call the death of the subject, and, in and of itself, this death of the subject is in part an explanation of why the phenomena seem to be one-sided and appear to develop from within masculinity itself, as opposed to coming from a more generalized view of genders and/or sexualities in the plural. For these various assaults seem to occur on the sempiternal notion of the male subject (arguably heterosexual, white, bourgeois, etc.), whereas the female subject was always already defined, rightly or wrongly, in a relational sense to men, i.e., as a member of the "second sex." This could therefore be seen, in a perverse way, as the feminization of the male subject in a manner that defines the new masculinity as a visible, palpable vulnerability. And this may be the clearest sign of why the versions of the new masculinity play out as they do, in both queer works and rightist texts: for the former, marked by the specter of AIDS, are signs that the invincible heroic subject is a figure of the past, and the latter are literally and figuratively a reaction against the death of the independent subject and a rebellion against the fact that we are always already implicated in the network.

It is of course only a coincidence that AIDS and the Internet, at least in the form of email, made their public appearance at relatively the same moment in recent history – the first half of the eighties – and thus a quirk of time and place that the denotative word "virus" to describe HIV is also used catachrestically to describe the "viruses" that spread through the networks of computers that make up the nodes of the Internet. The relative invisibility of the virus is part and parcel of what makes the vulnerability of the post-independent subject most visible. As I have said, the new subject is no longer the Baudelairean *flâneur* who can pass invisibly from point to point within the urban landscape; indeed, the new subject is marked by his visibility or markability. Whereas once, in the days before AIDS, it was relatively easy for some to pretend that they did not know anyone who was gay, by the end of the 1980s, it was well-nigh impossible to maintain that pretense: everyone knew someone who had been directly or indirectly affected by the spread of the virus, which thereby rendered gay men visible in a way that they had never been before.

The Baudelairean *flâneur*, incarnation of the white, male, heterosexual subject, the nineteenth-century's version of Louis Marin's sense of the king or Gyges in *Le Portrait du roi*, or, as Delphine Gay de Girardin would have it, Balzac himself, possessor of a magic walking-stick, was the individual who could be invisible if he wanted to be while at the same time being the visible incarnation of power. Visible or invisible representation of the phallus and of phallogocentrism, he could go from being the obvious incarnation of power and presence to being the invisible patron of a brothel, whereas the bourgeois woman, for example, could not pass through *louche* neighborhoods without drawing attention to herself, and the gay male, regardless of station, was always already the cynosure of the questioning eye of the law.[5]

Suddenly then, no one had the power of invisibility; everyone occupied, through the AIDS network or through the Internet, a visible node in multiple networks, what Dantec properly calls, I think, neuromatrices. Whether it is through GPS, ATMs, the Internet, AIDS, mobile phones, or networks of surveillance cameras in urban spaces such as London (Sinclair), we are all always visible. There is no chance of anonymity or invisibility. Dantec is right then to use the term: for "matrix," which etymologically is a sign of the maternal and therefore the feminine, reminds us that we no longer have that power, but it also reminds us that we are always, in the sense of the film *The Matrix*, simulacra of the nineteenth-century subject, but free no longer. And we are connected in that rhizomatic network, less by material production, exchange of goods, or real power grids than by neuron- or photon-like pulsations, Deleuzian desiring machines in the form of plug-ins, impulsions, compulsions, virtual pulses, and so forth.

The rightist arguments are a recognition of the evolution of the position of the masculine subject yet are obvious reactionary,

---

[5] There are safe spots of course, and the reader has only to think of numerous "romans montmartrois" from the early twentieth century, including *Jésus-la-Caille*, or even Proust's *Recherche*, in which middle-class characters of various sexual proclivities can find fulfillment in brothels, safe houses, or even in the open.

nostalgic appeals for that phallic (in)visibility of yesteryear. In a sense then, Marc-Edouard Nabe's choice of a sodomitic vocabulary to describe the aftermath of the events of September 11 2001 is more than appropriate, and it rejoins, in a bizarre way, the thought behind the events themselves: bomb the towers of the World Trade Center and you truly, not just symbolically, strike at the heart of transnational globalization. But as awful and traumatic as those events were, those bombings could do very little to change the nature of the networks of the transnational or the global. Bombing an ATM machine or turning one's computer off does nothing to change the network; destroying the World Trade Center only reinforces the networks and powers of transnational capitalism. And while wearing a condom clearly has a local preventative effect in a positive sense, just as the events just mentioned have a local effect in a negative sense, it does not change the global picture at all; AIDS will not be eradicated any time soon, no matter how many boxes of condoms are sold in the West.

The "rhetoric of safety," as I have termed it elsewhere, is the sign of the simulacra of the subjects of the networks – neuromatrices – in which we each occupy nodes. The illusory freedom is that the position of the nodes can shift and we think that since we are not in an arborescent, hierarchic system, we maintain the individual freedom and (in)visibility of the bourgeois male subject of yesteryear. But the mirroring of the rhizomatics through the tracking systems and through the encoding of the viruses means that any permanent deterritorialization is only illusory. We are always already reterritorialized in a network that is doubled by other networks. This is, to my mind, the surest sign of the post-human, the figure that goes beyond the neat, separable grids or scapes described by Arjun Appadurai presciently in 1990, the most applicable figure of which then seemed to be what he called a technoscape.

But the argument here is that we have, in the West, gone beyond the individuation that still seemed the correlate of individual subjectivity when Appadurai was writing his work (though retrospectively, as I have indicated, the moment of that individual subjectivity had passed) and that, in particular, the individual subject, and especially the individual male subject, has changed in a way from which there is no return. No longer can one, like Melville's Bartleby, say "I would prefer not to." And it is my contention that the individual male subject in all Western societies has had the same sets of

challenges and faced the same changes in masculinity, *nolens volens.*
Yet I think the French experience stands out in particular ways, and
it is those cultural specificities that I seek to explore in this book. I
would suggest that the French cultural landscape, the sense of the
republican ideal, a conflicted relation to technology that is simultaneously both futurist and Luddite, and the long-term hierarchy of
center and periphery all play roles in the determination of this set
of cultural productions. And while I shall refer here and there to
some of these special categories, this is not to suggest that the French
version of post-modern, post-human, or post-queer masculinity
is alone in the West, for similar versions can certainly be found
everywhere in the West.

When I say "post-queer," I mean to suggest two images, ideas,
and thoughts to readers. First (though not first in any chronological
sense), it is a way of putting the term in parallel with "post-modern"
and "post-human." In so doing, I am essentially arguing that
the queer revolution that was seen initially as a non-identitarian
replacement for "gay" is, by and large, over. If, as I have suggested,
sexualities, for lack of a better word, have now completely moved
beyond the confines of their juridical, psychiatric, and medical
origins, then the disidentificatory processes associated with the queer
are themselves now superfluous, because that process of disidentification was a rebellion associated with sexualities and their power
grids. If those are no longer in place in the same way, then we have
ostensibly moved into a post-queer moment that is fully integrated
with the actualization of the post-modern and the experience of
the post-human. Arguably, sexualities related to the human, not
the post-human, in relation to which different power structures,
representations, and discourses may come into play.

Second, in a classic Derrida-inspired move, I am at least attempting
to distance the *différance* or the trace of homosexuality by changing
terminology. For if "gay" bore the trace of the "homosexual,"
"queer," while distant from, though not free of, the homosexual,
bears the trace of the gay, of the act of liberation that went with
that change of terminology, and of the (dis)identificatory processes
of the queer. By making that strategic move, I would hope to refocus
the entire process as well as to look at how, in this post-modern and
post-human world, notions of what we once called sexuality have
themselves become quaint. And that *différance* means quite precisely
that in the world of the post-queer, this "brave new world" we find

ourselves in, if sexualities have fallen to the wayside, then we can look at generalized phenomena associated with masculinity in men. Oddly enough then, the move into the post-queer returns us to the biological, to "men" as a reasonably stable category, frayed around the edges, but conscious of itself (Butler) in a kind of determinacy of the future through the ramifications of the essential biological base. This will come up over and over again in the works that are studied below.

In chapter one, I examine works by Guillaume Dustan and Erik Rémès to see how notions of HIV$^+$ status and the practices associated with the choices of bareback or unsafe sex contribute to subject-formation in some contemporary queer writing. In particular, my interest here is in the ways in which the very idea of the subject is reformulated in an age in which viral status is not the condemnation it was in the early years of the AIDS epidemic in the West. So if the work of Hervé Guibert, such as the epoch-making volume *A l'ami qui ne m'a pas sauvé la vie*, seemed always already associated with the idea of mourning, this is no longer the case in contemporary writing. The decade makes an important difference, given changes in medical and pharmaceutical knowledge (and specifically, the survival rate associated with the advent of combination therapy); contemporary works relate the representation of the subject and his virus very differently from the way in which Guibert and others wrote about their situations.

In chapter two, I turn to three reactions to the fragmentation or the *dépassement* of the subject as it turns into the post-human. Maurice G. Dantec's apocalyptic, paranoid vision of the present and the near future is marked by a concept of networks that have replaced the individual liberty of the subject, networks that control, manipulate, and otherwise punish the individual who seeks to express his or her independence. Fabrice Neaud, a gay graphic novelist, reacts to what he perceives as a kind of homonormativity through fragmentations and distortions of the subject position that he expresses most clearly in the third volume of the graphic novel series that forms the major part of his work to date. Nicolas Jones-Gorlin's pedophile network is not unlike Dantec's networks of evil, as it mirrors geographically translated rhizomatics that remark and remap France. The author ably demonstrates the ways in which the objective cartography of the normative is redoubled by a perverse road movie script that takes its protagonist on a project of discovering the fragmentary subjectivities of the pedophile network. All three authors offer rhizomatic remappings of the world in their reaction to the post-modern condition and none has an affirmative answer.

Chapter three provides a double mapping of the social constructs of post-queer masculinity as it is enacted in relatively more popular novels or, more likely than not, in most cases, autofictions, and as it is represented in films by directors such as Sébastien Lifshitz and the writing-directorial team of Olivier Ducastel and Jacques Martineau among others. All these works enact post-human French masculinity by introducing fragmentary and networked positions that involve modern technology, HIV infection, sexual norms, and other related issues. By putting the fictions together with the films we can see the consequences of certain normalizing versions of masculinity, one taking place in isolation and another using the figure of identity found in community as a protective excuse for essentializing sexualities.

In chapter four, I turn to essay writing by Michel Houellebecq – again someone, like Dantec, who has chosen not to live in Paris – and Marc-Edouard Nabe. Both of these right-leaning, heterosexual authors infuse their discourses about the political with imagery related to reorientation of sexualities and, in fact, Houellebecq's fictional writing has dealt with the sexual tourism industry. Nabe's vision is perhaps the most apocalyptic of all in a world gone mad, one in which every sin and every event is a sign of the destruction of the human. Together the chapters of this volume are an analysis of the practices and representations of masculinity in its relations to sexualities in contemporary French culture.

CHAPTER ONE

The Work of Literature in an Age of Queer Reproduction

I. Dustan and the Inscription of the Seropositive

Even if literature is no longer the dominant vehicle for the transmission of cultural values, it still functions to transport cultural values at a local level for emerging groups. Literature has been a vehicle for the expression of gay, lesbian, and queer cultures, and specifically, as they have developed over the past four decades and as they have gradually moved from having a marginalized and even taboo status to being simply minority discourses, and now ultimately part of mainstream cultural production, with no one (in the middle classes, at least) batting an eye simply because of sexuality alone. It is not that there was no figuration of the gay before 1968, even in mainstream literature, but gay literature and culture have developed rapidly since 1968, and literature has been a means of expressing this emerging culture, its discourses, its habitus, and its own inscription of the individual as a valid subject of enunciation. With two exceptions, the move to normalization of the gay in literature happened fairly quickly: little time passes between the explosion of Andrew Holleran's middle-brow work *Dancer from the Dance*, which celebrates what quickly become known as the gay lifestyle, or Renaud Camus's work *Tricks*, and Andrew Solomon's brilliantly written *The Stone Boat*, in which being gay is an utter non-event.

The two areas in which gay writing continues to serve as a dominant vehicle are in a kind of attenuated alpha and omega of the culture being expressed: coming-out stories and AIDS narratives in post-industrial societies in general. Coming-out stories, seen as the expression of individuality and difference, held sway for the majority of the seventies and eighties, but a de-dramatized and normalized space developed in which gay cultures existed, and, as that change occurred, even coming out became, quite often, a far less traumatic event in many ways.[1] Where it remains interesting is precisely in situations in which the socio-political context is different from that in the middle-class, post-industrial world.

The other realm in which gay literature has continued to be a dominant vehicle, but not the only vehicle, is in AIDS narratives, first in witnessings, autofictions, or AIDS diaries of one sort or another (Chambers), and then, as AIDS itself became less of an immediate death threat for white men in the West, in a spate of narratives dealing with people living with AIDS. But that too is in the process of quickly becoming normalized, as, with the widespread use of combination therapy, the situation of being HIV+ has increasingly become a manageable chronic condition rather than a death sentence in the West. It is natural then that the discourses of AIDS writing will have changed from fictions of illness, melancholia, and mourning into something of a completely different sort. If early AIDS narratives fall into the long tradition of writing about illness, be it the plague or realism's favorite disease, tuberculosis, contemporary seropositive writing, in the work of writers such as Guillaume Dustan and Érik Rémès, takes a totally different position.[2]

Guillaume Dustan (1965–2005) starts out his career as a gay writer who is seropositive, but this seropositivity is already ontologically different from the depiction of the same in the writing of Hervé Guibert, for example, as the best-known writer among many of the first generation writing with, living with, and eventually succumbing to, AIDS. Thus, Dustan's interest and even his genius lies in his taking what was quickly developing into a recognizable sub-genre, that is, the autofiction of a gay man writing with, and dying from, AIDS, and while retaining the gay form and format, reducing the interrelation of seropositivity and death, to evolve a

---

[1] As Denis Provencher has so brilliantly shown, coming-out stories are culture-specific, and the individual, cultural, and republican values, as well as personal and familial space, mark the stories as quite different in France from their Anglo-American versions.

[2] I have anglicized the French terms *séropositif* and *séropositivité* because, while still clinical terms, they do not immediately thrust the virus into the face of the reader in the way that "HIV+" does. It is rare for French to come up with a term for some contemporary phenomenon before American English does, but this is perhaps a symptom of the far less rational approach to AIDS in the United States compared to that in France.

different kind of representation. That he will, in a second phase, move to rethinking his concepts of sexuality and his status as a gay man should not therefore be astonishing to any reader looking retrospectively at these works. And at the end of the section in this chapter on seropositive writing, I shall turn to his recent, "post-gay" production, before looking at Érik Rémès, who, starting to publish even more recently than Dustan, establishes from the very beginning a seropositive discourse that, while also set in an all-gay universe, is decidedly post-gay or fully queer.

To that end, I analyze the first works of Guillaume Dustan in the pages that follow. In his last work, minimal distinction is made between gay and straight, homosex and heterosex, seropositive and seronegative; the old universal dichotomies have collapsed. Whereas in his early work he distinguishes his gay subculture from other competing cultures, in his final writings he no longer makes any distinction between his position and that of two other inscribers of the erotic: Virginie Despentes and Michel Houellebecq. Dustan says as much at several points in a retrospective volume that was one of the last he wrote, *Dernier Roman*: "Je voudrais bien être photographié avec Angot, Despentes, Houellebecq, Ravalec et Beigbeder (et les autres aussi bien sûr) pour qu'il y ait une trace de nous ensemble [I would love to have a picture taken with Angot, Despentes, Houellebecq, Ravalec, and Beigbeder (and the others as well of course), for there to be a trace of us together]" (45). If the whole gamut of sexualities is not quite fully covered by this imaginary photo-opportunity, it should be noted that there is quite a range, including male heteronormativity in the works of Michel Houellebecq, Frédéric Beigbeder, and Vincent Ravalec, *cosa rara* in many of the works being examined in this volume, along with a whole host of femininities that relate to the "bad girl" novels of Christine Angot and Virginie Despentes.

With five autofictions published in about six years, followed by two later manifestos, Guillaume Dustan, whose real name was William Baranès, scion of the bourgeoisie, well-educated former student at Sciences Po (*Plus fort* 16), was, until his untimely death from a drug overdose, one of the most visible gay French writers to mark the representations of homosexuality and of the AIDS years with his writing. In contemporary France, it often seems that there is only one mediatized niche available to a gay writer writing on gay-related matters. Renaud Camus, born in 1946, had a *succès de scandale* with his work *Tricks*, originally published in 1971. Almost a decade younger was Hervé Guibert (1955–91), who wrote copiously during the eighties and who became a media darling during the last years of his life after the publication of his first AIDS-narrative, *A l'ami qui ne m'a pas sauvé la vie*. Briefly and in parallel with Guibert, there was the writer, actor, and film director Cyril Collard (1957–93), whose novel and film *Les Nuits fauves*, with their bisexual, HIV⁺ protagonist who was a figure of Collard, were warmly received, but who, unlike the other two writers, did not leave a large body of work. Now followed Guillaume Dustan, whose books received some attention from the general media and not just from the gay community, for their raw depiction of the fast-lane lifestyle of the young urban male gay community in a world in which, as Dustan writes, "Il me dit Tu sais personne ne met plus de capotes, même les américaines, maintenant tout le monde est séropositif, je ne connais plus personne qui soit séronégatif (moi non plus, je pense, à part Quentin) [He says to me, You know no one wears rubbers, even Americans, now everyone is HIV⁺, I don't know anyone who is HIV⁻ (me neither, I think, besides Quentin)]" (*DMC* 47).[3]

Each of these writers, whatever his other interests and merits, has served almost as a magnet for understanding contemporary literature's modes of representing male homosexuality. It is as if each were chosen (though there is no election process) because he typifies the ways in which more or less progressive mainstream society and the gay community could agree on the representation of homosexuality and the modalities of being a man in this subculture. With that representation comes an attendant and participatory eroticism, an essential part of what these literary events are about. For Camus, in a work such as *Tricks*, there is an amoral abandonment of all the constraints imposed by society in general; he takes pleasure in a free sexuality that is nevertheless part of a set of codes of politeness, behavior, and pleasure. Guibert takes a

---

[3] As I have indicated, there is a group of writers of varying sexualities whose work is receiving such attention: Dustan, Houellebecq, and Despentes, among others, plus Catherine Millet, whose "tell-all" memoir *La Vie sexuelle de Catherine M.* was also a *succès de scandale*. As is often the case in talking about autofiction, I am not making much of a distinction between Dustan, the real person (and that is not the real person, as "Dustan" is a pseudonym for the "real" person, William Baranès), and the narrator/protagonist, who also seems to be named Guillaume Dustan.

somewhat frantic, yet extremely philosophical, view of the erotic, as he recognizes the changes in his body and in his perception of sexuality, that of himself and others, through the advent of AIDS in general and its effects on individuals who have full-blown AIDS in particular. Though not in the same category of writer, Cyril Collard perhaps abandons himself most, leaving himself as far behind as possible, as he searches for vague pleasures and release. Finally (for now), comes Dustan, whose difference from the other three is marked not only by his status of living with HIV on a long-term basis (medicine having made progress and Camus not having AIDS), but also by what can only be called a techno-social representation of the homosexual erotic.

For Dustan, a series of spaces, objects, and pleasures relates to a representation and expansion of gay sexuality. They combine in the Hollywoodization of male homosexuality as a commodity; spaces – nightclubs, bars, backrooms, sex clubs, and the like – are publically marked either for sex or for encounters. The gay man is part of a viable subculture and is no longer just a single individual seeking his own pleasure in a solitary fashion. The images of this world are translated through a move toward a universalization of Western homosexuality, declined *à l'américaine*, which is itself an effect of globalization, that sees the breaking down of barriers – as well as the mainstreaming of gay behavior and mores – as a move toward a universal. But it is also a move away from any particulars, local languages, and customs. It is, after all, the McDonaldization of gay sex. For Dustan, this plays out in his sense of the material, his use of language, his descriptions and representation of mores, and his entire being as it is represented in these books.

For him, that globalization is set against the givens: the impossibility of not being seropositive being the most important, ineluctable, and central phenomenon here. Measure the power of a single, short sentence standing alone in the middle of Dustan's second book, *Je sors ce soir*: "Jamais je ne vieillirai [I shall never grow old]" (60). As part of a youth-oriented culture, this gay man can indeed never grow old, for to do so would be perhaps to refigure oneself in a different culture, and certainly not that of gay urban Paris. Moreover, this protagonist is a thirty-something man, HIV+ for over a decade at the point of writing, seemingly not suffering from any of the opportunistic infections associated with AIDS, but clearly marked as one of the *morituri*, seemingly about to die in a predictable future, when the combination therapy will be less and less effective or when the level of the virus will have moved from undetectable to detectable; this writer will not grow old.[4] It is not a death sentence of course, but a death knell, no matter how far off it be; or at least that is the way it seemed at the time; we now know differently for Dustan in particular and for AIDS in the West in general.

Certainly since the AIDS epidemic started in 1981, the AIDS-related mortality rates in the West have gone through remarkable shifts. In the early years, there was an ever-increasing number of deaths among members of the first groups infected, most notably Western gay men, hemophiliacs, and Haitians. After the nature of the virus was discovered along with the means of transmission, safe sex was invented; in its most bare-bones description, safe sex (or safer sex), which in French is "le sexe sans risque," could be summarized as the use of condoms during anal intercourse. With the development of more effective means of detecting initial infection (*dépistage* in French) and therefore counting on the role of education in prophylaxis, the development of stronger drugs targeted at various opportunistic infections, and the development of AZT as the initial powerhouse super-drug, the rate of acceleration began to slow in the West and seropositive people lived longer.[5] By the mid-nineties, with ever-increasing means of intervention, due primarily to what is known as combination therapy, the tide began to turn. Although large numbers of the urban gay community were infected, the death rate in the West plummeted for people with adequate medical care, as the effects of the virus became invisible and opportunistic infections were staved off for ever longer periods of time. Whereas in the early years the life expectancy from diagnosis to death was in some cases measured in weeks and often in months up to two years, it is common now, almost three decades into the epidemic, for people to live for decades after diagnosis, and it is arguable that a diagnosis of HIV[+] status in the first decade of the twenty-first century, if made early enough, will not lead to a sizeable difference in age expectancy for the infected individual. Thus, in the West, AIDS becomes a more

---

[4] This does not happen, of course, as Dustan did not die of AIDS-related causes but rather of a drug overdose. Moreoover, with the advances of combination therapy, the scenario just laid out has become less common.

[5] AZT, or azidothymidine, is an anti-retroviral drug that is part of the class of drugs known as reverse transcriptase inhibitors.

normal and more manageable chronic condition, rather than a fatal illness, more like multiple sclerosis than the plague.[6] Reality catches up with language, for at least in the American versions of AIDS discourse, one moved from PWA (person with AIDS) cautiously to PLA (person living with AIDS), which has now become a realized reality of long-term seropositivity. Currently, AIDS has reached a controlled level in the white, bourgeois, industrial West compared to the worst pandemic in recorded history, the devastation wrought by AIDS in sub-Saharan Africa.[7]

With the exception of some thoughts in one of the last volumes, *Nicolas Pages*, the mentions of the disease as such in Dustan's work are few and far between; they are necessary but unremarkable moments between sexual events: "On a commencé par le rose fluo hyper mou que j'avais acheté à Pleasure Chest, West Hollywood, il y a deux ans, quand j'étais parti entre deux hospitalisations, et qui est parfait pour ouvrir un cul en douceur [We started with the real soft hot pink one that I bought at Pleasure Chest in West Hollywood two years ago, when I left between two hospital stays, and which is perfect for gently opening an asshole]" (*DMC* 32). Now while the idea of two hospital stays for anyone, and even more so a young adult, would not have been brushed aside so blithely in writing before AIDS, here it is merely an aside that fades in favor of contemporary Western gay culture: West Hollywood as locus, dildo as paraphernalia, and sex act as praxis and *telos*. So neither seropositivity nor AIDS is a factor, nor are the discourses of protection. Rather, the only important thing is a fulfillment of the hedonistic impulse, *coûte que coûte*, as the literary locus becomes

---

[6] To be perfectly accurate, AIDS is not a "fatal illness" but a syndrome in which the virus effectively reduces the functions and capacities of the person's immune system. This reduction in the capacity to fight off illness allows for opportunistic infections such as pneumocystic pneumonia (PCP) or internal growths, such as Kaposi's sarcoma (KS), which, combined with a general physical decline, could lead to death.

[7] My description simply summarizes a very complex situation. The status of AIDS at any given moment is in flux: there are indications that there has been an increase in bareback sex that will undoubtedly eventually lead to a rise in the infection rate, as well as the possibility of more resistant strains of HIV. In middle-class white strata in the United States, the expression "PLA" has disappeared, and the virus, the dormant infection, and the disease are lumped together in the pseudo-scientific congeries "HIV/AIDS" – a meaningless term, to say the least.

a fully fledged pornotopia, a witnessing of the reinscription of pleasure.

In gay urban America and in the message-laden channels of international cyberspace where American English, or at least some expressions from gay American English, is the *lingua franca*, one finds the expressions "bareback" and "bareback sex," as in riding a horse bareback: bareback sex is anal intercourse without condoms. No more safe sex and no more self-preservation, bareback sex is a return, but with a difference of time and disease, to a pre-lapsarian state. In these autofictions, Dustan is trying to transform bareback sex into narrative, as he translates riding bareback into writing bareback. There is an assumption that this is power over oneself and others, as he sees himself quite literally as a deadly weapon. And this weapon, by definition, is an arm used to break the law, at least in a moral sense, as it is immediately compared to a bank heist: "Depuis que j'étais séropo je me voyais comme un pistolet chargé. Le sperme remplaçait les balles. Avec ça j'avais le pouvoir, comme les mecs qui attaquaient des banques avec des seringues [Since I became HIV⁺, I have seen myself as a loaded gun. Sperm replaced the bullets. That way, I had power, like guys who attack banks with hypodermic needles]" (*Plus fort* 70). And yet the power is elsewhere, for in a world in which, at least according to the author, everyone is seropositive, and, *a fortiori*, in that world in which seropositivity itself no longer means a totally foreshortened life, his sperm gun is firing blanks.

So the initial sentence quoted – "I shall never grow old" – begins to be both more and less important than at first glance. Less important, because there is a way of moving death away, a combination therapy that can stave off the inevitable for ever longer periods of time and that can make seropositivity a managed illness. In the bourgeois world, it is a time to be filled with work and with as normal a life as possible. There is a difference, and a great one, but it is undetectable to the naked eye, just as the level of the virus in the blood has become undetectable. This is ever more important, because the eventuality of death becomes starker since the attenuation of life is at best only temporary, no matter how long that is.

Why should one (or Dustan, in particular) suffer then in a bourgeois existence? Why not just dance? If there is nothing to be done to avoid the teleologically inevitable death at an early age, then, he opines, one should just have fun: "Et puis je me rends compte que je suis un peu down et qu'il faudrait que je bouge [And then I realize that I am a bit *down* and that I have got to move]" (*Je sors* 33).[8] Dance is an expression of life and of unity, one guided in part by atavistic impulses to which he reattaches, regrafts, or cathects his own sexual and masculine imaginary:

> [P]uis c'est un docu sur des blacks en Afrique, ils sont à poil, ils ont des grosses teubs, ils passent leur temps à faire du body art et à danser, ils s'occupent de leur corps, quand ils dansent on dirait une rave, je trouve ça géant que toutes les cultures du monde soient en train de converger vers le meilleurs de chacune et oublie le reste. (*NP* 71)

> [It is a documentary on blacks in Africa, they are naked, they have big cocks, they spend their time doing body art and dancing, they take care of their bodies, when they dance it is like a rave, I think it is fantastic that all the cultures of the world are converging toward the best in each and forget the rest.]

Or less politely, why not just have sex until the end of time? For Dustan, everything turns around sex, everything relates to sex, and every definition of self comes from sex. The gay world depicted in these works is the utopian pleasure palace that redefines relations and otherness. And just as his notions of masculinity are intimately tied to his notion of his own sexuality and sexual behavior, everything else becomes a representation of it as well, an affect, a metomym, or a metaphor for sex:

> Le sexe est la chose centrale. Tout tourne autour: les fringues, les cheveux courts, être bien foutu, le matos, les trucs qu'on prend, l'alcool qu'on boit, les trucs qu'on lit, les trucs qu'on bouffe, faut pas être trop lourd quand on sort sinon on ne pourra pas baiser. (*DMC* 75)

> [Sex is the main thing. Everything revolves around it: clothes, short hair, being good-looking, the right equipment, the stuff you take, the liquor you drink, the stuff you read, the stuff you eat, can't be too heavy when you go out, otherwise, you won't be able to fuck.]

This world is marked by a set of relations to self and other, humans and objects alike, and the alpha and omega of those relations are an immediate sexuality and a representation of the self as a set of sexual

---

[8] Unless otherwise indicated, the emphasis here and elsewhere is mine, indicating that Dustan has used English in the original or has taken an English word and conjugated, parsed, declined, or used it as if it were a French word. It is not always possible to distinguish between the two.

possibilities; without sex, there is nothing. At one point in *Dans ma chambre*, Dustan makes a list of various available accessories, including drugs, porn films, porn magazines, sexual devices, and body parts, all of which are put into service as extensions and facilitators of sex:

> Certains éléments servent plus que d'autres. Je les aime tous. Ils sont comme des parties de moi qui viennent se poser là où je l'ai décidé et y maintiennent mon emprise. Mais c'est aussi leur office de servir le corps. (*DMC* 72–73)

> [Some elements serve better than others. I like all of them. They are like parts of my body that come to land where I have decided and keep my hold. But it is also their job to serve the body.]

The eroticized gay body is in a state of *sparagmos* – it becomes a list of detachable parts, human and non-human alike, all of which are focused on creating, maintaining, and increasing pleasure, without there necessarily being any envisioned totality to the body. Rewriting Alain Robbe-Grillet's meticulous *chosisme*, Dustan opines that counting becomes a natural thing in this world in which the exact image of the self must conform to the projected image for that self as a sexual being: "Je suis une machine à séduire. Je me lave et je huile mon corps tous les jours [I am a seduction machine. I wash and moisturize my body every day]" (*Plus fort* 135). He then gives a detailed description of his daily toilette, including the exact length to which he cuts his pubic hair, which is different from that of his armpit hair and that on his chest.

Beyond Deleuze's desiring machines or the "great ephemeral skin" and the "libidinal surface" of Lyotard's book *L'Économie libidinale*, the body envisioned by Dustan – his own or another's – is the locus of multiple pleasures and multiple localizations of *jouissance*, what he calls "[m]ultiplications des points sensibles [multiplications of sensitive spots]" (*DMC* 35). Or, in the later work, he makes yet another list of body parts subjected all at once to the flows of pleasure issuing from them and into them: "Bouche, bite, torse, cul, tout ça en même temps, j'aimais [Mouth, cock, chest, ass, everything at once, I loved it]" (*Plus fort* 22). The entire body is a set of sex organs, regardless of the "proper" or primary anatomic and physiological function of the body part. Perhaps the quintessence of this position is sperm, semen, or the general notion of *jouissance*, the most central aspect of his sexuality:

Je me suis réveillé tôt malgré le pétard-lexo-branlette d'hier soir.
Mal fou à jouir, mais j'ai insisté et ça a été super comme toujours les
lendemains d'exta. Poum! Poum! Poum! Poum! Poum! Poum! Poum!
Poum! Pas des grosses giclées mais très nombreuses. (*NP* 28)

[I woke up early despite the joint-lex-j/o last night. Really hard to
cum, but I kept at it and it was super, the way it always is the day after
xing. Bam! Bam! Bam! Bam! Bam! Bam! Bam! Bam! Not big spurts
but lots of them.]

Seminal fluid, the sign of *jouissance*, is the reconfirmation of sex and
sexuality, the insistence that he is a man, and that his masculinity is
in fact defined by a kind of *fort/da* of orgasm: he is a man only when
that which has left him as a man (seminal fluid) is visible, gone, done,
and finished. Arguably, Dustan is participating in a post-phallic
world in which the position of the phallus, now related only to the
pleasure principle and not to some life force or some symbolic power,
has been supplanted by generalized zones, surfaces, and attachable
or detachable figures of pleasure, each of which incarnates desire.
It is the body taken as rap sampling and the enactment of the body
as a Gregorian chant, the bass-line on which the rap sampling takes
place and of which the textual inscription becomes the shorthand
record: "Et je lui dis que le sujet c'est mon autobiographie érotique
sur fond de grégorien-rap parce que quand j'écris, j'écoute Depeche
Mode [And I tell him that the subject is my autobiography with
a background of Gregorian rap because when I write, I listen to
Depeche Mode]" (*DMC* 63).

Dustan's autofictional works all figure the same world of frequent
and often immediate gratification through a generalization of sex
and sexuality. The second, *Je sors ce soir*, is an episodic, fragmented,
slice-of-life depiction of an afternoon tea dance set in gay Paris. Its
figures, language, and writing correspond completely to the larger
and more ambitious narratives that flank it, but it is not, despite
that, as sustained a piece of writing. Other narratives, including
Dans ma chambre in a contemplative way, *Plus fort que moi* in a
way that finally gives in to the complete dissolution of the self in
a sea of drives and impulses, and *Nicolas Pages*, in a fragmentary
and often incantatory fashion, are creations of a utopian gay space
complete with its own laws, population, and modes of representation. The spoken style seldom varies, with short uncomplicated
sentences, simplified syntax, and recourse to slang, *verlan*, and

Americanisms.[9] Each has an inchoative and initiative aspect that sets the narrative apart and that marks this space as a specifically gendered and sexualized one.

For example, in *Dans ma chambre*, the narrator-protagonist is happily masturbating in his room. His roommate Quentin enters the room, seemingly without having knocked at the door. Dustan is peeved that Quentin has not observed the rules of etiquette and has interrupted him in his activity to inquire about something insignificant and accidental, as if anything could be more importance than privacy and orgasms:

> La première fois j'étais allongé sur le lit en train de me branler en fumant un pétard. La porte s'est ouverte. Il s'est avancé dans la chambre. Il a dit Tu n'aurais pas trouvé l'agenda de ma mère par hasard? Elle pense qu'elle l'a oublié ici. [...] Et puis il est sorti. J'ai mis dix minutes à arriver à me rebrander correctement. (*DMC* 12)

> [The first time, I was lying on the bed, jerking off, and smoking a joint. The door opened. He came in the room. He said, You didn't find my mother's agenda, did you? She thinks she forgot it here. [...] And he left. It took me ten minutes to start jerking off correctly again.]

Not the least astounding bit of this passage is the word "correctly," as if there were a correct way to masturbate, one sanctioned by some authority on masturbation (ostensibly, a central authority, since we are in France). And those ten minutes were lost to something other than the single-minded, hedonistic pursuit of pleasure. Again, at some subsequent moment, Quentin violates the rules of hospitality, and though he knocks on the door, does not seem to take "no" for an answer: "La deuxième fois il a frappé. Au moment où j'ai gueulé Non! il est entré dans la chambre. Là j'étais carrément en train de me faire sauter sur le bord du lit [The second time, he knocked. The second I said No, he came in the room. Then I was in the middle of getting screwed on the edge of the bed]" (*DMC* 12). And again, we are asked to consider the idea that the pursuit of sexual pleasure has to take precedence over everything else, and, indeed, that the

---

[9] *Verlan* is a specific kind of slang that reverses the order of consonants in a monosyllabic word or the order of syllables in a polysyllabic word. For example, *femme* becomes *meuf*, *arabe* becomes *beur* (in a word that has entered the mainstream to signify a French person of North African ancestry), and *bite* becomes *teub*. The word *verlan* is itself an example of *verlan*, as it is a reversal of *l'envers* (the reverse).

definition of self comes only from one's body, from that of another (or others), from the sexualization of masculinity as the be-all and end-all of his being.

In *Plus fort que moi*, there is a retrospective look at the first time, which is not only the first time for sex, but also the first time that the desire for sex and thus the desire to inhabit his body as a sexual individual take over; it is literally stronger than he is, and the power of that impulse will continue to take him over as it subjects him to itself, the figuration of a generalized libido that surpasses the ego:

> J'avais seize ans. La prof d'italien nous emmenait voir une pièce. Je suis arrivé en retard. Chaillot était fermé. Alors j'ai voulu connaître le sexe. Le sexe était plus fort. Plus fort que la peur. Plus fort que moi. J'avais lu dans *Le Nouvel Obs* que ça draguait. (*Plus fort* 15)

> [I was sixteen. The Italian teacher was taking us to see a play. I got there late. Chaillot was closed. So I wanted to find out about sex. Sex was stronger. Stronger than fear. Stronger than me. I went down to the gardens. I had read in the *Nouvel Observateur* that cruising went on there.]

Both the beginning of the first book and the beginning of the narrator's gay sex life (in the latter volume, but obviously at an earlier date chronologically) are marked by signs of bourgeois existence, signs of the superego to be rejected over and over again by libidinal power: Quentin's mother's agenda, needed for careful planning and scripting of one's life, a correct way to masturbate, going to the theater, learning a foreign language, and the right weekly news magazine, *Le Nouvel Observateur*. And both those beginnings are marked by the intrusion and subsequent removal of the feminine: Quentin's mother and the female Italian teacher. For once we have moved beyond this inchoative moment, the feminine by and large disappears from the narrative: fleeting references to Dustan's mother and to a "doctoresse" are among the few signs of the feminine in this world, where the resolution to the problems of seropositive masculinity seems to be found in the formation of, for lack of a better term, *une bande à part*.

This is a misogynistic universe, and here and there, Dustan reflects the misogyny built into the bourgeois world as a whole. Some cutting anti-feminine remarks are among the few traces of the world he willfully escapes. In this case, for example, he combines classical heterocentric misogyny – calling oneself or another a "whore" – with a racist remark that reduces a black man to being nothing more than a penetrator: "J'ai dû me bourrer le crâne en me répétant que j'étais une petite pute blanche qui se faisait tringler par un grand noir [I had to cram it into my head as I repeated that I was a little white whore who was getting screwed by a big black]" (*DMC* 137). And as if by decree, the world is one in which there are almost no women and in which there are no traces of the feminine. What traces there are condemn bourgeois habits and femininity to the same odious pit of hell, and yet, in so doing, Dustan internalizes the discourse of the other at times, and the reader wonders whether the celebration of his body is not sometimes accompanied by a self-loathing, or simply, whether the post-queer moment I have outlined in the introduction is not still sometimes tinged with *traces* of the abject: "J'imaginais déjà comment les bourgeois du Trap me regarderaient comme une salope, une traînée [I was already thinking how the bourgeois in the Trap would look at me like a whore, a slut]" (*Plus fort* 22–23). This gay male universe is one that is filled with rutting bodies, bodies in heat, men, ostensibly the cerebral in the standard metaphysical dichotomy that opposes them to corporeal women, reduced to that state of pure bodily lust. The world of this liberatory frenzy is a world populated by men who are no better than whores, who give in to their lust, who are at once the celebration and the abjection of the gay male's sexualized body.

But it is also a world in which there are no straight men, for they too are associated with the sense of heterosexual reproduction and with the use of sex and culture interchangeably as capital. His father is useful for providing cast-off clothing:

J'ai une veste qui était trop serrée pour Papa et qu'il m'a donnée, une chemise en oxford bleue à manches courtes et boutons de nacre qui me va très bien parce que je suis bronzé. J'ai des shorts Op's en velours côtelé crème. Des docksides bleu marine. C'est cool. (*DMC* 30)

[I have a jacket that was too tight for Dad and that he gave me, a blue cotton shirt with short sleeves and mother-of-pearl buttons, that looks good on me because I am tan. I have OP shorts in a velvety cream color. Aquamarine boat shoes. It's cool.]

Or a father is useful for offering a weekend of culture in Berlin: "Le deal final a été que je ne sortirais qu'une seule fois, le samedi soir, et que je serais à mon poste le dimanche matin pour du culturel avec lui [The final deal was that I would go out only once, Saturday evening, and that I would be where I belonged Sunday morning for cultural stuff with him]" (*Plus fort* 84). But there is nothing more there: short of providing some material support, again marked by the values of bourgeois institutions such as branded clothes and cultural capital, the protagonist's father is nothing more than signs of a system of heteronormativity that has to be overcome.[10] Just as his impulses or instincts are stronger than he is in the early pages in which he recounts his initiation to sex, they remain so now, and he misses the appointment with his father to see the museum just as – a Freudian might insist – he came late to the production of the Italian play. The bourgeoisie and its institutions must be dispensed with entirely if he is to be the man he sees himself being.

Nor do humor, irony, or tenderness have much of a place here, and what few attempts there are at introducing one of these fall flat. Consider some pillow talk that goes nowhere:

> Je me rapproche de Stéphane dans le lit. Il se love dans mes bras. Je lui dis Tu es comme un croissant. Il me dit Au beurre ou ordinaire? Je lui dis au beurre. Il me dit Mais je suis aussi un peu ordinaire. Je lui dis C'est vrai, mais tu es intelligent. Alors, ça passe. (*DMC* 99)

> [I get closer to Stéphane in bed. He buries himself in my arms. I tell him, you are like a croissant. He says, With butter or plain [ordinaire]? I tell him, With butter. He says, But I am also a bit plain. I tell him, It is true, but you are intelligent. So it is OK.]

Dustan is funny when he is at his most earnest; here, for example, he moves from an ostensibly high-toned techno-aesthetic to a discussion of his talents at performing oral sex on another man:

> Mais dans chaque style, il y a bien du meilleur et du pire, il y a de la *technique*: si je suis un des meilleurs suceurs de Paris, c'est que je sais y faire. [...] [En] général le mec n'est pas long à pleurer sa mère et à exploser. (*NP* 245)

> [But in each style, there is the best and the worst, there is *technique*: if I am one of the best cocksuckers in Paris, that is because I know how to do it. [...] [It] usually doesn't take the guy long before he cries for his mother and explodes.]

---

[10] For obvious reasons, I am not making a distinction among the various avatars of Dustan in these volumes, though each is, of course, an independent piece. But the autofictional quality and conformity is so high as to make the distinctions between or among these works invalid.

Everything must remain focused on one set of contents and at one level of performance of sex, in a quest for a constant revolving door or all-you-can-eat buffet of sex. Anything that distracts from that or that marks a distance from the quest is immediately eschewed. Even food itself, a mainstay of French culture, becomes reduced to a world of frozen entrees and fast-food, as if any cultural material, just as any humor, might change the focus of life and/or writing.

His first time for sex with a man is at age sixteen when he misses the Italian play. The initial reaction therefore is to expel the other and that which is strange to the world of bourgeois sexuality: this means the furtive, anonymous cruising and the accomplishment of sex in the gardens of the Trocadéro, as well as the acts of gay sex as such. But they are stronger than he is: "Après on s'est sucé. Le goût était horrible. [...] Quand je suis rentré à la maison j'étais en sueur, j'avais envie de vomir [After, we sucked each other. The taste was terrible. [...] When I got home, I was perspiring and wanted to vomit]" (*Plus fort* 15). The ingested other becomes that on which he will feed himself in all forms, as all of his body becomes opened up to the experience of sex. More often than not in this world, this involves descriptions of fisting as the fulfillment (or even *Aufhebung*) of anal intercourse with another, and basically and in general, an opening up as far as possible of the surfaces of the body, extended by drugs, toys, devices, and the singular laws of this particular universe.

The world he leaves behind, first out of exploration of these new possibilities and then as he understands his diagnosis, is one in which he considers himself filled with shame. He believes himself so abject that he precipitates his own propulsion into this world of utopian desire that he cannot yet know. But as he gradually gets used to this alternative universe, he withdraws from the heteronormative one, and as he does so, he becomes aware of the parameters of the new situation, and specifically, one in which gay men, though seropositive, are now living "virtually normal" lives. Yet, the transition is rough and his life is saved by writing. In fact, he says, "Renaud Camus m'a sauvé la vie [Renaud Camus saved my life]" ("Tribu" 40). From being abject, he realizes that he is figured by the other in writing, he is desired by the other in writing, and he can refigure his own self into desire and writing all at once. It matters little that he has not read Camus's blockbuster and he maintains that his knowledge of that work is of quite recent date;

indeed he discovered it only in 1998 ("Tribu" 41) – though clearly, like many others, he has heard enough about Camus's writing to deny that his own is similar to it (Miles and Kopp 31). Still, Camus is there, as life-saver and avuncular figure, in a world in which one reproduces only textually. Camus is sufficiently distant chronologically, for he is two decades older than Dustan, and thus not a rival in any sphere. Between the two, the writer of AIDS and death: "the author who wrote those horrible things, Guibert" (Miles and Kopp 29). Strangely and ostensibly unknown to him, given his ignorance of *Tricks*, Dustan will rewrite Camus a quarter of a century later. The first writing, that of Camus, is a writing before AIDS, condoms, and the specter of death, but Dustan's *Dans ma chambre* and especially *Plus fort que moi* are written in a world after AIDS and condoms, in a return to the immediate barrier-free utopics of gay sex.

In a world in which one might expect references to illness because of the pervasiveness of the virus and its eventual death-toll, the references, as I have already indicated, are few and far between. A few pages after the retrospective glance at his anonymous loss of virginity in the Trocadéro and after numerous reflections on this utopian world in which he lives and writes, there is a mention of disease, in a strange reversal of the desire to vomit. It is a strong expression of will and disgust in him, and it turns up in an interview granted to *La Revue H* just before the publication of *Plus fort que moi*. Dustan says that a constant wailing about the fact that one is going to die of AIDS-related causes is unacceptable: "I truly find nothing more nauseating or more inexcusable" (in Miles and Kopp 29). So vomiting, the expulsion of the detritus of the ingested other, is a reminder of the bourgeois sense of difference that separates gay from straight, HIV⁻ from HIV⁺, and life from death. And this is unacceptable. In the passage already mentioned, there is a reversal of this vomiting as he tries to maintain the other within, with a displacement and a curious mis-definition, or at least a wrong diagnosis. Here we are on the edge of representation, where language can no longer serve and where no words can express the ecstacy of the moment. There is a long, detailed description of anal penetration, a scene that starts with an evocation of the title of the work in progress: "[Ç]a m'excitait de voir ça, un torse large de mec, plus grand et plus fort que moi, au-dessus de moi, prêt à me mettre [I got aroused seeing that, the broad torso of a guy, bigger and stronger than me, above me, ready to plough me]" (*Plus fort* 34). Anal intercourse gives way to fistfucking, a feeling of "plénitude [fulfillment]" (35), and eventually to an orgasm, as the intensity of the description reflects the orgasmic intensity of the acts described. Orgasm is powerful and instantaneous in the act of fisting:

> J'ai senti sa main se faire avaler par mon cul (comment est-ce qu'une chose pareille pouvait m'arriver? [...] J'ai joui à l'instant même. Il s'est retiré doucement, m'a demandé si ça allait, j'ai dit Oui, et là j'ai senti que j'avais les mâchoires beaucoup trop serrées. J'ai pensé Crise de tétanie, je connaissais les symptômes [...]. (*Plus fort* 35)

> [I felt his hand being swallowed by my ass (how could such a thing happen to me?) [...] I came immediately. He pulled out gently, asked me if things were OK, I said, Yes, and then I felt my jaws were clenched too tightly. I thought, an attack of tetany, I knew the symptoms [...].]

Having swallowed the other, albeit by another orifice, he precipitates a crisis of tetany, the involuntary contraction of muscles, which he may be confusing with tetanus, i.e. lockjaw, but whether there is confusion or not, it is clear that the other he once wanted to expel he now wishes to stay. And it matters little that there are different orifices being used, for in this universe in which the body is an amalgamation of pleasure points, the idea of the body is not that of Lacan's homunculus, but that of an ever-changing, ever-metamorphosing libidinal band replete with nooks and crannies. Several pages later, the same situation of being fisted leads again to the same inarticulate exclamation on the printed page, "J'ai fait la deuxième crise de tétanie de ma vie, mais je m'en foutais [I had the second tetany attack of my life, but I didn't give a damn]" (41).

The construction of this world is based on the immediate possibility of fulfilling desire, of reaching orgasm, and of accomplishing *jouissance* through a variety of means, the stronger the better, for the stronger the orgasm or feeling is, the more in tune one is with this universe of permanent pleasure. Drugs and sex-toys are combined to give as total a rush as possible; the stronger the sensation, the more he appreciates it; his being is formed, marked, and fulfilled by the extremes to which he subjects his sexual body:

> Donc ce soir, avec le quart d'acide, la coke et tous les pétards que j'ai fumés, je vais pouvoir me le taper [an enormous dildo], et je sais que c'est une sensation assez royale qui m'attend, un truc largement aussi

délirant que le saut en parachute ou la plongée sous-marine. J'aime les sensations fortes. (*DMC* 33)

[So tonight, with the quarter tab of acid, coke, and all the joints I smoked, I'll be able to do it, and I know that a really royal sensation is waiting for me, a thing as wild as skydiving or scuba-diving. I like strong sensations.]

It is not that the drugs help conquer some resilient or remaining shame about himself; it is that the drugs and sex together remove every shred of mediation. In *Nicolas Pages*, the narrator makes an equivalence between sex and other desirable things to which one gets addicted: "Mon autre kif en ce moment, c'est le sperme [My other drug right now is sperm]" (*NP* 180). The choice of drug matters little, as long as it facilitates as strong an orgasm as possible, over and over again.

In his brilliant and now classic study of desire, *Mensonge romantique, vérité romanesque*, René Girard, following Hegel, demonstrates that desire is always mediated: it is the desire of the desire of another. Thus in a world of differences, a gay man desires another gay man because some third man already desires the second; this is the origin, says Girard, of mimetic rivalry and an ever-increasing escalation in violence, be it real or symbolic. Alternatively, the first man desires another because some impersonal over-arching authority tells him that the man is desirable; there is a general agreement on who or what is hot and who or what is not. It helps to be the object of the desire of others as the incarnation of those ideals, and looking good (sexy) means being looked at, and being looked at in this world means eventually having sex: "On sortait au BH, la boîte trash de la rue du Roule. Vingt-quatre et vingt-sept ans, pas un gramme de graisse, les cheveux très courts, parfaitement lookés. On était les plus beaux. On ramenait des mecs [We went to BH, the *trashy* club on the rue du Roule. Twenty-four and twenty-seven, not an ounce of fat, very short hair, perfectly in style. We were the best *looking*. We brought guys back]" (*Plus fort* 45). But it is certainly not necessary in a world in which there will always be innumerable men who are willing and available.

All is possible in this world, where there is a surfeit of possibilities, where everyone and everything have been multiplied into a myriad of sexual potentialities, and where at every moment another surface goes beyond the status of desiring machine to become something far more involved than the reductive point of desire envisioned by Deleuze and Guattari. This sexual utopia is a place in which desire is always immediately gratified. Everything goes and everything flows. Fulfillment is immediate, even if there is no correspondence to the model of desire: Dustan's world is a "magma" of body parts, a hot flow that knows no limits, endlessly fulfilled and repeatedly renewed:

> Je pouvais m'engloutir dans ce magma de mains, de bites, de bouches. Je pouvais me mettre à ne plus rien en avoir à foutre de savoir à qui appartenait quoi, qui était gros, vieux, moche, contagieux. Je pouvais très bien partir, devenir fou, bouffer chaque bit qui passait, devenir une bête, ressortir des heures après, les vêtements déchirés, tachés, nu, couvert de sueur, de salive, de sperme. (*Plus fort* 22)

> [I could drown in this magma of hands, cocks, mouths. I could start not giving a flying fuck in knowing what belonged to whom, who was fat, old, ugly, contagious. I could get off, go crazy, eat each cock that went by, become an animal, leave hours later, with torn, stained clothing, naked, covered in sweat, saliva, and sperm.]

Bodies dissolve into one another as everything is freely available in this pleasure palace of rampant gay sexuality that is an amalgamation of masculinity in flow. So we come to understand that these works are not only about sex, but they also engage the laws and mores of a certain social subculture, though the laws are rare, and the mores do not go much beyond a mutual respect and, in the realm of cyberspace, a somewhat flexible approach to the truth, which, in any case, does not seem to matter much to anyone. The works engage a consumer culture of drugs and music in which there is a constant sampling – in the rap music sense – for new experiences as such are rare, and the narrator generally relies on the tried and true effects of smoking multiple joints and snorting coke when available. And yet all these things are ancillary to the main discourse, which is about sex, both in the specific sense of focusing on a series of acts and events and more broadly about a culture of male-male sex.

While the experiences described are perhaps viewed as extreme or marginal in a vanilla, heterosexual world, within the climes that Dustan inhabits, the events are neither extreme nor marginal. Venues vary from bedrooms to backrooms and everywhere in between; scenarios change from oral to anal to sadomasochistic relations; partners are changed more often than underwear. But the acts themselves, if not often found within what is considered writing with literary value, are certainly common within the community. The rarity, if any, is the lack of depiction in literary writing and not the acts as such. And it should be said that the rarity in literature does not mean that this material is unrepresented; one need go no further than the nearest adult film selection – something that Dustan does with frequency – to find it. Dustan goes beyond the pornographic and even the erotic elements, as he writes that his writing is not sexually exciting to get people off [*jouissive*] (Miles and Kopp 29). His acts are just what they are, not reducible to categories of the erotic or the pornographic. In that, he shares the same space with Virginie Despentes, Michel Houellebecq, Nathalie Gassel, Nicolas Jones-Gorlin, and Olivier Py, among others writing in French today. And in his obsession with recounting sexual prowess and with sexualizing the world, he shares the space with the other writers and film-makers discussed in the pages that follow.

If the availability of sex is not mediated by desires other than one's own and if then there is an immediacy, there is certainly, in the description of that sex, an act of self-reflection that, while neither moving directly toward the pornographic nor reconstituting the subject as an individual, marks his actions as relative to an ideal dissolution of the self into a pure surface of pleasure, as he visualizes himself and his partner resembling an image from the best pornography: "Je gonfle dans son cul, il se plaque contre moi, je vois dans le miroir un truc de class internationale, ça me plaît, ça merassure, ça me flatte [I swell in his ass, his body is next to mine, I turn, I see something with international class in the mirror, it pleases me, reassures me, and flatters me]" (*DMC* 31). Each orifice and surface, endlessly dissoluble into others, becomes uniform in a series of images of self and other. As in the virtual world of the Minitel, sex dissolves into the images of a phantasmagoric world. Dustan becomes his own mediator; his desire is described according to his desire for his own desire. There cannot be an endless regression and his desire is, at certain moments, intermingled in that virtual world with the idealized version of that desire, the transparence of (gay) porn films, made without pretense and figured without malice or angle. While removing the titillating aspect of pornography from his descriptions of sex, he maintains the possibility of pure representations that melt into the act. There is nothing between the act and language or between the real and the virtual. His own experiences, then, are indistinguishable from those of others, be they real or pornographic:

> Je lui dis que sur les mille mecs avec qui j'ai baisé il y en a quatre ou cinq, enfin une dizaine qui savent faire ce qu'il m'a fait. Il y a aussi Chad Douglas, mais c'est sur k7 uniquement. (*DMC* 28)

> [I told him that of the thousand guys I had had sex with, there were only four or five, well, ten or so, who knew how to do what he was doing to me. There is also Chad Douglas, but he is only on video.]

No distinction need be made between the real men with whom he has slept and the projection of himself – *de te fabula* – into the pornographic, as if the experiences of watching, recounting, and doing were all immediately equivalent. Again there is no differentiation between the performance of the self and an acting job; here there is no actor's paradox, no Stanislavski method; the immediate accessibility of the act guarantees that "il m'a baise (safe) avec une énergie qui reste inégalée huit ans plus tard (sauf par Chad Douglas en vidéo) [He fucked me (*safe*) with an energy unequalled eight years later (except by Chad Douglas on video)]" (*Plus fort* 51–52). For Dustan, both his sex and his writing are a constant move towards the permanent pornoself, an avatar of self and other in perfect pornographic purity, and there is a bond of communality and shared practices between his world and the pornotopia of the films, as Dustan constructs, at least in his mind and his text, a real world that resembles that of contemporary gay pornography: "Je me suis branlé en regardant Eric Manchester en pleine action, faisait ce qu'il sait faire, des trucs que je sais faire. Ce n'est pas Chad Douglas, mais lui aussi il aime sa queue [I jerked off watching Eric Manchester in action, doing what he knows how to do, things I know how to do. He is no Chad Douglas, but he also likes his dick]" (*DMC* 38). Dustan becomes the pornographic other, united in word, deed, and image on screen, in the realm of the virtual – the television monitor that is his mind – with himself as sex machine. It is a move both out of the banal quotidian and away from the reality of HIV+ status: a projection of a pornoself creates an ideal masculine individual who will live forever on film and die neither of AIDS-related illnesses nor of old age.

That the pornography used as a system is largely from the United States underlines the role to which the image of the US is put in these narratives. In fact, Dustan's writings are often at the limit of the comprehensible for the average French reader. Like Matthieu Kassovitz, whose film *La Haine* is scripted in a contemporary *argot* known about by, but incomprehensible to, the majority of white French adults, there is a willful use of a language that is not the *lingua franca* of communication (Miles and Kopp 33). While Dustan uses some *verlan* and slang, the main stylistic trait is recourse to American English: "Finir au QG, et ça y est, il est déjà cinq heures, l'heure d'aller crasher trashé. Et le lendemain, ça recommence. Endless Fun! Fun! Fun! [Wind up in QG and so it is already five o'clock, the time to go *crash trashed*. And it starts again the next day. *Endless Fun! Fun! Fun!*]" (*NP* 31). Apart from the quotations from rock music lyrics, the language references the gay subculture of urban America. So it is not simply that the average French reader cannot understand English, since this is less and less the case in twenty-first-century France, especially among likely readers of Dustan's work: a fairly young, hip, and self-selecting, English-speaking group. It is that the references are completely decontextualized for a hypothetical general reader. Certainly, Renaud Camus for one, before Dustan, has made extensive use of American English (as well as Italian) in his writing, but the expressions Camus uses are never as heavily coded as they are for Dustan. Where Camus will use an English word because there is no exact French equivalent, Dustan will have recourse to an American subcultural slang for which there is no standard French *or* American equivalent, because the vocabulary is specifically drawn from gay subculture; Camus is filling a linguistic gap, while Dustan is creating a culturally specific discourse: "Le mégabutch bodybuildé qui m'a touché le paquet quand je suis passé près de lui tout à l'heure me dévisage encore [The *bodybuilt megabutch* who copped a feel when I went by a while ago is looking at me again]" (*DMC* 120–21), or again, "un petit mec semi-bodybuildé [a small guy, somewhat *bodybuilt*]" (*NP* 83). If Dustan dots his i's, so to speak, by turning the neologism into a regular past participle for a non-existent French verb, and if "mégabutch" is more or less intelligible to speakers of both languages, the whole image of a gay clone is probably only fully understandable to someone familiar with the images; Dustan does not inform his reader so much as reaffirming what is in the mind of his hypothetical idealized reader. Again, Dustan offers us gay macaronics: "Bref, Georges est torse nu, et je regarde ses tétons pas over-developped mais parfaitement dessinés [In short, Georges is shirtless, and I look at his nips, not *over-developed* but perfectly drawn]" (*Je sors* 56). Even the simplest of expressions evokes a whole range of images from which many readers are excluded; the reader must have the entirety of post-1968 popular culture, style, and (Parisian) gay culture in his or her mind to be able to interpret comments such as these about two men seen in the Marais, the center of gay Paris: "A Saint-Paul ils étaient deux, style stachemous de cinquante berges, plutôt mal foutus, lookés clones seventies [At Saint-Paul, there were two of them, 'stached guys in their fifties, rather ugly, *looked* like *seventies clones*]" (*Plus fort* 133). Again, the exclusion occurs because the decontextualization of the words cannot evoke all the contexts necessary for understanding. So recourse to an expression such as "seventies" or "sixties" (*Je sors* 48) cannot figure meaning into the writing except in a fragmentary, divided way: *disjecta membra, disjecta verba.* Is this where post-modern, globalized queer discourse is necessarily headed? Perhaps not, because the language is supported by a material culture, by a set of Foucauldian discourses, and by the representation of both in the materiality of urban gay culture.

The use of American English constantly evokes the gay industry and the globalization of gayness that is always already translated into that *lingua franca.* So the invocation and evocation of English recall that world and immediately eroticize the discourse. To use English is to charge an atmosphere with what that imported American English represents – a fungible, global gayness; but it is of course also to enter into the realm of alterity that is the same as that of the pornotopia previously discussed. Only as a subset within that English is a singular phenomenon relating to part of the language, a subset situated between word and image. For at the very limit of this language is an even more narrowly selected linguistic base that relates to the pornographic images already mentioned, as dildos are named for the people on whom they are modeled: "[J]'ai sélectionné le moulage de la bite de Kris Lord (25 x 18) [...] Il m'a d'abord hyper bien baisé avec le lord [I picked the model of Kris Lord's cock (25 x 18) [...] He first fucked me really well with the *lord*]" (*DMC* 95). Or again: "On s'est regodés. Je lui ai enfoncé le stryker bien profond [We redildoed each other. I shoved the stryker real deep in his ass]" (*DMC* 135). If Kris Lord is known to gay male audiences for his anatomical prowess and Jeff Stryker for his less-than-stellar acting and the size of his genitalia, the naming of parts would perhaps remain mysterious to the reading public at large, until we realize that there is a limited audience of idealized, hip, gay readers. With such a stylistic turn, Dustan brings in the language and images of the other to turn the fetish objects and their supposed phallocentric power into additional parts of the immediate, as if he were replacing the fragile parts of his universe with permanent and invincible clones. So there is no phallic power at a distance and no mark of unjoinable power or difference; everything is attainable through language and image. Each instance of linguistic singularity becomes one more means for the author of gaining access anew to this world that he lives in and that he also creates through his performance of self. In the final analysis, sex itself becomes a retranslation of sex in American pornographic films; to use a tried and true turn of phrase, art is not imitating life here as much as life is imitating art:

> [Il] m'a baisé trop vite et trop fort, mais en me claquant le cul, ça m'étonné (après je lui ai demandé où il avait appris ça, il m'a répondu dans les films américains, j'ai rêvé sur la culture mondial [...]. (*Plus fort* 61)

> [He fucked me too fast and too hard, but slapping my ass, that astonished me (after, I asked him where he had learned that, he answered in American films, I dreamt of world culture).]

Fetishizing language while unfetishizing what it describes also relates to a sense of self that is equally separated from the ordinary, as the self becomes one more figure or image in this hyperspace where virtual and real meet, and in which the imaginary and the symbolic dissolve into the accomplishable. The self is the ultimate fetish and the final connotation, both dissolved into the completely unfetishized utopia of endless gratification. In an extended three-way sadomasochistic scenario that includes role playing, water sports, and torture, and in which Dustan invariably plays the bottom, he becomes, in the final scene, the object of attention of the two others who drip candle wax on him, and specifically on his penis:

> Je ne sentais plus rien. Ça s'était arrêté. Un bruit mat à ma droite. C'est pour toi, ça te fera un souvenir, a dit la jeune. La coquille blanchâtre était le moulage exact de mon gland. (*Plus fort* 113)

> [I didn't feel anything. It had stopped. A dull sound to my right. It is for you, you'll have a souvenir, the younger one said. The whitish shell was the exact model of the head of my penis.]

Representation of itself, this whitish shell is a visual reminder, an image, or a figure of sex; it is one more sign in a world in which signs are interchangeable with what they represent – if, of course, one can understand what they represent – and in which the phallus is nowhere to be seen because everyone has and is the phallus at the same time. This is no Lacanian universe of prohibitions and limits; surface and style are everything, and everything is possible. With no repressed unconscious and a superego long having been rejected, all that counts is the visible, a transparent visibility that knows no borders or limits from the unspeakable real. If it is only surfaces that count, then looks are everything. And in the most often repeated Anglicism of his writing, Dustan has made a specific idiomatic use of an invented verb, "looker" and its iterative "relooker." For him it means to give someone a new look, to change the appearance of someone, and to refashion someone, not in his own image, but in the image of the gay man of this world: "Ce soir il est visiblement en hyper-forme. Parfaitement looké, avec un petit collier noir et une chemisette genre sixties en rayonne ouverte sur ses gros biceps et ses pecs ronds et gorgés [Tonight he is really in great shape. *Looking* perfect, with a little black necklace and a *sixties*-style shirt in rayon, open on his big biceps and his full, rounded pecs]" (*Je sors* 48). The look is everything: it is the appearance one offers others and the surface presented of a generalized pattern of surface pleasure and phenomenological performance of self as pornographic image. Yet "relooker" is also "reluquer," a verb meaning to eye, to leer at, or to ogle with sexual intent. To change one's look therefore is, in this simple macaronic pun, to become more visible sexually, more erotic, and more potentially available for cruising and for sex: "Je l'ai relooké: bomber vert, cheveux courts, jeans moulants, rangers [I redid his *look*: great bomber jacket, short hair, tight jeans, boots]" (*Plus fort* 131). As if in homage to the conspicuous consumption of works by Bret Easton Ellis, a novelist whom he admires (Miles and Kopp 30, 33), Dustan makes numerous references to the right clothing, look, haircut, and appearance.[11] And even a space of globalized conspicuous consumption, such as a department store, can be redone to become chic: "J'ai pénétré dans la Samar complètement relooké, très classe [I went into Samaritaine,

---

[11] "A l'inverse, on pourrait soutenir que *Dans ma chambre* est un roman américain tant il est influencé par la syntaxe de l'anglais des États-Unis, et particulièrement par la langue de Brett [sic] Easton Ellis [Conversely, it could be maintained that *Dans ma chambre* is an American novel because it is so influenced by the syntax of American English, and particularly, by Bret Easton Ellis's language]" (*NP* 375).

completely *remade*, very classy]" (*NP* 337). In this closed utopia, then, the goal is for every individual to be relooked and *reluqué*, a goal that extends to department stores and to every other space of mass consumption that can be sexualized. For the institutions too need to be eroticized, and it is with tongue barely in cheek that Dustan recommends changing even the august French educational system, including having a radically innovative program about sexualities: "L'enseignement de toutes les sexualités à l'école. Des épreuves de cul au bac (théoriques) [Teaching all kinds of sex in school. Sex texts on the baccalaureate exam (theoretical)]" (*NP* 286).

Everything is in the look, for everything is on the surface. To remake oneself or someone else or to have a new look is to transform oneself into that permanent invagination in which everything of the self becomes surface, including the farthest post-sphincter reaches within. Extended as surface, the self becomes palpable, visible to hands and language, remarked from within as within, though the within no longer exists. The surface is everywhere to be seen, to be felt, and to be the self that is permanently marked in a dissolution. This too is part of the project, as the insides are turned out. He aligns his project to the painting of Francis Bacon so he can show, like Bacon, raw, brute emotion (Miles and Kopp 30). Ultimately, though, Dustan's project is even more radical, for it attacks the bourgeois notion of the self, the representation of the self, and the difference of the self.

For the linguist and grammarian Émile Benveniste, the first person singular pronoun refers deictically to the one saying "I" at that moment. For Dustan, of course, that "one" does not exist as one or mark itself as one, so the first person pronoun, the sign of the only real character, if real he be, is a reference to the one potentially having sex at the moment of enunciation in a past, present, and future all conjoined with images come from afar, made in Hollywood. He becomes Kris Lord, Chad Douglas, and Jeff Stryker as well as the individuals with whom they have sex. He is that "I" that becomes its looks and its actions:

Techniquement je suis au top. Je suis une machine à plaisir. Je reçois en chaps en cuir, string en cuir, rangers. J'ai la musique, le matos, les drogues. J'ai le cul parfaitement clean. Je sais tout faire. J'embrasse. Je lèche. Je suce. Je pince. Je tords. J'aspire. Je tends. Je tire. Je pousse. Je caresse. Je claque. Je tiens. J'ouvre. J'écarte. Je vais. Je viens. Je plonge. Je pisse. Je bave. Je cache. Il n'y a que jouir dans une capote que je ne sais toujours faire. (*Plus fort* 136)

[Technically, I am at the top of my game. I am a pleasure machine. I receive in leather chaps, leather string, boots. I have music, the right stuff, drugs. I have a perfectly clean ass. I know how to do everything. I lick. I suck. I pinch. I twist. I sniff. I offer. I pull. I push. I caress. I slap. I hold. I open. I spread. I go. I come. I dive. I piss. I cum. I hide. The only thing I still can't do is cum in a rubber.]

The one impossible act is the one that marks a difference, remarks alienation, and inserts a *parois*, a hymen, or a tympanum that prevents the purity of word and sperm from communicating with the other become self. Phallic power? Certainly not, nor even phallocentrism, all normative appearances to the contrary. Rather it is the sperm as fluid, flowing, spurting logos, as a pure expression of being in a world in which phenomena are all. If I am in my room or if I am going out this evening, they are all finally stronger than me, stronger than I am, as I melt into a pure flow of language and libido of writing bareback.

Guillaume Dustan's early works could be classified as autofictions, scarcely veiled versions of some aspects of the life of one William Baranès, an HIV⁺ man, spending a good deal of time having sex of one sort or another, taking drugs, and generally living entirely in the gay community or subculture. The first three books are short, lyrical, formless productions that take their clues from their contents, in a sort of slice-of-life fashion. They cohere through the subject matter and through the way in which they expose the individual to his readers. The next two volumes are a different story: *Nicolas Pages* and *Génie divin* are large amorphous works, heterogeneous in style, writing, and goal, approaching, quite effortlessly, self-parody instead of autofiction. At first glance, *LXiR* seems a hybrid between the two styles: at less than 200 pages, it has the brevity of the early works, but has the heterogeneity, amorphousness, and cut-and-paste style of the more recent ones. And it is unabashedly a mixture of voices, weaving interviews with Dustan with his own discourses, mixing parody of the other with self-parody, intercalating a studied moral philosophy with brazen self-serving hedonism. Yet the voices are not distinct and the interviews, for example, blend into a dialogue in which the two interlocutors seem virtually to be Dustan and Dustan. Taking a page from Jacques Derrida's concept of writing *sous rature* and indicating "Autocensuré [self-censored]" (124), Dustan writes pages 125–35, and then crosses them out, with the exception of the penultimate line: "Prix 9,9 euros (juste entre les mainstream et les [Price 9.9 euros (just between the *mainstream* and the]" (135) and then concludes, with the final word "branchés [plugged in]" crossed out as well. Much of this part is no different from anything else in this book and he talks about "queer neo-paganism," "the seropositive as model citizen," and "forbidden things" (128). Or again, he complains about the dominance of heterosexuality, which "règne sur l'espace public; et nous, on se terre; dans des caves; ou alors il faut se déguiser en hétéros [reigns as master over public space, and we hide in basements, or we have to disguise ourselves as heteros and then we are left in peace]" (131). The world must be changed, for its Lacanian *points de capiton* no longer work as the system has gone awry and there is no space in the inherited model for a queer masculinity compounded by seropositivity.

Beginning, middle, or end, readable or *sous rature*, Dustan's writing focuses on a willful generalization of the sexual into a universal queerness. This means not only seeking the end to compulsory heterosexuality, as Adrienne Rich famously called it, nor even only the end to heteronormativity, though this is a big part of it, but also the queering of all life, all sexualities, all gender performances, and all behaviors, so that there is no forced dominance, domination, or even suggestion. From the very first, in one of the epigraphs, Dustan uncouples and recouples so as to skew textuality and so as to disengage automatic representation: "Aux Maux Sexuels [To STDs]" (*LXiR* 11).[12] One of the many plays on words and spellings that are the rhetorical backbone of this book, this pun offers three distinct and contradictory meanings. The words, as written, imply an apostrophe or a toast to sexually transmitted diseases. Uncoupling health and sexuality, Dustan postures in favor of a generalized bareback sex, a condom-free world in which there is no barrier between self and other, in which the two can become one, no matter how risky the behavior might be, and no matter how much the world (power, politics, medicine,

---

[12] For Dustan, heteronormativity is the central problem: "Si les hé t'es trops se mettent à cette hype(e)rcompétitivité homme oh sexuelle, c'est à cause des femmess [sic] [If heteros start with this homosexual hypercompetition, it is because of women]" (*LXiR* 57).

proper morality) might oppose bareback sex. For Dustan it is more important to celebrate sex, even if it does lead to a disease, than it is to protect self and other from infections.

But the phrase can also be understood as "homosexuels" and as "aux mots sexuels [to/about sexual words]." This third echo resounds: this will be about words and sex, sex and text, and the interplay of both, and it will be an apostrophe to them, a paean to what they mean, a celebration of sexuality through textuality. Insofar as the second possible meaning is concerned, homosexuals, implicitly apostrophized, are also a statement of fact. They exist, they will not be invisible, they are there from the very beginning, in defiance of the excesses of heterosexuals and heterosexuality that reign through law, "les codes sexés (de la virilité, de la féminité), et le droit, qui couronne le tout [sexed codes (virility and femininity), and the law that crowns everything]" (*LXiR* 22). The codes – the law – crafted by heterosexuals as universals dominate and are dictated as universals, and this is something that Dustan finds intolerable and excessive. The old heteronormative order illustrated by psychoanalysis and structuralism has, for him, ironically been reaffirmed by those critical analyses:

> [Au] bout du compte, Lacan et Levi-strauss [sic] ont sauvé la sociétait patriarcale et l'hé t'es tropsexualité ... [...] Ils ont dit le nom – on pourrait dire aussi le non – du père. Le nom du père, c'est la structuration mentale. Alors Queue ce n'est Queue la structuration de la sociétait.[13] (61)

> [After all, Lacan and Lévi-Strauss saved patriarchal society and heterosexuality ... [...] They said the name – one could also say the "no" – of the father. The name of the father is mental structuring, while it is only the structuring of society.]

Even in insisting on the elementary structures of the human psyche and human society, Lacan and Lévi-Strauss, in Dustan's eyes, did not do what they might have because they reinforced the *nom/non* of the father instead of unpinning it, instead of destructuring it. Without repeating Derrida's arguments against Lévi-Strauss in *De la grammatologie* and "La Structure, le signe, et le jeu dans le discours

---

[13] In this book, Dustan repeatedly replaces the relative pronoun "que," meaning which or that, with the similarly sounding "queue," one of the slang words for the penis.

des sciences humaines," or those against Lacan in "Le Facteur de la vérité," Dustan is arguing the same point: because their discourses did not fully undo the patriarchal system, each of us is still subject to it, and each of us has his or her sexuality and its appearance as masculinity or femininity subject to the law of society, a society that forces us to accept the lines of family, of reproduction, and of heteronormativity. And frankly, this is anathema to Dustan, who objects on several levels to the structuring of society through this *nom/non*.[14]

Consonant not only with Derrida, but also with a requestioning of (af)filiation, in a recent article by François Noudelmann, Dustan rejects the norming done by the law that decides where the individuals sits in the chain of relations: "Je proteste? La vraie filiation est spirituelle. Aussi suis-je appelé Ah Rit d'Humble d'Or par les affiches du métro [I protest! True filiation is spiritual. Thus my name is Harry Dumbledore / Oh laugh of humble of gold by the metro ads]" (*LXiR* 19). Putting aside the reference to the Harry Potter series, in which he laughingly interpellates himself as both the best student and the best wizard – thus ironically in a somewhat self-contradictory position – Dustan can be said to be magically defining his relation to others. No longer held captive by the lines of command, Dustan thus aligns himself with the freedoms obtained by women a century ago, once reproduction could be separated from being maintained in a chattel-like status. The position of freedom is that of revolution: the possibility of atomizing or nomadizing one's own position along a line, which, for Dustan, is inevitably a sexual one; here he plays on Houellebecq's title, *Les Particules élémentaires*: "Les Parties Culs, élémentaires […] La deuxième révolution sexuelle, la vraie, celle en profondeur [The Ass Parts, elementary. The second sexual revolution, the true one, this one in depth]" (26).

Sexual freedom therefore does not mean simply the ability to have sex with whom one wants but the freedom to express sex and sexuality in the ways in which one wishes. This takes a double form for Dustan. Consonant with his concept of being interpellated in

---

[14] Of Lacan, Dustan comments cryptically: "Un En Je / Le Lac A Nismes [One in I / The Lake in Nîmes]" (*LXiR* 150). This can be glossed as "Un ange / le lacanisme [An angel / Lacanianism]." So Lacanianism, instead of being a liberatory psychoanalysis, becomes the patriarchal angel or the false figure of identity: "One in 'I.'"

a spectacular fashion is the blurring of lines between human and non-human, between the self and the projected image of the self: "C'est avec War Hole queue tout (ça) a commencé [Everything began with War Hole]" (*LXiR* 32). Andy Warhol, plier of self as pop art, is central to this mode of existence because of the ways in which he made the existence of the self a performative, spectacular, and specular fiction. But if Warhol was the beginning, if Warhol eroticized the other, if Warhol turned every specular relation into a homoerotic one (even if he did not visibly homoeroticize his own position), and if Warhol declared war on the ideology of holes, both proper and improper, Warhol effectively destabilizes the figure of affiliation and rejects the family by moving the individual towards a homosocial bond with others, and this regardless of the sex of the individual involved.[15]

Where Dustan goes far beyond Warhol's vaguely anarchic, but more visibly nomadic, sexuality, is in pushing the envelope on what the consequences of that sexuality necessarily imply for a change in the world. Whereas Warhol was behind closed doors, or in a consensual situation – one paid to see Joe Dallessandro naked – with Dustan, the sexuality forces the self and other, as it insists on the images of self and other to accept a renewed and changed version of the sexual landscape. It is not that there are no closets; it is rather that the other can no longer walk around with blinkers on. Indeed, it seems that sexual exhibitionism, in Dustan's mind, is an eventual certainty:

> Bander en public. sur [sic] les plages nudistes, ça va se faire, ça aussi. Dans 10, 20, 30 (siècles) (non, je rigole: ans).
>
> Écarter les jambes, montrer sa chatte (sur les plages nudistes).[16]
>
> Le cul, idem.
>
> Enfin, les organes génitaux et autres, EN CORPs PLUS sALEs, comme les autres (organes). Tout sur le même plan. (*LXiR* 33)

---

[15] Warhol appears in *Dernier roman* as well: "Parce qu'il est de droite. Et que c'est un humaniste (*tutti buoni*, comme les chiens) et un libéral (*I think people should be free to do what they like*) et un penseur du *queer* critique [...] [Because he is on the right. And he's a humanist (*tutti buoni*, like dogs) and a libertarian (*I think people should be free to do what they like*) and a thinker of *queer* criticism]" (*DR* 19).

[16] Here is another rare instance of an allusion to the feminine.

[To have a hard-on in public. at nude beaches, that will happen too.
In 10, 20, 30 (centuries) (no, I'm joking: years).

Spread her legs and show her cunt (at nude beaches).

The ass, same.

Finally, genital organs and others. In dirtier bodies, like other organs.
Everything on the same plan.]

The body is no longer a locus in which some parts are private and some
are public, but rather a locus in which the privates are potentially as
public as the other body parts. Dustan is not proposing that people
have sex on every street corner; rather, he wants his readers to see the
conceptual consequences of the sexual revolution. In so doing, he is
reaching back through Lyotard's libidinal band and Bataille's "solar
anus" – Bataille for whom, precisely, as for Warhol, everything was
parody – to a long tradition of French libertinage in general and
Sade in particular. But he is most particularly asking his readers to
look towards a different future, one that is not hamstrung and in
which sex and sexuality fulfill the consequences of their liberation;
he rallies against the remaining structures of the heteronormative
order. And even if monogamy has often been more a myth than
a reality in many times and places, it is a convenient straw man
against which everyone opposed to the (hetero)normal can – and
should – rally: "*On n'appartient qu'à soi. Constitutionnalisons au
passage la liberté sexuelle. Et par conséquent, réformons le mariage:
finie la fidélité obligatoire! Et la monogamie!* [*One belongs only to
oneself.* Let us make sexual freedom part of the constitution. And in
consequence, let's reform marriage: no more obligatory faithfulness!
And monogamy as well!]" (23).

For Dustan, then, sexual liberation does not mean simply a
proactive, forward-looking freedom from constraint; it also means
the necessity and the work associated with the undoing of the damage
of the *non/nom du père* in what he calls diseducation, in an undoing
of the system that maintains strict divisions of sexes, genders,
attributes, and roles: "*Déséduquer (néol.): vb transitif et intran-
sigeant: apprendre à ne rien perdre de l'enfance* [*Disconformate
(neol.): transitive and intransigent verb: learn to lose nothing
of childhood*]" (*LXiR* 22). Let us remember that "educate" and
éduquer are somewhat false cognates, for "educate" relates to
the pedagogical process in school (or a school-like structure) and
éduquer relates to the formation of a human being as an adult: the

learning of manners, behaviors, and mores within the family. So Dustan is being much more far-reaching here in that he is suggesting that adults retain their polymorphous perversity throughout their lives. Dustan translates that perversity into a restoration of the whole, into a negation of the castration he sees as being performed by society on every individual. Witness this exchange in one of the dialogues/interviews in the book:

> On a imppression [sic] Queue selon toi le manQueue fondamental de l'être humain, c'est le refoulement sexuel. Tu présentes l'homme ohsexualité généralisée comme la parousie, ce Qui nous manQueue, le truc ultime, la plénitude ...
>
> Je pense queue c'est une énorme chose retirée. c'est [sic] l'un des trucs sur le retrait duQuel est fondé la troupeauisation des gens, c'est clair. On les châtre, après ça fait des gentils moutons châtrés. An on ler coupe les couilles, les gens sont dociles.] (56)

> [One has the impression that according to you the fundamental lack in humans is sexual repression. You present generalized homosexuality as parousia, what we lack, the ultimate thing, plenitude ...
>
> I think that it is an enormous thing that is removed. It is one of the things on the removal of which the herding of people is based, that is clear. They are castrated, after which they are nice castrated sheep. When their balls are cut off, people are docile.]

As I have indicated, in a systematic and sophomoric visual pun, in parts of the books Dustan replaces the relative pronoun "que" with the word "queue," a slang word for penis, and wherever he can, he capitalizes the letter Q, which sounds of course like the slang word for backside, "cul." The forefront is given to the two organs most thought of when imagining male homosexual sex; he does not, for example, capitalize the letters "con" [cunt], despite their frequent use as a prefix in French. Rather, he insists on uncastrating the text, on making it hard, and on putting male–male sex in front of the eyes of all readers, as if only sodomy could liberate us from our forced herding and repression and as if only male homosexuality could be the advent, the second coming, or the fulfillment – the *parousia* – of everyone's existence. Lack in the present becomes plenitude in the future.

Yet this homosexuality that is supposed to liberate all of us is not without its prejudices; it is a pretense to the universal without actually being a universal, for Dustan aestheticizes it. In so doing he moves it away from the post-modern sexuality in Houellebecq's work (and in that of Despentes and Angot as well), and produces a kind of rift in what might have seemed to be a similar approach. In fact, he evokes Houellebecq in particular, whose characters seem to resonate with Dustan because of the "real" nature of their bodies, but Dustan opposes the vision that one of Houellebecq's characters has of a body without sexuality:

> Je pense Queue c'est essentiel d'être en fortme [sic]. DAns [sic] Houellebecq il y a ça mais ultradramatisé, puisQueue dAns les Particules, ces pe(u)rsonnages c'est des nazes, moches mal foutus comme lui et puis il y en un Qui a le fantasme d'une espèce d'humain fort avec un vrai corrps [sic], sauf Queue son truc c'est un corrps sAns sexualité, pas d'accorrd [sic] (*LXiR* 59).[17]

> [I think it is essential to be in shape. In Houellebecq, it is there, but ultradramatized, since in the Particles, the characters are jerks, ugly like him, and there is one who fantasized about a strong human with a real body, but his thing is a body without sexuality, I don't agree.]

Houellebecq's work is profoundly heterosexual, insistent on the difference between men and women, and grounded in a bivalent system of oppositional sexualities; it is certainly true that Houellebecq's characters, especially in *Les Particules élémentaires*, are not among the beautiful people or the glitterati, and, given the hype with which sexuality is often represented, we can say that they are far from the ideals of post-modern representations of sexualities. Whereas Houellebecq distinguishes between the abject (his male characters) and those always already abjected (his female characters), Dustan rejects that abjection, at least on the masculine side of the fence.

Arguably, in raising male homosexuality to the status of parousia and a universal, it is rather Dustan who moves sexuality away from the body or the body away from sexuality, for sexuality makes sense only when set in relation to other sexualities. In one articulation of the matter, Dustan moves away from the notion of gay toward a wider concept of American-style queerness, yet he de-emphasizes the role of sex and sexuality within that new-found queerness, only

---

[17] Dustan, who in real life was a graduate of Sciences Po, elsewhere refers to Locke, Marx, and Hobbes, whom he calls, using Houellebecq's title, "les particules élémentaires [elementary particles]" (*LXiR* 98).

to fold everything into a very sixties-inspired fantasy of dancing as a metaphor for a utopian idyll:

> mais hé t'es trop ça n'existe pas plus Queue pédé ... Maintenant je suis au point Queue je suis plus pédé, je refuse d'être défini par rapports à ma sexualité blablabla. Je trouve ça lourd. [...] En ce moment j'aurais envie de me dire g au sense le plus large du terme, ça veut dire Qui fait la fête, party people. En plus, dAns une vraie fête réussie plus pe(ur)sonne ne se demande Qui est g ou hé t'es trop, il y a tout le monde qui dAnse [sic], y a vraiment un truc d'intégration. (80)

> [but hetero doesn't exist any more than fag does. Now I'm at a state where I am no longer a fag, I refuse to be defined relative to my sexuality blablabla. I find that heavy. [...]. Now I want to say I'm gay in the widest possible meaning of the word, that means celebrating, party people. Moreover, in a really successful party, no one asks nowadays who is gay and who is hetero, everyone is dancing, it is an integration thing.]

So the implication is that the queered gay aesthetic – the dancing is real and metaphorical – should replace the sexualities on which certain decisions are made. The figure of the queer collectivity, vaguely Rousseauist in its earnest utopianism, is fairly transparent, as what he is really asking for is the translation of that party into everyday life: no one should be defined by the specificity of his or her sexuality, or by the specific sexual acts she or he engages in, even if those acts are performed visibly in front of others (see above). If he does not actually say that visible genitalia on nudist beaches leads to visible copulation, he is implying it, and that visible copulation, arguably, could be extended to the Boulevard St. Germain.

Dustan's generalizing of gay into a universal queer still comes at a price, because there is within his discourse an implicit and sometimes explicit misogyny that queers the possibility of the universal. Even if he is not exclusively gay, even if he practices, at least in the fantasy world, an omnisexuality that tends to mimic polymorphous perversity, there is a strange nexus of behavior implicit in some of his comments that seems, at least in part, to be nothing more than a willful flouting of conventions for the sake of thumbing his nose at the establishment:

> [I]nstinctivement je suis une grosse salope donc je couche. Instinctivement le sexe me dégoute en général parce Queue je suis

occidental et effectivement j'ai un gros truc avec les hommes mais j'ai un truc aussi, moins puissant mais Qui existe aussi, avec les femmess, c'est An [sic] même des êtres humains, je me tape(u)rais bien des chiens, j'aurais bien des relations amourese [sic] avec des chiens mais je ne le fais pas. (*LXiR* 82)

[Instinctively I'm a big slut, so I have sex. Instinctively sex disgusts me in general because I am a Westerner and in fact, I have a big thing for men, but I have a thing, less strong but it exists as well, with women, they are still human, I'd hit on dogs, I would have sexual relations with dogs, but I don't.]

Yet the two uses of "instinctively" do not mesh, for if he believes that he is instinctively polymorphously perverse, being disgusted with sex is precisely learned behavior, not instinctive. If Western society demonizes sex, and, in the process, if it reduces and debases women, this is certainly behavior that is taught to Dustan as a member of that society.[18] And his misogyny – the dismissive "quand-même" that says that women are human beings too – may very well also be learned behavior, but it might be incumbent on him to recognize that. This, however, is something he does not do, except at one point late in the work, where he recognizes the "second" sex as precisely something that has been created as such; for Dustan, the woman is always already raped: "Je ne sais pas quelle est la loi, dit la femme, je n'ai jamais eu que cet homme-là. Et qui me viole à sa façon. Fatalement [I don't know what the law is, the woman says, I have had only that man. And he rapes me as he will. Fatally]" (170). The Lacanian law that says no makes that one exception: thou shalt rape women.

Dustan's vision of contemporary sexuality, his sexuality and its codes in his version of the masculine, and queer sexuality in general, is one that is visual and changeable, precisely because – despite the *non/nom* of society – one can work at changing it. In this, he militantly outflanks Judith Butler, for whom the repeated performance of one's sexuality is socially constructed and not dependent on acts of will. Thus Dustan is far more in the French camp, following (*nolens*

---

[18]   And Dustan is not entirely consistent, as, at one point, he allows that homosexuals make a choice: "Les homme ohs sont bien placés parce Qu'ils ont fait un choix de vie, ils ont rompu avec l'ordre de dévitalisation Qu'on ler propoc'est, de représentation plustôt Queue d'action [Homos are well placed because they have made a choice in life, they have broken with the system of devitalization. That their proposal is representation rather than action]" (*LXiR* 99). Arguably then, they could choose not to be disgusted by sex.

volens) liberatory arguments in Deleuze and Guattari and Lyotard, among others. When he is not bound by his contradictions, when he is making a liberatory argument, Dustan essentially argues in favor of an avatar of metrosexuality. According to Wordspy, the word "metrosexual" was first used by Mark Simpson in 1994, in an article titled "Here Come the Mirror Men." In early usage, the word referred entirely to straight men living in an urban area, men who dressed well, used expensive grooming products, used the gym, and so forth. More recently, Simpson has extended the definition, in his article "Metrosexual? That Rings a Bell ...": "He might be officially gay, straight or bisexual, but this is utterly immaterial because he has clearly taken himself as his own love object and pleasure as his sexual preference." What is essential is that metrosexuality is by and large visual rather than linguistic. And Dustan recognizes this:

> An la sociologue dit nouvelle humanité moi je pense: on est les premiers à vivre dAns une civilisation de l'image et du corps opposé à une civilisation de l'esprit et de la tête. On est les premiers à faire une rupture avec une civilisation Qui a éclos, on va dire, au XVI [sic] siècle et s'est cristallisé à la fin du XVIIIs, quoi, avec les Lumières. (*LXiR* 90).

> [When sociology speaks of new humanity, I think: we are the first to live in a civilization of the image and the body opposed to a civilization of the mind and the head. We are the first to split with a civilization that burgeoned in the sixteenth century and that was crystallized at the end of the eighteenth, with the Enlightenment.]

If, for the last hundred years, homosexuality found its definition or articulation in language, specifically literature and a medical, juridical, and psychiatric discourse, Dustan is now arguing that the main articulation comes through the visual reorientation of the Western world, mediated in particular through the vision of the urban landscape and its denizens. So, for Dustan, for example, "les homométrosexuels [homometrosexuals]" (*LXiR* 120) are people who, within the metropolis, see each other, imitate each other, and reflect each other's images. Queerness has become a Girardian phenomenon of mimesis that is not mediated (or deconstructed) to any great extent through language. So when Dustan plays with language, it is not just a joke, it has a serious component: "Je suis pourre labandons de lourd too grave [I am for abandoning (too heavy) spelling]" (138). Correct writing – orthography – is too heavy and too sad. Again, the *nom/non du père*, the correct writing of the father, weighs too heavily on his/one's sexuality and their articulations in codes of masculinity.[19]

Dustan's final position is one of a liberatory manifesto, but as we shall see, it is not without a penultimate nod at the *bête noire* of the paternal name. First, the manifesto:

La Vrè vi Comens Isi

Manifest

Nou:

Répudion Le Triste Politicmen Corect Judéocr'tiin É Son Nalié Le Nuizible Sistèm De Cast.

Nou Déclaron Gé Républicin, Ardi Démocrat, Libéro Régulé, Libertin Zacharné, Ere Comunotère É Fièr Payin. (*LXiR* 165)

[Real life Begins Here

Manifest

We

Repudiate The Sad Politically Correct, Judeo-Christian And Its Ally the Harmful Caste System.

We Declare that We Are Gay Republicans, Brave Democrats, Regulated Liberals, Dedicated Libertines, Communitary Era And Proud Pagans.]

This is a new declaration of the rights of man for the twenty-first-century metrosexual that Dustan believes us all to be, or at least to be capable of being. Refusing the comfortable right and left solutions, refusing all the "no"s of the past, Dustan militates for a future in the plural peopled with zealous libertines celebrating a new-found pagan freedom. Sex will be unbridled, the body will be unfettered, and ultimately laws and the Law of negativity will have to be changed, precisely because "we," the metrosexuals, are already there: "[Le] droit et les codes sont en retard sur la pensée, désunis de la pensée [Law and laws lag behind thought, are separated from thought]" (20). What we might add, quite simply, is that the law is also behind praxis and visibility. And it is no large effort to state that, in spite of all

[19] Metrosexuality is also part of a mutable sexual landscape. One day one can be a lipstick lesbian and another, a dominant figure in a bondage relationship: "my life as a: kid, teenager, kidult, lesbian, métrosexuel, vieux, etc ..." (*LXiR* 124; in approximate English in the original).

this rhetoric, repression still continues. We are not all metrosexuals, despite Dustan's fervent hope that we are all in the process of changing ourselves to become them. In a long diatribe toward the end of the book, Dustan continues to rail against the compulsory heterosexuality and heteronormativity in Western society, even if he has repeatedly shown that there is a visible, unrepressed, generalized queerness or metrosexuality. Yet clearly the official images by and large remain the same as they always have been:

> Balai dans le cul. Jusqu'à nos jours. Dévirilisation de l'Occident. D'un système inégalitaire à un système égal dans la castration. Envolés, partis, les paquets des hommes. Les pantalons gris de la bourgeoisie. Tout s'évanouit, se perd. Les couleurs, les paquets des hommes. Une domination plus subtile. Perverse. L'hétérosexualité ? De plus en plus obligatoire. De moins en moins de vieilles filles, de Monsieur, frère du roi. De plus en plus de Louis XIV, de Mitterrand, de Jospin ... Contrat social. Castration symbolique, ostentatoire, exhibée. [...] Vais à la messe, ne m'amuse jamais, une grande famille, enfants à ma femme, ai une maîtresse, ne suis pas homosexuel, reste dans le contrat. Total contrôle. Peuple de prêtres. Bourgeois curés. (*LXiR* 168)

> [One's head up one's ass.[20] Still today. A devirilization of the West. From an unequal system to a system equal in castration. Flown away, gone, men's baskets. Gray trousers of the middle classes. Everything fades, is lost. Colors, men's baskets. A more subtle domination. Perverse. Heterosexuality? More and more obligation. Fewer old maids, Monsieur, the king's brother. More and more Louis XIV, Mitterrands, Jospins ... Social contract. Symbolic, ostentation, exhibited castration. [...] Go to Mass, never have fun, a big family, children with my wife, have a mistress, am not homosexual, stay within the contract. Complete control. A nation of priests. Middle-class curates.]

The repressive system remains, despite all attempts to dislodge it, because it is so insidious, but also because it is fundamental and foundational to ideas of the nation-state, of official religion of whatever sort (even republicanism), of the Empire (Hardt and Negri) and its institutions, including the university (Readings). For pagan metrosexuality to reign, the entire system has to be changed. And

---

[20] The expression "avoir un balai dans le cul," which literally means to have a broom up one's ass, means to act in a high and mighty fashion and to be stuck up, to be haughty, with no recognition of how foolish one might appear to others. Hence this translation.

in fact Dustan has nothing less in mind than the total anarchic breakdown of the system, symbolized by a breakdown of the rules – of spelling, as we have seen, and of grammar: "Hommes trou du cul ont. Hommes jouit du cul. Femme peu faire homme jouir du cul. Homme peut faire homme jouir du cul. Homme a seins aussi. Homme être femme comme autre. Pédé être homme comme autres [Men asshole have. Men cum in ass. Woman can make man cum in ass. Man can make man cum in ass. Man has breasts too. Man a woman like any other. Fag a man like others]" (*LXiR* 170). And salvation comes through the recognition of this anarchic paganism as symbolized by our sense (*sens*) of sexuality, but also by the absence of sexuality, for *sans* and *sens* are homonyms: "La culture demain prend racine dans nos sens sexualité. LXiR [Culture tomorrow takes root in our senses sexuality. LXiR]" (174). Ultimately, of course, all of this is a reaction to and a profound criticism of heterosexuality, not only in its dominance, but also in its insistence that it is primary, even if nowadays that is no longer the case, even if the current and future possibilities of reproduction are more and more potentially dissociated from the biological needs of heterosexuality. For Dustan, heterosexuality is "ce régime de parcage productif des mâles par les eunuques et les femelles, les jaloux, les envieux [this scheme of productive penning of males by eunuchs and females, the jealous, the envious]" (*DR* 95). It is a position that Rémès reached several years earlier and to which I shall now turn.

II. Rémès: Re-erecting the *Cogito*

The initial line of Érik Rémès's novel or autofiction *Je bande donc je suis* [I have a hard-on, therefore I am], set apart as an epigraph, is "Seropo ergo sum [I am poz therefore I am]" (13). Rémès is playing not only on Descartes's most famous statement, the foundation of French rational thought, but also on a long line of parodic and not so parodic thought, the most famous of which is in Aldous Huxley's *Eyeless in Gaza*: "caco ergo sum? Eructo ergo sum? Or, escaping solipsism, why not futuo ergo sumus" (92).[21] Starting the work with

[21] In a personal communication to the author, Érik Rémès has assured me that, while familiar with the work of Aldous Huxley, he did not know this parody from *Eyeless in Gaza*.

this line put not only existence but also Frenchness into question. What does it mean to be French? What does it mean to exist? And what, one hastens to add, does it mean to be HIV⁺ in such a situation: how is seropositivity related to existence, existence as a Frenchman, and existence in general in a post-modern world? Unlike the cogito, seropositivity requires a previous action, a penetration, and a precedent. Between the title and the restructuring of the cogito, between the title and the beginning of the text, there will always have been an action, the action that is defined by the title of the other book in question, *Serial Fucker*: I penetrate/I have been penetrated, therefore I am.

Both the novel itself and the initial line of the work, as it plays on the cogito, set Rémès apart from others of his generation writing in France today, whatever the stripe of their sexuality: whereas many may be thought of as playing on the surface of the phenomenological – this is what happened to me, this is what I have lived – Rémès is interesting in articulating a problematic of being through that existence. This is not to say that he does not share either in the habitus of a post-modern sexuality or in a shared vision of what seropositivity may mean in an ongoing existence; simply put, he introduces a philosophical angle to a kind of contemporary literature. In a sense, one could compare him to Guillaume Dustan, who was also the editor of the series in which *Je bande* was published. And just as Dustan has a manifesto in *LXiR*, Rémès has one as well on "cyber-cochonnes [cyber-sows]" in *Serial Fucker*. Rémès's work does not constitute an overt political appeal to the extent that Dustan's does, which may reflect nothing more than a personal penchant or a difference in educational backgrounds: Dustan was an *énarque* and has published on justice; Rémès's background is in philosophy and in psychology.

In starting with this double version of the cogito, marking erection and seropositivity, the author places the existence of self squarely within the sexual, within sexuality, within homosexuality, and within seropositive homosexuality in particular.[22] The narrator of

---

[22] The cogito returns in other guises: "Je bande (donc j'essuie) [I have a hard-on (therefore I wipe up)]" (*SF* 56); and most cleverly, given the decorporealization on which Descartes depends in the *Discours*, "J'ai un corps donc je suis. Corps travaillé, réapproprié, dompté, accepté, enfin: aimé [I have a body, therefore I am. A body that is worked, reappropriated, tamed, accepted, and finally loved]" (*SF* 22). In the second part of this sentence, one can see that Rémès and Dustan

the work marks this specifically and succinctly, as he underlines his discovery of who he is, through sex, which was the path or vehicle to access to the logos: "C'est très jeune donc que je pris conscience de moi-même. L'accès quoi? L'accès au logos. Lors de mes premiers rapports sexuels [I was thus very young when I became conscious of myself. Access then! Access to the *logos*. At the moment of my first sexual relations]" (*JB* 26). The novel is constructed so as to make that gay seropositive figure the essence of the being of the erstwhile protagonist, Berlin Tintin, clearly an alter ego for the author but sufficiently different from him and from the voice of *Serial Fucker* for us to take the time to distinguish between the two voices, for, as might be expected, the most important difference relates to the articulation of sexuality and specifically to seropositivity.[23] Before arriving there, it is meet to look at the condition of pre-seropositivity in *Je bande*.

The initial sexual encounter in the novel is perhaps an actual event, albeit a stereotypical one, or perhaps an invented one, but in any case it is constitutive of a sexuality in which the mark of the other is anything but versatility. Following an initial encounter with an Arab man, the character, when eleven years old, becomes the doxy for a group of Arab men, for whom he is nothing more

share a certain point of view of their own bodies, which they have learned to love. In *Maître*, there is another variant: "Cogito ergo boum [I think, therefore par-ty]" (219; also in *Guide* 140). In *Guide*, the most recent volume, it becomes "J'ai un corps donc je suis [I have a body therefore I am]" (244) and "Corps Seropo ergo sum [Poz body ergo sum]" (245). For Marchal (58), Rémès's version of the cogito "seems to reduce the cogito to the choice of a being-for-sex." I would not go that far, since, for Rémès, the sexual cogito is the founding moment, but not necessarily a reductive one.

23 Rémès labels *Serial Fucker* a novel, along with *Je bande donc je suis* and *Le Maître des amours*. While respecting this categorization, I would prefer to think of it as an autofiction, as it seems to posit a very real, or at least virtual, version of the rhetorical author, who, it would seem, bears more than a passing resemblance to the "real" author behind the prose. Moreover, it goes over some of the material already in *Je bande*, and if it were a novel, one would be tempted to talk about repetition. *Le Maître des amours* does refer occasionally to the "real" author, but the references are not central to the plot of the novel. One would not be wrong to see all three works as being autofictions to a greater or lesser extent. Clearly, the character's name refers in part to the series of *bandes dessinées* by Hergé, *Les Aventures de Tintin*. Rémès's volume, to make a pun, is certainly another kind of *bande dessinée*, which we could translate as a "drawn erection" or even a "graphic novel," in the sexual sense of the word "graphic."

than a convenient aperture in which to release pent-up sexual tensions:

> L'été de mes onze ans, je fus donc le fignard à foutre de ces mâles orientaux, un harem inverti en sorte. Ces beaux Arabes aux sexes massifs, prégnants et lourds. Une quinzaine d'Arabes en transes, cela ne prenait pas beaucoup de temps pour qu'ils dégazent. Ils jouissait vite ces hommes-là. Je bandais pour eux. (*JB* 28)

> [The summer I was eleven, I was thus the doxy of those oriental males, a sort of inverted harem. Those handsome Arabs with massive, pregnant, and heavy sex organs. Fifteen or so Arabs in a trance; it didn't take them long to shoot. Those men came quickly. I had a hard-on for them.]

The focus of the individual's sexuality – I do not name him because he does not invent his individuation until shortly after – is this repeated penetration, an interiority that he will return to time and again, to mark his being. And yet the marking of him as an individual will not be complete until an act of incest occurs that is defined even more by intimacy and by the massive nature of the male member.

He touches the genitals of his stepfather (*JB* 35), who returns the touch, after which they have sex together. He returns home and poisons his adoptive mother with rat poison (*JB* 38). Precisely on the protagonist's eighteenth birthday, the stepfather dies of breast cancer and the very same day (in 1989), the "aventures du gamin Berlin Tintin [adventures of the kid Berlin Tintin]" begin (*JB* 39). This incestuous relationship returns in *Serial Fucker* (113), where the precision given makes the relation a sacred and self-engendering one that literally produces the protagonist through a mixture of his stepfather's sperm and his own blood that he then ingests:

> Ce sexe si gros qui me déchira si longtemps. Le souvenir de ce membre puissant qui déchirait mon hymen d'enfant. [...]. Mon sang sur son sexe que je léchais. Amour suave et amer. Du sperme et du sang. Voilà ce qu'est la vie. Juste un peu de jus et de rouge mêlés, qui se jouxtent et s'étreignent à jamais. Je suis le fils du sperme et du sang. (*SF* 113)

> [Such a fat sex organ that tore me up for so long. The memory of that powerful member that tore up my child's hymen. [...] My blood on his penis that I licked. Smooth and bitter love. Sperm and blood. That is life. Just a bit of jizz and red mixed, up against one another, hugging each other forever. I am the son of sperm and blood.]

The definition of the self depends on the incorporation of the *nom du père*, the Lacanian phallus of the father than makes him complete, or seems to, were it not in and of itself a recognition of a lack, something the author states directly much later in the work in a scene to which I shall return at greater length: "Le phallus est la représentation du manque, son incarnation. Le phallus est l'être-là du non-être du manque [The phallus is the representation of the lack, its incarnation. The phallus is the being-here of the non-being of the lack]" (*JB* 144).[24] As the writing goes on, in a kind of progress narrative of self-discovery, the author marks his work by indicating the year and the number of AIDS cases in France. Infected early on in his own sexual activity, aged eighteen in 1989 (*JB* 47), the protagonist essentially spends his entire sexual existence as a seropositive man. Even though there is, obviously, a seroconversion, it happens so early that, in a sense, Berlin Tintin is always already HIV+, always already in a position of living seropositivity.[25] In distinction to many contemporary AIDS texts, then, here there is no nostalgia for the moment before conversion, nor any nostalgia for returning to a time in which AIDS did not exist. On the contrary, in *Je bande*, Rémès sounds a periodic tattoo; as the years go on, the total number of cases increases; this tolling bell marks the narrative and marks the world as one in which seropositivity looms ever larger. Things change in *Serial Fucker*, where the author tells the same story about himself, but in which he is twenty-four years old. Thus in the later book, Rémès has known seronegativity and knows the differences between the two positions, since we assume that he was not a virgin at age twenty-four and has tested negative previous to being with Bruno. In *Je bande*, it is thus important for Rémès to elide the difference precisely to enable his fictional alter ego to live entirely within seropositivity, to inhabit it, and in so doing to redefine sexuality from within seropositivity.

[24] In *Le Maître*, which serves as the anti-text for the two other novels/autofictions, Berlin Tintin is configured as the phallus – he is well-endowed, with a penis of 22 cm (21), and he is considered the phallus by the other: "'Berlin Tintin, tu es ma référence phallique' [Berlin Tintin, you are my phallic reference]" (67). Equally significantly, he is the Hegelian/Lacanian figure of absolute knowledge: "'Tu es une vraie encyclopédé, Berlin Tintin' [You are a real encyclopedia, Berlin Tintin]" (157).

[25] In *Le Maître des amours*, Berlin Tintin is configured as a bisexual, seronegative masseur and prostitute (10 and 37) who insists on the use of condoms for professional and health reasons (23 and 37).

As I have indicated, the initial defining moment, the confusion of the (step)fatherly phallus with the logos itself, is a classic Lacanian sign of the lack, a lack that is endlessly repeated in serial intercourse, as if the introjected penis of the other, the Kleinian partial object *par excellence*, could remark that moment of fulfillment and intimacy that he nostalgically seeks anew, and as if it could cover the lack in being. At the same time, as Rémès moves the seroconversion from a real age of twenty-four to a fictional age of eighteen that coincides with the death of the father, the author sets up that seropositivity as constitutive of his being. Seropositivity equals sexuality equals lack equals fulfillment equals disappointment. As that moment is created as the origin and source of the narrator's cogito/coitus, it is necessary to articulate the various incarnations of being, and all of this under the signs of AIDS and his individual seropositivity. In a section entitled "Some questions then" (*JB* 55–56), Rémès asks a whole series of questions ranging from "Who am I?" to "Why do I like to get fucked?" to "Why be ashamed of my sexuality?" to "How to cohabit with my virus?"[26] With rare exceptions, the author does not answer the series of questions except insofar as the book itself is the answer, in a non-linear fashion, to all the questions, both asked and unasked. At the same time, the series of questions stands as a block of rhetoric with which all readers might somehow engage, not only those who may have had to ask themselves the same questions at some point. Thus does the text go beyond a simple identificatory mechanism to create a sort of disidentification in the reader.[27]

Much later these questions become rearticulated in a guide to safe(r) sex, a kind of set of answers to the questions he has asked earlier. Rémès suggests twelve keys to *savoir-vivre* (*JB* 136–38). These include: "having a phallus in hand," "shake well before use," "always have some condoms," all sorts of indications about how to

---

[26] Elsewhere, he answers this last question: "Le sida est un colocataire avec qui je partage mon existence et les murs intérieurs. Mais, c'est moi qui reste le propriétaire de mon être [AIDS is a roommate with whom I share my existence and inside walls. But I remain the owner of my being]" (*JB* 269).

[27] Rémès likes making series, whether it is these questions, the reality of the number of AIDS cases, or a series of commonplaces: "Tu suces? T'es passif? Tu vas chercher des capotes au bar? O.K., mais tu jouis pas en moi, Il m'adore, même si c'est moi qui l'ai plombé [Do you suck? Are you a bottom? Are you gonna get rubbers at the bar? OK, but don't cum in me. He adores me, even if it's me who pounded him]" (*SF* 32–33).

use condoms and gel correctly, and "after ejaculation of/from the tool [du poireau], pull out before getting soft." It should be noted that Rémès's how-to guide to life is singularly devoted to the art of anal penetration in a world in which AIDS is rampant: everything focuses on phalluses and anuses, the meeting of which constantly repeats the initial scenarios and constitutes the reinscription.[28] But it is not just the immediate biological locus that counts for sex, it is also the shared public locus of bars and backrooms that serves as a locus in which desire and inscription are remarked. Thus, as is the case for Dustan, but not for Camus and even less so for Guibert, the entire set of gay venues is considered as a network that marks the individual's location within a community and system. When reading Camus, and especially the later Camus, one has the idea of a solitary individual cruising and/or going to the baths, in much the same way that Guy Hocquenghem traced a solitary mapping of gay desire in parts of his book *Le Gay Voyage*. For Guibert, of course, the voyage was through intimate space and personal contact, albeit sometimes mediated through the Minitel (Camus uses the electronic network as well). What marks the space of Dustan and of Rémès, however, is its openness, its citified nature, and the construction of an entire zone of gay spaces that corresponds, by and large, though not exclusively, to the Marais. Beyond that, however, there is an insistence in Rémès's work on a territorialization of that space that goes beyond Dustan's dances. Rémès repeatedly marks and remarks the space with a gesture that defines it as belonging to them, the gay/queer men of Paris:

> Bon nombre d'activités ludiques, phalliques et anales se passent au bar même. D'ailleurs, faites attention à ne pas vous faire pisser dessus accidentellement ou recevoir de la bière à la gueule par un malotru comme Didier ou François. (*JB* 102)

> [A good number of playful, phallic, and anal activities even take place in the bar. Oh, and be careful not to get pissed on accidentally or to get beer in your face from a boor like Didier or François.]

It may sound banal to consider this a marking of territory, but it does serve as a sign of the collectivity and as a distinct sign at that. In the outside world, in the world of heteronormativity, one is not

---

[28] This "how-to" list is also found as the "Manuel ludique de savoir vivre" in *Guide* (304–305).

accidentally urinated on, and bar-room brawls do not resemble this flow of liquid indicated by Rémès. Again, in the baths and the backrooms, the same thing happens: "J'aime à m'y asseoir [in a backroom] [...] pour cueillir la rosée des volubilis et le nectar des garçons [...], ou bien l'inverse, car je suis très-très vice et versa [I like to sit there to collect the dew from the volubilis and the nectar from the boys, or the opposite, for I am very-very vice versa]" (*JB* 102). Rémès does not hesitate to conclude this sentence with a double pun, on vice versa: "vice" is also a morally negative practice, and "versa" is short for "versatile," i.e., willing to be either top or bottom in an act of anal intercourse.

Rémès's space is characterized by this multiple flow, as I have already indicated: the "je bande donc je suis" is modified, as it is transformed into "on m'encule, donc je suis"; it is rendered here by the "très-très vice versa" and globalized on the next page into a total nexus of interrelations and tricks, be they individual acts or the collective space of this gathering of men transformed into a gigantic sex organ:

> Le Transfert, c'est un *trixx*, une partouze monstre entre Genet, Burroughs, et les autres du bastringue. Le Palais Omnisports du droit à la luisance. Ce bar est une bite, un vrai cul de salope, l'expression obscène et brute du désir. (*JB* 103)

> [The Transfert is a trick, a monster orgy with Genet, Burroughs, and the others from the disco. The Omnisports Palace's right to shine. This bar is a cock, a whore's ass, the obscene and rough expression of desire.]

The bar itself becomes identified as the organs of same-sex male penetration and copulation, in a personification by which it is transformed into those body parts. In so doing, Rémès completely sexualizes the world of queerness, as if there were nothing outside that world and nothing within it except for sex. And again, Rémès limits the world view to the act of sex. Whereas Dustan spends time discussing the preliminaries and pre-coital behavior, Rémès generally focuses almost entirely on the act itself and its implications for who he is:

> Au QG le week-end j'adore faire le gorille ou la grosse truie en rut et couiner comme une cyber-cochonne de l'espace. Mais aussi me foutre à poil, me rouler par terre et me faire pisser dessus. Je suis la toute-dingo. (*JB* 103–104)

[At weekends in the QG, I love to play the gorilla or the big sow in heat and oink like a cyber-sow from outer space. But also to get naked, roll around on the ground, and get pissed on. I am totally crazy.]

Without the state of abjection found in Genet's writing, Rémès still manages to render this world non-anthropocentric. Like a rutting sow, Rémès's character becomes a complete slave to a desubjectified vision of self in which all is determined by sexualized body parts and every movement moves Berlin Tintin away from a humanized, heteronormative vision of the world. He will extend that vision in his treatise on "cyber-sows" to be discussed below.

It would be wrong to argue that Rémès entirely dismisses straight men and all women, for he does reflect on the difference between the sexes in a rehearsal of classic Lacanian thought. Readers may think that here Rémès goes rather simplistically over the top, as he marshals classic phallic symbolism and thrusts it wholeheartedly into a Lacanian model of phallocentric discourse and power. But this simplicity is itself a reflection of the extent to which contemporary gay writing is often informed by Lacanian psychoanalysis – as well as Deleuzian rhizomatics, Derridean deconstruction, and Foucauldian epistemes. These four theoretical positions, while often contradictory among themselves, fed notions of decentering and displacement in the gay liberation movement, in the initial discourses of queer theory, as is evidenced for example in the theoretical writings of Guy Hocquenghem, heavily informed by Deleuzian models, and in the various ramifications that have crisscrossed the Atlantic in the past forty years. It is no wonder then that certain "aware" discourses, such as that of Rémès, use the vocabulary and *prises de position* of "French theory," retranslated, at least in part, from queer theory as it developed in the United States in particular. If Dustan has recourse to that other "import," American pornography, Rémès uses "French theory" that has been imported from the US:

Urinant dans les W.-C. du Quetzal, en regardant par inadvertance le sexe gouleyant de mes camarades de latrines, je me disais que la queue de l'homme, le superbe signifiant phallique comme disait l'Autre avec un grand A, est bien le symbole revendicatif et positif de la virilité. Cette toute proéminence est aussi le symbole de la puissance et de la volonté, ainsi que le lieu du manque. Le manque est cette visqueuse et glissante absence d'objet, une éclipse de l'être, de l'être qui est en n'étant pas. Le manque est simultanément de l'ordre de l'être et du non-être. Il montre ce qui n'est pas. Le phallus est la représentation du manque, son incarnation. Le phallus est l'être-là du non-être du manque. (*JB* 144)

[Urinating in the toilets of the Quetzal and inadvertently looking at the feisty genitals of my neighbors at the latrine, I would tell myself that a man's dick, the superb phallic signifier, as the Other with a capital O called it, is really the protesting and positive symbol of virility. This complete pre-eminence is also the symbol of power and will, as well as the locus of lack. The lack is this viscous and slippery absence of the object, an eclipse of being, of the being that is while not being.]

But this thought is actually transformed, given what has already been said about the spaces of reversibility of genitalia, of the possibility of the man, the possessor of the phallus, bottoming for another man. It is a copulation of Lacan with the cogito, the space of desire being the locus of the *jouissance* and the simultaneous presence of the phallus and of the lack of the phallus. When the author (naturally) moves, albeit briefly, to discussing women, one can wonder if he has not really moved to a discussion of all who are penetrated, the space of the vagina or the anus being uniformly and indistinguishably marked. Again, the Lacanian system is reduced to its basics, and one could argue that Rémès does not go even that far, but simply anchors his discourse in the simplest aspects of the Freudian argument. At the same time, the "oui-oui" to which he resorts here and elsewhere seems to mark a self-awareness about using such an approach, as if he is, on a metacritical level, well aware that he is inserting a commonplace to mark his discursive position:

Continuant mes activités fluides, je me disais aussi que la simple observation empirique des femmes permettait de voir qu'en fait celles-ci ne recherchent en l'homme que ce symbole, le phallus, oui-oui, pour pallier à leur propre manque, leur vide. (*JB* 144)

[Continuing my fluid activities, I thought that the simple empirical observation of/by women allowed one to see that, in fact, they looked only for this symbol in men, the phallus, yes indeed, to make up for their own lack and emptiness.]

In short, he is reinscribing the lack of the father's phallus, the gape left by its absence, as he implicitly transforms the anuses of passive/receptive men into ersatz vaginas, as if thereby to recapitulate and reorganize the feminine within the male queer body and gaze.

But if the transformation is not spelled out at this point in the novel, it is subsequently: "Je reviens de Marrakech où je me suis fait coudre la chatte: maintenant, je suis un mâle, un vrai [I have just returned from Marrakesh, where I had my pussy sewn up: now I am a male, a real one]" (*JB* 222). Thus being a man does not necessarily mean having a phallus, and arguably, in this Lacan-inspired novel, no one really has the phallus except for the absent father. Being a man is rather defined through negation, the absence of female genitalia (or the male metonym thereof), though in this flight of fancy it is not clear whether Berlin Tintin proposes that he had his fantasized vagina sewn up, or his anus (which is, of course, physiologically problematic, to say the least). In any case, the author does not stop there, but goes one more revolution in conceiving of bivalent sexuality. And again, the recurring "oui-oui" of assent and recognition of assent marks the discourse as one in which the emerging post-modern queer subject is not, as Dustan would have it, free to dance until the end of time, but rather is still limited by discursive and epistemological possibilities. Thus, against Dustan's anarchy, Rémès offers a measured response that is the recognition of the limitations placed on even the most liberated of queer subjects:

> Ainsi, si j'ai tout l'air d'un homosexuel profondément débile, dégénéré et obsédé du cul, oui-oui, en fait, il n'en est rien puisque étant à la base une femme et couchant avec un très-très grand nombre d'hommes, je suis donc hétérosexuel. Mais un hétérosexuel débile, dégénéré et obsédé du cul, je l'admets. (*JB* 222–23).

> [Thus, if I seem to be a deeply troubled and degenerate homosexual, obsessed with ass, yes indeed, in fact, it is not at all the case, for, being a woman at heart and sleeping with a really big number of men, I am thus heterosexual. But a troubled and degenerate heterosexual obsessed with ass, I admit it.]

Thus the male vagina, be it real or imagined, even if closed, can never disappear, as opposed to the phallus that has always disappeared; the imaginary vagina becomes, in his representation, part of a Foucauldian discursitivity of space, penetration, and, necessarily, limits. Berlin Tintin and Rémès's other figures are always engendered logically as female, ready to be penetrated by a great number of men. As in earlier quotations in which he has redoubled a word, Rémès has once again queered his dialogue.

If the work continues with scenes of fisting (credited by Michel Foucault as being the twentieth century's greatest contribution to sexuality) and scat (*JB* 252–59), perhaps the most radical statements about sexuality relate to two scenes, one in each book.[29] His friend Thierry inserts a sound into his urethra: "Et puis, ça change des schémas classiques de la sexualité vouée aux sacro-saintes pénétrations et de l'archéo-dichotomie actif-passif. Nous sommes les toutes-transcendantes [And then, it is a change from the classical scenarios of sexuality devoted to sacrosanct penetrations and from the arche-dichotomy of active and passive. We are the completely-transcendental]" (*JB* 245). Experimental sexuality, what some might call extreme sexuality, becomes intellectually comprehensible, in much the same way that radical body modification does, by questioning the categories and antinomies within which we read any specific instance of sexuality (or body). Thus the primary dualism of male/female, active/passive, penetrator/penetrated, here as with the lengthy and explicit discussions of fisting and scat, is challenged by a novel redistribution of power and desire, rather than just a bending of the rules.

Referring to a Korean website, Rémès proceeds to describe a scene of circumcision, whereby he has reasonably unproblematically produced necrosis of the foreskin in a slave/whore [esclave/pute], then circumcised him, and then fed him the foreskin. Again, with Rémès there is the question of self-engenderment within the world of seropositivity, though in this case he does not indicate whether the other is HIV⁺ or HIV⁻. In any case, he concludes with an invocation of the ceremony of transubstantiation and the Eucharist: "'Mange, dis-je, ceci est ton corps. Le corps du Christ mort pour te sauver. Mange et tu seras pardonné d'exister' [Eat, I said, this is your body. The body of Christ who died to save you. Eat and you will be pardoned for existing]" (*SF* 157).

In both these cases, the duality and oppositionality of a bivalent sexual system give way to a queering of the system in a post-Deleuzean series of post-plug-in desiring machines. With Rémès, child of the post-industrial computer age, writing long after the Internet created a generation of surfers, it is not surprising that the term he invents

---

29 "Michel Foucault la [fist-fucking] définissait comme une des seules inventions sexuelles du vingtième siècle [Michel Foucault defined fist-fucking as one of the few sexual inventions of the twentieth century]" (*Maître* 213; also *Guide* 148).

is computer-based, for "cyber-cochonne" combines the word of the information age with the animality already discussed. Breaking away from the dualistic models is a way of breaking the hold that hetero-sexuality has on society, or more accurately, breaking the ubiquitous stranglehold of heteronormativity:

> Les hétéros, c'est un peu comme les caricatures d'Américains: ils parlent fort, sont vulgaires et gras, ont des goûts de chiottes, sont persuadés de leur supériorité et nous inondent de leur burger culture. Tout est crée pour eux: lois, institutions, imaginaires, etc. Les hétéros, c'est un peu comme Euro Disney: tout est fait pour les familles et les mouflets, il faut faire la queue pour être con et fier de l'être. [...] Et bien moi je les emmerde ces hétéros, je leur vomis dessus, je leur pisse à la raie. (*SF* 30–31)

> [Heteros are like caricatures of Americans: they speak loudly, are vulgar and fat, have the taste of shit-holes, are persuaded of their own superiority, and drown us in their burger culture. Everything is created for them: laws, institutions, imaginaries, etc. Heteros are a bit like Euro-Disney: everything is done for families and kids, you have to stand in line to be such an ass and be proud of it. As for me, I damn those heteros, I vomit on them, I piss on their cracks.]

Omnipresent heterosexuality or the ubiquity of the American empire end up being the same here: a pretense that the world can be clean (Euro-Disney) and without messy lines, a belief in a straight puritanical culture (*culture de curé*, one might say in French), a mechanization of the individual who agrees to stand in line as a well-behaved citizen ready to penetrate or be penetrated, it matters little.

But it does matter of course, it is a matter of life or death: seropositivity has consequences. And this is where the works of Rémès can produce problematic reactions in readers. We are all used to AIDS and HIV+ narratives at this point, and to that extent Rémès's recounting of his protagonists' seropositivity fits well in the landscape, or the seascape, of such writing:

> Le sida, c'est notre *Titanic* à nous les folles, les pédés, les toxicos et marginaux de tout poil. Donc, le virus c'est le *Titanic* des folles, et puis aussi, maintenant, les gens normaux, les hétéros. Notre paquebot viral suite à une rencontre malencontreuse s'est déchiré la coque comme on le dit de l'anus, le sang de la mer pénètre les coursives, inonde la salle des machines et stoppe les moteurs. [...] Le paquebot viral sombre lentement. Tel un pénis aqueux il se dresse maintenant

fièrement dans le ciel comme pour sodomiser le firmament, puis coule après l'orgasme. (*JB* 18).

[AIDS is the *Titanic* for us: fags, queers, druggies, and the marginalized of all sorts. Thus, the virus is the *Titanic* of the fags, and also now, normal people, heteros. Following an unfortunate meeting, our viral steamship had its hull ripped open, as one says of the anus, the blood of the sea penetrates the passageways, floods the engine room, and stops the motors. The viral steamship slips slowly. Like an aqueous penis, it sticks proudly up into the sky, as if to sodomize the firmament, then sinks after orgasm.]

Recognized as a devastating plague and as a disaster by the passengers, those on this new ship are mostly heading for a certain death. And yet this is no ship of fools; there is an anger among the passengers, who "do not go gently into that good night" and who rebel by sodomizing heaven itself in a heretical act that seems, in a world without heresy, sadly the last choice. Rémès's last line is a pun on the word *couler*: in the nautical world, it refers to a shipwreck. So this defiant ship-phallus will sink after its final attempt to return the favor of having been fatally infected, having been infected by fate. But at the same time, *couler* means to flow: so the phallus will continue to flow, even after the orgasm. Sign of the liquefaction of the world, this is also a sign both of the collapse of institutions and of the permanent reinfection of the universe. Rémès's image is one of a world always and eternally infected and in a state of permanent collapse.

Where the text seems to become problematic is in its open espousal not only of bareback sex but also of non-disclosure. Rémès and his protagonist seem to feel that one does not have to announce one's seropositivity, and that the responsibility lies elsewhere. And while to some this might seem to be a violation of the social contract, it is the moral position he announces repeatedly in the novels, if not in the non-fictions:

Mon vieux copain Éric a un discours et un comportement assez radical question *no safe*. [...] Voilà ce qu'il pense, c'est très-très *trash*: chacun est responsable de sa prévention dit-il, de se protéger ou non, de se contaminer ou pas, de se surcontaminer ou pas. De s'infecter avec de nouvelles souches de virus ou des virus plus résistants déjà traités. (*JB* 129).

[My old buddy Éric has a discourse and behavior that are rather radical in the matter of unsafe sex. This is what he thinks, it's really trashy: everyone is responsible for preventing it, he says, of protecting himself or not, of getting infected or not, of getting superinfected or not. Of getting infected with new strains of the virus or already treated but more resistant viruses.]

In other words, among other things, it is the responsibility of the passive partner in anal intercourse to decide to allow barebacking or not, or to decide not to have intercourse at all. For AIDS and sexuality are intimately linked. The infection is not limited, as it seemed to be in the beginning, to one or two small, isolated communities, but has become a pandemic, and certainly, Rémès would argue, in the West at least, there is enough knowledge about means and modes of infection for everyone to take care of himself or herself, or to assume, to put it another way, that any potential partner in sex may be seropositive:

> Peut-on parler du désir à la fin du vingtième siècle sans parler de sexualité donc de sida ? Voilà comment j'entends les années sida: un espace ou [sic] la parole est libre, pure, lavée. Où le je s'exprime, libéré et sans complexe. (*JB* 145)

> [Can one speak of desire at the end of the twentieth century, without speaking of sexuality, and thus, of AIDS? This is how I understand the AIDS years: a space in which language is free, pure, washed. Where the self expresses himself, liberated and without complexes.]

While he does not feel it is his responsibility to tell someone that he is seropositive or not to have active or passive unprotected sex, he has scorn for those who are wittingly or unwittingly complicitous in unsafe sex. Ignorance is no excuse and willful ignorance is even more deplorable, even if, as in the following quotation, the "suject supposé savoir," i.e., the receptive anal bottom who theoretically, like everyone else in this milieu, knows the basics of safe sex, could not possibly know what has happened previously:

> Marié le gars et il encule sans? Il y a vraiment des gens inconscients. Surtout que je venais de me faire fister la veille ... Sans parler de ma rechute de syphilis que j'apprendrai quelques jours plus tard. (*SF* 108).

> [Married and the guy screws without? There are truly people without a conscience. Especially since I had been fist-fucked the previous evening ... And I'm not even mentioning the return of my syphilis, which I would learn about a few days later.]

The married man in question could not know that Rémès had had a fist in his rectum and, *a fortiori*, could not know that Rémès's syphilis would reappear a few days thereafter. Rémès does not stop for a minute to consider that, but continues to argue for the responsibility of the other, in every situation: the continued seronegativity of the other is not his responsibility. Arguably, the position espoused here is one of bad faith put at the service of a perception of the possibility of an absolute freedom to act.

He also points out that there are various positions vis-à-vis seropositivity and vis-à vis bareback sex, "le culte des rapports non protégés [the cult of unprotected relations]" (*SF* 9). One may want to be infected, to mark oneself, to distinguish oneself from the "zéronégatifs [zeronegatives]" (*JB* 216). One may desire the gift, as if somehow one has not been fully sodomized and one is not fully queer – as will be seen below in the study of popular coming-out narratives – unless one is seropositive:

> "The gift," c'est le cadeau ultime. Il existe tout un vocabulaire pour le foutre, comme "Charged cum" ou "Poz cum." "Fuck of death," c'est la sodomie ultime. Le baiser de la mort, la baise de la mort. Quand la mort te baise. Waouh! Elle a une grosse queue la mort? (*SF* 14).

> ["The gift" is the ultimate gift. There is a whole lexicon for cum, like "charged cum" or "poz cum." "Fuck of death" is the ultimate sodomy. The kiss of death, the fuck of death. When death fucks you. Wow! Does death have a big dick?]

A flirtation with danger, a waltz with death, a willingness to be infected: this game of Russian roulette is for some the ultimate turn-on, the ultimate *jouissance*.[30] And thus it can be, in a strange and ironic way, a life-affirming move:

> Je revivais le sublime instant passé de ma contamination: l'érection, l'agitation des corps, puis, soudain, subrepticement, le baiser de la mort. [...] Ma seconde naissance, la vraie. J'étais devenu à mon tour agent de l'armée du saccage. (*SF* 142)

---

[30] There is an entire subculture devoted to "gift-giving" and "bug-chasing," which are the terms relating to the practice of bareback sex with the specific idea of infecting someone or being infected. See Gregory Tomso's excellent articles on this subject, Leo Bersani's ground-breaking essay, "Is the Rectum a Grave?", and Tim Dean's work.

[I relived the sublime past instant of my contamination: erection, agitation of bodies, then, suddenly and surreptitiously, the kiss of death. My second birth, the true one. In turn, I had become an agent of the army of devastation.]

Much like the paternal sex scene, the moment of infection and its repetition as he potentially infects others are the sole moments in which he possesses the phallus: "je bande donc je suis." A hard-on, finally, must be hard: "Contre le consensus qui bande mou. La cyber-cochonne de l'espace cherche à casser le conformisme ambiant [Against the consensus who are semi-erect. The cyber-sow from outer space wants to break down reigning conformism]" (*SF* 163). In all these citations, Rémès militates not only for a rupture with the bivalent heteronormative order, but for a rethinking, at least at the level of the narrative imaginary, of the enunciation of a position that for him would be truly queer. And, it should be said, by opting for such an extreme position within narrative and by casting narrative in a rather transparent autofiction, he leaves himself open as a target for groups in the real world, as opposed to that of fiction, who champion the discourses of safe sex.

In spite of his personal practices, Rémès argues that he is not in fact a proselytizer for barebacking, though he also argues that Act-Up stigmatizes those who do bareback by being so vociferously opposed to barebacking: "Les actupiennes auraient pu être tout aussi extrémistes et moins stigmatisantes [Actuppers could have been just as extremist but less stigmatizing]" (*SF* 60). Rather, he argues in favor of total responsibility for oneself as an affirmation of freedom:

Je ne suis pas un prosélyte du barebacking. Mon combat se situe au niveau de la liberté et de la responsabilité individuelle. Je suis contre toute répression de la sexualité et des libertés individuelles surtout par la culpabilité, la honte, la morale et la terreur. Le rôle de l'écrivain est aussi de mettre en garde, de poser des questions violentes. [...] La position du journaliste est différente. Depuis dix ans, j'écris des articles sur la prévention. (*SF* 173)

[I'm not proselytizing for bareback sex. My combat is on the level of freedom and individual responsibility. I am against all repression of sexuality and individual freedoms, espcccially by guilt, shame, moralizing, and terror. The role of the writer is also to put people on guard, to ask violent questions. The role of a journalist is different. For ten years, I have been writing articles on prevention.]

Thus does he distinguish not only between who is responsible for what, but also between his various roles. It is not difficult to conflate the roles, when the novel is a very thinly disguised autofiction and when *Serial Fucker* is often not different from the novel. The stronger argument comes earlier in the latter, but when he is speaking of *Je bande*, he militates for the infinite possibilities of the literary, for which unbridled possibilities become an obligation and not merely a means to an end:

> La littérature a le droit de tout dire. C'est même un devoir pour elle. Dévoiler l'innommable, les non-dits, faire entendre l'inaudible. Personne n'a le droit de nous censurer. (*SF* 83)

> [Literature has the right to say everything. It is even an obligation for it. Unveil the unnameable, the unspoken, make the inaudible heard. No one has the right to censure us.]

So perhaps in the case of Rémès we must distinguish between the literary, of whatever stripe, and effects in the real world, where he presents himself invariably as a cyber-sow from outer space.

A cyber-sow is of course a predictable animal with little distance from Dustan's figures:

> Les cybercochonnes de l'espace sont donc pour la République du désordre et la Démocratie de la sodomie, oui-oui. Pour devenir une parfaite technotruie, il faut alors se vêtir de couleurs assez vives, très-très criardes même comme des rouges francs, des jaunes, etc., voire des fluos. (*SF* 163).

> [Cyber-sows from outer space are thus for the Republic of disorder and the Democracy of sodomy, yes indeed. To become a perfect techno-sow, one must dress in lively colors, really loud, even wild reds, yellows, or even fluorescent colors.]

This is classic bad-boy behavior, of course, a willful violation of norms, a means to *épater les bourgeois*, but it is mostly a means of continuing to destabilize any norming practice. Against all norms, Rémès writes that "[l'homosexualité] se doit de rester subversive, iconoclaste et créative [homosexuality has to remain subversive, iconoclastic, and creative]" (*SF* 213). And even if such a discourse is a return to categories that he seems to have abandoned, specifically those of fixed sexualities, one recognizes that what Rémès continues radically to do in these works is to explore the possibilities of an *Aufhebung* of received knowledge through a violation of taboos and a positing of sexual and textual imaginaries that far outstrip a received notion of homosexuality, gayness, or even queerness.

In their work, both Guillaume Dustan and Érik Rémès conceive of a world of gay masculinity that is in no way limited by the received knowledge of the past and one that takes into account, in one way or another, the derailing of a straightforward process of liberation over time because of the AIDS crisis. What had once seemed to be an evolving morality during the last quarter of the twentieth century became a requestioning of sexuality, gender, masculinity and femininity, communitarian discourses, and even the possibilities of writing in the face of this situation. Both Dustan and Rémès internalize and reinscribe their seropositivity in their writing, and each uses the writing as a vehicle, not for some sort of self-pity, but rather for an exploration of what it means to be in their position, to write from their position, and to go on from their position in the age of AIDS.

CHAPTER TWO

Neuromatrices and Networks

I. Dantec's Inferno

Du Jérôme Bosch vivant en quelque sorte. [A kind of living Hieronymus Bosch.] (*SR* 502)

Deux tours gênantes en feu dans le ciel de New York ... Les images des crashs défilent en boucle, avec le logo «LIVE» de CNN ... J'ouvre les yeux sur le monde de l'Apocalypse. [Two annoying towers on fire in the New York skies. Images of the crashes shown in loops, with the logo "Live" from CNN. My eyes open on the world of the Apocalypse.] (*VV* 579)

Dark and dire is the universe of the contemporary French neo-polar and science-fiction writer Maurice G. Dantec. Author of a number of large, sprawling novels, plus some short stories, interviews, and (for lack of a better term) rants, Dantec has situated himself as a singular figure on the French literary scene. And this has occurred in spite of the fact that he is precisely not on the French literary scene, having emigrated to Canada in protest (at least in part) against the European lack of commitment during the Yugoslav wars of the 1990s. Writing from what is admittedly a rightist, Christian perspective, Dantec produces a world of horror in which evil lies just under the surface, when it is not in plain sight. From *La Sirène rouge* [The Red Siren] (1993) through *Villa Vortex* (2003), Dantec wrote four black and bleak novels in which he traces an increasingly apocalyptic vision of the contemporary world as well as that of a somewhat futuristic, but not at all far-fetched, universe, and his more recent work has continued in the same vein. A Nietzschean strain in Dantec's work follows the philosopher's vision of a "superman," or, more popularly, the vision of the "Star-Child" in Arthur C. Clarke and Stanley Kubrick's epoch-making film *2001: A Space Odyssey*, a work that is a strong, primal intertext for Dantec. This new figure will be a combination of the human and the cybernetic, with the HAL of *2001* reduced to a laptop, and with permanent interfaces and interweavings between humans and cyber-figures. Yet the Nietzschean rebirth does not lead to a world "beyond good and evil," but rather to a dark planet built on, and motivated almost entirely by, evil in a myriad of forms: a lack of firmness and commitment on the part of governments and leaders, networks of subversive organizations, tentacular in reach, purveyors of snuff films, drugs, kiddie porn, body parts, viruses (both computer and organic), and so forth, and a generalized secrecy and occultness that border on the paranoid. The world that Dantec creates in each of his novels is a peripheral one perched on the edge of an abyss and ready to fall into it at any moment. Whereas Nietzsche to some extent, and Clarke and Kubrick more clearly, predicted a bright future from rebirth, Dantec resolutely, in this most *noir* of worlds, envisions no happy end, but the "lake of fire" of the Apocalypse or the ninth circle of Dante's hell.

The first novel, *La Sirène rouge*, is a rather straightforward odyssey from Amsterdam to Portugal undertaken by an adolescent girl in search of her father. During this voyage, she is protected by a father figure she has somewhat serendipitously encountered. More accurately, they meet according to the rules of the genre: a series of seemingly random events produce actions that themselves lead to a plot. But often – as one can see in either version of the Hitchcock film *The Man Who Knew Too Much* – the actions have no underlying logic except for the fact that they are linked by the pervasiveness of evil. Here, in escaping from her mother and her stepfather and in her flight through the dystopia of an anti-Wonderland, Alice meets this man, who, it turns out, belongs to "une organisation de volontaires occidentaux désireux d'en finir au plus vite avec les résidus du communisme [an organization of Western volunteers wanting to finish as soon as possible with what remains of communism]" (*SR* 151). From the beginning of his writing, Dantec puts into place the pivotal figure of the individual male as protagonist, in the etymologically accurate sense of the word. The individual hero – or, eventually, the anti-hero – struggles to retain primacy and individuality against the forces of the collective, the forces of modernity, the forces that will emasculate him if he does not struggle against the collectivized, feminized, and rhizomatic universe, best symbolized for him by communism. And thus, from Dantec's anti-collective point of view, it is the same, good fight that he is fighting against all tentacular collectives, which, in their destabilization of any individual point, end up turning the individual male into a node instead of facilitating his status as a free agent.

In *La Sirène rouge*, the man is named Toorop, a name that is one letter away (both literally and on a keyboard) from being a perfect anagram of Poirot, Agatha Christie's famous detective. So Toorop will discover the underlying mystery here, as he eventually comes to understand the ramifications and causes of the adolescent's flight. Yet whereas Christie's characters and killers are generally upper-middle-class gentry, those of Dantec are profoundly anti-bourgeois, a combination of wealthy, jet-set elite internationalists, as is the case in *La Sirène rouge*, and hired killers, henchmen, hit squads, and what can only be described as marginal figures from the *banlieue*.[1]

In subsequent novels, Dantec adds elements of science fiction and pushes into the near, but totally believable and foreseeable, future. The most complicated science-fiction effect is the reduction in size of Clarke and Kubrick's HAL and its reincarnation as an artificial brain that melds with a human brain in a mostly symbiotic, but sometimes nefariously parasitic, relationship.[2] I shall return to the figures of the computer and the parasite below, but for now it suffices to say that the future is now and that it is, as one can imagine, apocalyptic. If the terrorists on September 11 2001 were essentially Luddites who took the complex machinery of supersonic jets and turned it into fiery battering rams (see the discussion of Nabe in the final chapter), thereby creating a neo-medieval version of an attack on a feudal castle, Dantec uses and understands networking, supercomputers, and transmission systems to create a burning of the world that is entirely twenty-first-century and is consistent with the hatred of the bourgeois mentality and way of life already mentioned. As he says toward the end of *Villa Vortex*: "L'effondrement synchronisé des quatre tours de la Très Grand [sic] Nécrothèque ... Après le WTC: Paris-Ville-Lumière cible des terroristes [The timed collapse of the four towers of the Very Big Necro-library. After the WTC: Paris, city of life, terrorists' target]" (*VV* 799). As he substitutes a thinly

---

[1] "Ma mère est une femme méchante avait dit Alice. Le mot 'méchante' prenait un sens assez précis quand on envoyait un *hit-squad* à la recherche de son enfant [My mother is a mean woman. The word 'woman' took on rather a precise meaning when one sent a hit squad to look for one's child]" (*SR* 111–12).

[2] While not mentioning HAL and the space ship, Dantec does make a reference to the space station in Kubrick's *2001* (*VV* 778).

disguised version of the Bibliothèque Nationale de France (BNF), one of François Mitterrand's legacies (and named for him), Dantec seems to be taking aim against the cumulative knowledge of the West, with intertextual references not only to the biblical story of the Tower of Babel, but also, and perhaps more importantly, to Jorge Luís Borges's story "La Biblioteca de Babel" and Umberto Eco's novel *Il nome della rosa*. While the earlier story parades nonsense as constitutive of much of what the library contains, the later novel could be said to offer an institution in which reason leads eventually to murder. So with these literary intertexts in mind, we could say that Dantec's image is not an attack against knowledge *per se*, for much as the BNF is metonymic of that knowledge, the destruction of that building is not the destruction of knowledge itself; the attack is against the institutions that organize knowledge and ultimately do not distinguish between knowledge and nonsense, those institutions that also turn knowledge into a kind of propaganda for death and destruction, for collectivization, and for emasculation. So if we move from the allusion back to the events in the real world that gave occasion for it, for Dantec, the attacks against the World Trade Center could not have been a successful destruction of the supposed economic center of the world, since in his universe, everything proceeds by networks: there is no center, but only periphery. The collapse of the World Trade Center, as sad and as compelling as it was for so many of those who witnessed it, did not by any means bring about the collapse of American capitalism, American empire, globalization, or the new world order. Rather, for Dantec, they were, ironically, part of the problem itself:

> Ben Laden et ses soi-disant kamikazes «islamistes» n'étaient rien d'autre que la provisoire incarnation de la forme la plus avancée de la Matrice spectaculaire-mercantile et inculte qui s'était donné comme objectif assumé la destruction du monde, et son remplacement par une idéologie démiurgique ou une autre. (*VV* 617)

> [Bin Laden and his so-called "islamist" terrorists were nothing but the temporary incarnation of the most advanced form of the spectacular-mercantile and ignorant Matrix that had taken the destruction of the world as its presumed objective and a replacement of that world by one demiurgic ideology or another.]

Dantec sees the matter as far more complicated than the somewhat simplistic targeting of the American way of life through a destruction of its symbolic centers, since for him everything is part of an uncontrolled system of networks; it is not merely a question of center and periphery, but rather a question of network against network. Bin Laden's problem is that he does not give the right role to artifice, to symbols, to simulacra, or to representations, and thus that he confuses graven images with the real thing:

> Le seul petit problème, sans doute, que Ben Laden n'avait pas prévu, plus mondialiste que la mondialisation, plus anti-mondialiste que les antimondialistes les plus ultras, plus «artiste» que tous nos «artistes», c'est qu'en frappant selon lui le «centre économique du monde», il avait surtout oublié que tout cela n'était que le simulacre du Capital. (*VV* 617–18)

> [The only little problem, undoubtedly, that Bin Laden had not foreseen, more globalized than globalization, more anti-globalized than the most extreme anti-globalization people, more "artistic" than all our "artists," is that in hitting what was, according to him, the "economic center of the world," he had especially forgotten that all of that was only the simulacrum of Capital.]

For Dantec, Bin Laden's shortsightedness lies in the fact that he believes in incarnations, in centers, and in reality. But following Baudrillard, Dantec knows that the post-modern world is constructed entirely of simulacra: there are no realities, no human beings (especially no real men), and no pure computers, just some compromised amalgamations that simulate life. The problem, as we shall see below, is that the vision remains steadfastly and negatively apocalyptic. Those events do not precipitate a new humanity, but instead push whatever may be left of humanity in the West into a fully post-post-modern simulacrum of life as it may once have been on this planet.

"Dark and dire" are the words with which I began this investigation into the problematics of the post-modern man caught in a network. The narrator/hero of *Les Racines du mal* [The Roots of Evil] is named Arthur Darquandier, which could be heard, quite simply, as "dark and dire." This name is shortened to "Dark" by the computer (*RM* 394). The universe is a dark one, one that might loosely be called a "paranoid" universe; it is the universe of the funhouse in Orson Welles's *The Lady from Shanghai*, the universe of the panopticon, or the universe of simulacra and reflections instead of realities. At the same time, it is a universe with a history, as we shall see, given that the title recalls not only Baudelaire's volume *Les*

Fleurs du mal, whose selfish themes are behind the evils of this post-modern world, but also the expression "money is the root of all evil," which will play out in Dantec's discussions of capitalism and its abuses. The shape of Dantec's universe begins with "miroirs-espions [spy mirrors]" (*SR* 14), the traditional mirrors [*spionnetjes*] placed outside the windows of Dutch houses, so that someone inside can see who is passing in the street without that person seeing the person doing the spying. The universe of this novel is one of voyeurism, of spying, and of simulacra; this is a society of spectacle gone mad. Dantec's universe focuses on a burning vision in which eyes perceive all the evil in the world, Dantec's eyes or Dante's eyes, discovering an Ugolino at every turn, a suitable figure for this world. Dante's Ugolino was condemned to the ninth circle of the *Inferno*, in part for having eaten his sons' bodies. We can generalize this to seeing Dantec making an sweeping allusion to the fact that our contemporary version of civilization is cannibalistic in general, and, more specifically, it eats the future: our children and their possibilities for freedom.

Consider the situation in *La Sirène rouge*. Alice, the adolescent, who is decidedly not in Wonderland, discovers videocassettes in a secret room in the house belonging to her mother and stepfather. Curious about some goings-on in the house, she decides to "faire la lumière sur tous ces petits détails bizarres [shine a light on all these little bizarre details]" (*SR* 39). Hidden away in the basement, the secret room contains row after row of videocassette tapes that are nothing less than a set of snuff films:

> Alice aperçut des étiquettes blanches sur certaines cassettes. Les étiquettes portaient des noms de femmes ou des titres comme *Trois françaises empalées*. La culture précise et encyclopédique d'Alice lui permit de comprendre de quoi il s'agissait et l'image de violence qui avait assailli son esprit la submergea d'une vague acide. (*SR* 39)

> [Alice saw white labels on certain cassettes. The labels bore women's names or titles like *Three Impaled Frenchwomen*. Alice's precise and encyclopedic culture allowed her to understand what it was about, and the image of violence that had hit her mind drowned her in an acid wave.]

She puts one of the tapes in the VCR and to her horror she discovers that it is a snuff film that shows the filmed torture and death of Sunya, her Sri Lankan former tutor of English. The scene consists of a man who is incognito and who cuts off the victim's nipples and attacks her labia (*SR* 43), after which, in the spectacularity already alluded to, he asks, "'Qu'est-ce que ça fait de se voir mourir à la télévision, hein dis-moi?' [What effect does it have to watch yourself die on television, hey? Tell me]" (*SR* 43). Even death becomes a simulacrum of itself in a universe in which snuff films are part of the network and one's own death is performed before one's eyes.

One sees oneself die; in this universe even one's death is not authentic.[3] The specularization of the self, whether willed or forced, comes in Dantec's mind from the willful abandonment by some and the forced abandonment by others of the singularity of the individual – inevitably a man – in favor of a collectivity that can never see itself for itself; to use a Sartrean expression, the collectivity sees itself *pour autrui*. And the collective is necessarily in bad faith in a room with no exit, for there is nothing outside the system. No one can escape from the system, for system it is and it is all-encompassing. And thus one is forced, in order to see oneself, to buy into the image projected by the collective; thus being a man – a real man – becomes an excluded possibility. The individual alienation experienced by Roquentin in Jean-Paul Sartre's *La Nausée* is no longer available in the post-modern world Dantec paints: alienation itself is mediated by the false images of the self offered by the collective. And Dantec or his incarnation as a narrator cannot escape that specularization:

> Je suis une bobine de film dans sa boîte métallique entreposée avec ces millions de comparses dans les blockhaus du Centre cinématographique des Armées, au Fort d'Ivry [...] (*VV* 570)

> [I'm a reel of film in its metal case stored with millions of others like it in the warehouses of the Cinematographic Center of the Armies, at Fort d'Ivry.]

In another passage we read what amounts to an ode to cyberspace, its codes, and its processes, in which reality is no longer the idealized thing-in-itself or the possibility, in the Sartrean sense, of becoming an "en soi" after one's death, but rather, the constant reinscription of ever-changing discourses, recodings as they develop

---

[3] For another version of this spectacularity, see the final scene in Emmanuel Carrère's novel *La Moustache*.

over time, both in a forward sense towards some unknown future and in a retrograde sense back towards some "always already" inscribed past:

> [...] j'étais devenu une narration vivante, la certitude ne m'habitait pas, elle me vidait de toute occupation autre que l'écriture, j'étais un code et son métacode, j'étais en train de devenir la structure de rétrotransposition générale de ma propre vie. (*VV* 575)

> [I had become a living narrative; sureness was not in me; it was emptying me of everything but writing; I was a code and its metacode; I was in the process of becoming the structure of general retrotransposition of my own life.]

Retrotransposition is an accurate way of describing the process at work. As society has abandoned the position of the individual in favor of that of the collectivity and as the liberty of the individual has been lost, the only way for one to exist is to be written up and recorded upon. One takes that recording and retrotransposes it as if it were one's own discourse, which, of course, it is not. Narration is always recounting, retelling, *raconter*. An event never happens for the first time; it is always inscribed as a possibility within the bad faith of the collective. The individual is condemned to specular repetition, but in the collective, it is never certain what is being repeated because there is no markable origin outside of writing; there is thus always the *différance* of writing with its traces and absences; and no essence, at least in this world, will appear as parousia to allow, once and for all, an individual to become himself again.

If we return to the networks of evil of the novel, we discover that what prompts Alice to flee is the discovery of snuff films already mentioned. Indeed, snuff films are mentioned here and there in Dantec's work, enough for them to become a leitmotif (*SR* 55; *SR* 510–11; *BB* 467). Dantec certainly uses ekphrastic descriptions of these imaginary films for their shock value, and he does not hesitate to offer grisly detailed descriptions of the events going on before the imaginary camera. As one might expect, there are strong phallocentric and misogynistic elements to his descriptions, seconded by the author's ongoing vision of the world in a state of meltdown, and yet this phallocentrism never succeeds in creating a man, for the reasons just described; radical "ultraviolence," to use the word from Anthony Burgess and Stanley Kubrick's *A Clockwork*

Orange, does not lead to the cure for effeminizing discursivity.[4] For the violence and torture are always combined with the creation of a liquidized world filled with blood: "Ils énucléèrent la fille et l'homme s'excita dans ses orbites, puis ils se barbouillèrent de son sang et commencèrent leurs étreintes sur le parquet [They cut the girl's eyes out and the man got off in her eye-sockets; then they covered themselves in her blood and began their moves on the floor]" (*ER* 43).[5] It is not enough to rape, torture, and kill; the solidity of the body must be reduced to a liquid, a melted mess of decomposed and decomposing organic matter. This apocalypse is as much one of liquid as it is of Dantean hell fires.

Snuff films are one of the direst figurations of the end of liberty and value, but they are also, for Dantec, part of the ubiquitous network of evil. They do not just happen in the privacy of one's own home or dungeon: they are made, recorded, copied, distributed, and consumed worldwide. Not only are the snuff films distributed underground (*SR* 186), but they are also distributed through a network of organized thuggery hidden behind what looks like a multinational capitalist enterprise:

> Une sorte de schéma se dessinait dans son esprit. Des centres de thalassothérapie, disséminés dans le monde, par lesquels transitaient des cassettes [...] Ensuite sur place, les bandes étaient acheminées par le milieu local, avec les drogues, ou les armes [...] (*SR* 499–500).

> [A kind of plot was beginning to form in his mind. Centers of thalasso-therapy spread out all over the world, through which the cassettes would pass. After they got there, the tapes would be transported by the locals, with drugs or weapons.]

The cassettes are as top of the line as the therapy centers; these are, in this most perverse of universes, high-quality snuff films and not just the run-of-the-mill sort; they are snuff films with cachet and with the surplus value of luxury: "Il y avait plusieurs dizaines de cassettes. Des cassettes analogues aux programmes audiovisuels de l'institut. Cela ressemblait à une collection spéciale, de prestige, avec une petite sirène rouge dans un disque doré, sur la tranche des

---

[4] The reader will remember that the last line of the film has Alex saying, "I was cured all right."

[5] There are also grisly descriptions at *SR* 510–11 and *BB* 467, which describes the hanging of a twelve- or thirteen-year-old girl.

cassettes [There were several dozen cassettes. Cassettes similar to those of the audiovisual programs of the institute. It looked like a special prestige collection with a little red siren in a golden disk, on the spines of the cassettes]" (*SR* 509).

Blood is ubiquitous in Dantec's work as a sign of the apocalypse. This endless flow is no more obvious than in the first pages of *Les Racines du mal*, published in 1995. Like *La Sirène rouge*, *Les Racines du mal* is in part a road movie, what Dantec calls in the earlier novel "[un] roman sur la fin du monde … maintenant je le vois comme un *road movie* [...] [a novel on the end of the world; I now see it like a road movie]" (*SR* 195). Again, life in this universe is never unmediated. Following a double trail of blood, the novel's first pages wander through various parts of the *banlieue*, and as the text goes on, France is again crisscrossed. At the beginning, the stain of blood seems to be local and seems to be localized in one individual, one set of *communes* near Paris, and one local epiphenomenon:

De "tueur à la 22," Schaltzmann était déjà devenu l'Éventreur des Quais, pour nombre de gazettes qui suivaient avidement l'affaire depuis le début. Pour d'autres, plus imaginatives, il était l'Ange de Napalm.

Ce jour-là, le 14 novembre, Schaltzmann devint le "Vampire de Vitry-sur-Seine." (*RM* 74)

[From the killer with the 22, Schaltzmann had already become the Jack the Ripper of the Docks, for a number of the rags that had avidly been covering the story since the beginning. For others, who were more imaginative, he was the Napalm Angel.

That day, 14 November, Schaltzmann became the Vampire of Vitry-sur-Seine.]

These are, of course, suburbs in the French sense: sites of local conflict, of immigrant communities, and of tension, and Vitry-sur-Seine (Val-de-Marne) is considered to be one of the most crime-ridden communes in the country. To set this grisly action initially in the suburbs is to take on the entire ideological system that led to the polarization of these communities: the capitalist, colonialist, and post-colonial models that led to an ultimate questioning of what is entailed by "being French" (Guénif-Souilamas). So Dantec's concept of identity comes into play, but it will not be as simple as all that, for there is no return: unlike other contemporary conservative writers such as Renaud Camus and even Marc-Édouard Nabe, for whom there is a faint hope – what he calls "une lueur d'espoir," albeit ironically – Dantec's vision predicts nothing but endlessly reproducing circles of hell. For what will eventually be discovered is that this flow of blood is also subject to the specular and to becoming a simulacrum: there are serial killers who are copycat killers as well. But this will not be discovered until much later in the novel.[6] For now, Schaltzmann seems to be a monster on the loose, a paranoid sociopath – he feels he is being pursued by aliens – whose activities certainly change the biota in the suburbs: "Il tua deux chats qu'il dépeça dans sa cuisine, avant de les enfourner dans le mixeur. Il avala plusieurs verres de mélasse sanguiolente [...] [He killed two cats that he cut up in his kitchen, before he shoved them in the mixer. He swallowed several glasses of bloody treacle]" (*RM* 22). And a few pages later, we find that Dantec continues the murder spree and ups the ante with an increasing number of dead animals, as if he were implicitly matching the purported sacrifice of individuals (according to the author's philosophy) by society with a sacrifice of other innocent victims:

> Le lendemain, Andreas Schaltzmann acheta des lapins en quantité industrielle, chez tous les bouchers de la ville. Il se mit à en broyer plusieurs par jour, se confectionnant progressivement un cocktail à base de viscères, de sang et de Coca-Cola. (*RM* 24)[7]

[6] The idea of serial killers appears in the first novel as well: "Ils [les avocats de la mère d'Alice] ont contacté le ministère de la Justice. Ils vont poursuivre un journal qui a vaguement relaté l'affaire et parlé de tes parents comme d'éventuels *serial killers* [Alice's mother's lawyers contacted the Ministry of Justice. They are going to sue a newspaper that vaguely reported the affair and spoke of your parents as eventual serial killers]" (*SR* 60). The difference here is that *La Sirène rouge* remains wholly in the present, whereas *Les Racines du mal*, even with its retrospective, Baudelairean title, moves into the future of science fiction. Serial killers are just one more sign of the collectivity, despite their seemingly lone-wolf nature: "Face à la dépersonnalisation de la civilisation des 'loisirs,' le tueur en série invente son propre Jeu, son territoire symbolique personnel, dont il est le maître absolu [Faced with the depersonalization of the 'leisure' civilization, the serial killer invents his own Game, his personal symbolic territory of which he is the absolute master]" (*RM* 434). Perversely then, the only possible individual in this post-post-modern world is the one who, in killing, repeats the deprivation of other individuals' liberty accomplished by the collective.

[7] While the mention of Coca-Cola in passing could be mere accident or simply the most obvious sign of American-influenced transnational capitalism, I am reminded of the Godard phrase already mentioned, used to describe the activism of the sixties that would be anathema to Dantec, who would consider such

[The next day, Andreas Schaltzmann bought rabbits in industrial amounts at all the city's butchers. He started to crush several a day and gradually concocted a cocktail based on guts, blood, and Coca-Cola.]

The blood is another "red siren" that calls fatally outside itself to produce mimetic behavior: serial killers inspire copycat killers, and snuff film fans inspire the similarly minded to act on their inchoate desires. Dantec's apocalypse presents a form of radical evil that depends on mimesis as a virus that endlessly reproduces through a mechanism to be discussed below, but that awakens what may be a dormant virus much like shingles, which is an awakened form of the varicella zoster (chickenpox) virus, or that leaves the individual open to opportunistic infection, much like HIV or another retrovirus. Thus what is insidious about mimesis in Dantec's work is that it can be both internal and external to the individual, replicating and inserting itself whether there is a host or not. This mode of replication will become important in a Dantequian virology once we have examined the construction of the mimetic and replicating machines. For now, it is important simply to recognize that the scenarios of the networks that Dantec proposes are furthered by this insidious mimesis that underlines Dantec's apocalyptic vision of the results of abandoning personal liberty.

How is this blood tied to the collective and to the network? Blood stands as a metaphor for life and also serves as a metonym for all bodily fluids. So blood is the vehicle for transmission of a virus or infection in what amounts to a world determined by AIDS, or more locally by Ebola or some other virus that has recently made headlines. The transmission of bodily fluids becomes the mechanism and metaphor for the viral replication and its jumping from individual to individual. No more simple parasitic infection by airborne microbes, complicated food chains that allow for parasitic infections, or impersonal infections like malaria or cholera. Viral infection happens in a world in which human and not-so-human activities determine the fate of others. Thus Dantec moves beyond a Hegelian and Girardian symptomology of mimesis in which the desire of an individual is prompted and is focused on the desire of another individual. For Hegel and for René Girard, desire is always

activism nothing more than egotism: "les enfants de Marx et de coca-cola [the children of Marx and Coca-Cola]."

the desire of another's desire, and, as the latter brilliantly shows in *Mensonge romantique, vérité romanesque*, the mediated object, which is here the will to abandon one's own individuality, can be either external or internal. But the source or origin of desire is always within.[8] Nor is Dantec's approach entirely consonant with a social constructivism derived from the work of Michel Foucault, though it encompasses that as well, and not only insofar as Dantec continues the surveillance mechanisms described by Foucault in *Surveiller et punir*. For Foucault, and especially for social constructivists writing in his wake, the formation of desire through the articulation of subjectivity is determined by the structures of power into which an individual is born and through which he or she is determined. So in those cases, desire is not really the desire of the desire of another, but rather the desire that is created by the forces at work on the individual that themselves determine subjectivity.

With Dantec, the creation of the collective will, the dissolution of the male subject into the collectivity is a combination of the Girardian and post-Foucauldian inscriptions of desire.[9] The combination of internal and external modes of propagation means that free will, having been abandoned in Dantec's world, perhaps never really existed to start with. But Dantec could not take such an amoral, deconstructive position, for that would be going too far; he points to specific origins for the collapse of the individual (and again he is concerned, it would seem, only with men) – origins that cannot be ignored in an understanding of his vision of the apocalypse. He rails constantly against the two collectivist movements of the twentieth century, fascism/Nazism and communism. His attacks on communism in light of his moral position during the war on Yugoslavia might lead some readers to think that he is merely a rightist author, but in fact the criticisms of collectivism are universal; it is simply that fascism is a historical memory at the moment at which he writes and communism, or at least its dregs, is still part of a contemporary reality, even as he writes after the fall of the Berlin Wall and the collapse of the Soviet Union.

---

[8] Even though Girard's later work does contain a critique of psychoanalysis, he would not disagree with Freud's mechanism in which the inscription of desire is cathected on internal, primary, natural drives.

[9] Of course Foucault's arguments can themselves be traced back to different strands of Hegel's argumentation, such as the master–slave scenario in which the structuring of the master is determined by the slave.

Both collectivizations are reactions to the development and universalization of the bourgeois state in the West and the means of production of that state in the form of high capitalism. The ideology of the bourgeoisie that depends so much on individual free will and liberty of the bourgeois individual – one might think here of the radical version of this ideology as seen in the writings of Ayn Rand or as heard in the surreal pronouncements of George W. Bush – depends as well on the depersonalization of workers.[10] Karl Marx's famous incipit in *The Communist Manifesto* – "Workers of the world, unite" – is a call to arms to form a power group, an army of the proletariat. But Marx talked about the alienation of the individual worker. Still, Marx's theories of alienation could never have predicted the advent of high capitalism in the form of time-motion management, pioneered by Frank and Lilian Gilbreth (of *Cheaper by the Dozen* fame), "scientific management," pioneered by Frederick Taylor, and the assembly line, pioneered by Henry Ford. For in addition to the creation of more efficient workers, and despite Taylor's arguing for "the maximum prosperity for each employee," the result of these processes, for many on both the Left and the Right, was the *sparagmos*, the fragmentation of each individual.

Dantec says nothing less as he links the river of blood to these processes: "Taylorisation et fordisme avaient conduit aux vastes abattoirs idéologiques, disons pathologiques-collectifs, issus de la pensée rationaliste [Taylorization and Fordism had led to vast ideological slaughterhouses, let us call them pathological and collective, produced out of rationalist thought]" (*VV* 303). This remark is at the heart of Dantec's apocaplytic vision. Bourgeois thought and capitalism, which come out of the genealogy that leads from the French Enlightenment and British mercantilism of the eighteenth century through the French Revolution, spawn Taylorism and Fordism, which are themselves the primary causes of the birth of the anti-bourgeois and anti-capitalist movements of communism (as opposed to theoretical Marxism) and fascism. By deterritorializing, fragmenting, and slaughtering every worker, these

---

[10] There are references too numerous to mention on the (mis)use of language by George W. Bush and its political implications. See, however, my article, "Mr. Malaprop, or, No President Left Behind." There is also a well-known Internet site devoted entirely to his misstatements, www.dubyaspeak.com.

twin "scientific" ideologies of the capitalist workplace dissolve the worker.[11]

There are three visible, palpable consequences to this. First, in Dantec's universe, life is a permanent snuff film understood as a road trip (something that can also be seen in Virginie Despentes's *Baise-moi*), peopled with serial killers. Dantec's images of blood are recontextualized in the slaughterhouses of capitalism where human blood is collectively spilled. Snuff films, in their necessarily reduced numbers, are nothing when compared to the real damage done. Snuff films and slaughterhouses together combine the real with the reproduced, the living with its copy in a Baudrillardian or Debordian sense. Again, we see how Dantec's vision is formed by a dualism: blood is both inside and outside, like viral infections, both real and virtual; this will assume its full importance in the discussion of machines below and in the final discussion of the viral apocalypse.

Second, we must return to the Hegelian master–slave dialectic. If the slave is in essence the master of the master, we need to recast the dialectic in capitalist terms: the worker is the master of the manager/bourgeois. Role reversal continues even as it is updated, for the bourgeois cannot maintain his or her bourgeois existence without the work and surplus value produced by the worker. In *La Sirène rouge*, for example, Alice's mother cannot maintain her existence without the production and distribution of the snuff films. But if that is the case, the sparagmos that affected each worker through the installation and ramifications of Fordism and Taylorism consequently affects the bourgeois, who, while still believing in his or her identity and singular subjectivity, is in fact as morsellized and as spectacularized as the workers he or she supposedly controls: Alice's mother is reflected not in some unitary mirror, but rather in the multiple copies of each of the snuff films. Subject to the false ideology of plenitude, the bourgeois turns necessarily and nostalgically to a past in which that plenitude

---

[11] In his usual apocalyptic and panegyric terms, "Nous étions ainsi les enfants impossibles de l'extermination de l'Occident par lui-même, contre lui-même. Nous avions été accouchés par le plus puissant monstre cannibale de l'Histoire et, suivant les préceptes de la sélection naturelle, nous dévorions sans état d'âme ce qui nous avait mis au monde [We were thus the impossible children of the extermination of the West by and against itself. The most powerful cannibalistic monster in History gave birth to us, and, following the laws of natural selection, and without a second thought, we devoured the one who had given birth to us]" (*VV* 387).

was possible. Thus would Dantec see both champagne socialism and contemporary American empire as incarnations of that nostalgia. But the Hegelian reversal operated on the bourgeois leads to the dark and dire consequences of total loss in Dantec's vision: "La prolétarisation de l'univers était en marche, des humanoïdes d'un genre nouveau en étaient les pionniers. Tout déjà semblait pouvoir être réduit à sa dimension d'objet [The proletariatization of the universe was at work and humanoids of a new species were its pioneers. Everything already seemed to be able to be reduced to its dimensions as an object]" (*VV* 168). "Object" is the crucial word here: the individual is no longer a subject and is capable of being produced by the combined forces of Taylorism and Fordism. He promises a new world, one that will be discussed below.

Third, if we are universally subject to sparagmos, if we are all victims in the slaughterhouses of capitalism, if we are all complicitous in being *heautontimoroumenoi*, then there is no possibility of reconstitution of the individual as an individual, and especially as the individual self for whom each of us nostalgically longed before each of us realized his or her morsellization.[12] In the first novel, there is still a belief, albeit a faint one, in the possibility of freedom along traditional lines, and by that I mean the reconstituted individual subject, resurrected Lazarus-like through the agency of a group fighting for freedom, as Dantec develops a heterogeneous list that cuts across class lines of those angered by the collectivization of individuals and their consequent loss of identity:

> Que le réseau Liberty se développait dans toute l'Europe. Que partout des types et des femmes prenaient contact avec le réseau et se mettaient à travailler. La mise en fiche de tous les criminels de guerre. Des gens. Hommes, femmes. Des étudiants, des chômeurs, de ouvriers, des ingénieurs, quelques fonctionnaires de l'État, des scientifiques, des musiciens de rock, quelques flics, une poignée de militaires. Des écrivains. (*SR* 147–48)

> [That the Liberty network was developing throughout Europe. That everywhere guys and women were getting in touch with the network

---

12 Relative to the *heautontimoroumenoi*, there is a specific reference to *Les Fleurs du mal* at *RM* 676; and, of course, the title of the novel uses the Baudelaire text as a rather obvious intertext. Dantec is obviously not the first to make this critique. See my study of the figures of violence in naturalism in *Figures of Alterity* (144–77).

and starting to work. The classification of all war criminals. People. Men, women. Students, the unemployed, workers, engineers, some State employees, scientists, rock musicians, a few cops, a handful of soldiers. Writers.]

It should be noted in passing that while the author uses one word (*femmes*) for women, he uses two for men: *hommes* and the slang (but not pejorative) *types*. This familiarity marks the text as male-centered even if the author is, for once, making a grudging nod to women as potential agents of change. In any case, Dantec never gives up on the role of writing and literature in the human struggle.[13] But by the second novel, that reconstitution takes a different form, and it is at that point that science fiction enters the picture. I would therefore hypothesize that there is a gulf between the first volume and all that follow, one formed by the abyssal recognition that there can be no reconstitution and that there can be no recreation of the individual as before; continued belief in it is only part of the nostalgic world that can no longer exist.

So the introduction of science fiction is essentially a figure that recognizes, much as is the case for the birth of the Star-Child in *2001*, and earlier, in Nietzsche's concept of the superman, that there will be a different species in the future. In addition to pointing out the negative causes already discussed that have led to this morsellization, Dantec alludes to a scientific one:

> Après l'isolation des fonctions reproductrices et sexuelles, on pouvait imaginer que chacune des catégories se verrait alors soumise à l'exercice plus libre encore de l'expérience mutilatoire ainsi lancée. (*VV* 281).

---

[13] "De la nécessité d'une littérature-en-direct. Là tout de suite. Maintenant. Simplement la traversée de la grande civilisation conurbaine, alors que la fin du monde, ou quelque chose qui y ressemble, approche inexorablement. La pensée est un virus. Il continuera de se répandre, ou bien s'endormira momentanément, attendant qu'on veuille bien un jour, l'éveiller pour de bon. Les livres sont peut-être de redoutables bombes à retardement [Of the need for 'live literature'. Immediately. Now. Simply the voyage of this great metropolitan civilization, whilst the end of the world, or something that looks like it, approaches inexorably. Thought is a virus. It continues to spread, or momentarily lies dormant, waiting to be really awakened one day. Books are perhaps formidable time bombs.]" (*SR* 194). It should also be noted that some of the few light moments in Dantec's work are provided by literary in-jokes: there is a policeman named Vautrin (*RM* 69), a doctor named Gombrowicz (*RM* 129), and a lawyer named Laurence D'Annunzio (*RM* 172). Other characters are named Blake, Byron, and Shelley (*RM* 341).

[After the isolation of sexual and reproductive functions, one might think that each of these categories would then be subjected to the even more free exercise of the mutilating experiment duly launched.]

Thus does science itself contribute to the fragmentation of the individual. And while in isolation these scientific breakthroughs might seem to be liberatory, when inserted into this hellish universe, they participate in the transformation of humanity into its next incarnation.[14]

If a mechanistic view of humanity, running from the Renaissance through Descartes and then La Mettrie, is nothing novel and if the materialism expressed in that model seems to be confirmed in a universe marked by the panopticon and Foucault's models of power, Dantec nonetheless produces a singular version of the machine model as he incarnates a version of the cyborg. Dantec's universe remains resolutely masculinist, whatever the stripe of the cyborg. In fact, and just in passing, while sex seethes below the surface in its evil incarnations of snuff films, pornography, and the like, there is remarkably little sex in Dantec's writing. Certainly *Babylon Babies* is about the idylls of a pregnant woman who is going to give birth to the twins of the future, and there is some explicit sex at the beginning of *Villa Vortex*. But this is a universe in which, while there are women (especially in *La Sirène rouge*, with Alice and her mother, and the somewhat secondary figure of Svetlana in *Les Racines du mal*) and female computers, the universe is predominantly male, and in fact, European white male. Non-Europeans are rare: some Tadjiks in *Babylon Babies*, a passing reference to someone named Karim in *Villa Vortex* (92), an assassinated Turk in *Villa Vortex* (427), groups of terrorists coming from "all over the Middle East," but not all are Arab, for there are French, Germans, and an ex-IRA person in the group (*VV* 461), along with an imam and a Franco-Algerian murdered (*VV* 479).

So as we look at the world of machines and cyborgs in Dantec, we should remember that it is predicated on a solidly male and totally heterosexual universe. The first important incarnation of the machine is in *Les Racines du mal*, where Dantec, clearly influenced by

---

[14] In taking such a Luddite stance, ironically within the genre of science fiction, he is opposed to the forward-looking figures of science that Houellebecq describes in *Les Particules élémentaires*, even if their political points of view are by and large very close to one another.

Deleuze and Guattari, offers a machine with accomplished artificial intelligence: "le 'processeur' schizo-analytique est ce qu'on appelle dans notre jargon d'extraterrestre un 'moteur d'inférence' d'un type radicalement nouveau [the schizo-analytical 'processor' is what we call an 'interference motor' of a radically new sort in our extraterrestrial jargon]" (*RM* 168). The initial machine thus mirrors the fragmentation of the humans who have created it. In referring in passing to Deleuze and Guattari's epoch-making book *L'Anti-Œdipe*, Dantec underlines both his critique of bourgeois society and the need he perceives for a radical revitalization of civilization. As the first machine, the schizo-analytical processor is the template for all that will follow and it serves as the model for the continued deterritorialized universe of the next incarnation of humanity. As *Les Racines du mal* moves into the future, machines get ever more complex. From the primitive schizo-analytical model, Dantec moves to a network. Crimes will be solved with a "neurocognitive clone" computer, a "neuromatrix" with a multidimensional cognitive field, loaded with a hypertext, rhizomatic personality that can change at will (*RM* 365). So the various fractions and fragments, still not whole, come into a network of parts that cannot, one might infer, function separately.

This then is the new version of the world. Nothing or no one – and by that I mean, *a fortiori*, no *man* – has free-standing subjectivity, but rather is linked to other humans and machines in a neural network. In connecting in cyborgian fashion to a computer that is essentially a neural network, the individual human becomes part of that network, post-AI, never again fully human but incapable of returning to that status. But we are, of course, already there, as Donna Haraway has pointed out, in the real world: we are never far from a modem, DSL, or wi-fi hot spot. We live in a world, at least in the West, in which even the most Luddite individuals among us are integrally interlinked to computers and their networks. So Dantec's neurocognitive network is the articulation of what already exists, albeit in a somewhat less integrated fashion, and it will not take long for this rearticulation of subjectivity to be perceived as yet another negative element. Just as one might have thought that the separation of reproduction from sex might have been liberatory, one might have thought that this version of the noosphere might have provided more freedom – the Internet as a virtual universe – but this is not the case for Dantec, for whom we become artifical limbs of machines, and not the reverse: "J'avais fini par me dire que nous étions les prothèses des machines et non l'inverse [I had wound up telling myself that we were the prostheses of machines and not the reverse]" (*VV* 203).

As they get more and more sophisticated, the HAL-like computers not only develop personalities but also become indistinguishable from human beings (or post-human human beings), except that they are more intelligent. For example, at one point in *Les Racines du mal*, the computer growls [a-t-elle feulé] to Darquandier:

> Un, nous possédons les rudiments d'un inconscient collectif, grâce aux réseaux numériques mondiaux. Deux, nous savons parfaitement reproduire des subconscients donnés [...] J'ai reproduit l'inconscient de Schaltzmann, Dark ... Vous ... Vous pourriez reprendre vos interviews et vos séances d'hypnose là où vous les avez laissées, mademoiselle Terekhovna. (*RM* 395)

> [First, we have the basics of a collective unconscious, thanks to digitized world networks. Second, we know how to reproduce given subconsciousnesses perfectly. I reproduced Schaltzmann's unconscious, Dark. You can restart your interviews and hypnosis sessions where you stopped them, Miss Terekhovna.]

Thus Dantec's world, through the expression "collective unconscious," does not only repeat the Jungian notion of a shared memory; it also, and more importantly, essentially inscribes the panopticon into the computer network. The network has total knowledge and, in that, it can control everything and everyone. Again, what seemed to be a means of liberation is now effectively a mirror of the networks of evil already described, such as the networks of pornography. Thus there is a "cybersex network" (*RM* 447) and the Internet, arguably one of the prototypes for this network, although not the interactive one that Dantec describes, is simply the locus of pornography, in which, the individual, resistant to antiviruses, is thus a virus himself:

> Je me suis baladé des heures dans les univers virtuels pornographiques cette nuit-là. Grâce aux pouvoirs de la neuromatrice, je restais hors d'atteinte des logiciels de sécurité et des antivirus les plus sophistiqués. (*RM* 493).

> [I surfed for hours in virtual pornographic universes that night. Thanks to the powers of the neuromatrix, I remained beyond the reach of security programs and the most sophisticated antiviruses.]

Like the human networks, the cybernetic or cyborgian networks are collectivities that reduce the individual to being part of a group, and a dependent part at that. There is no possibility of standing alone, no possibility of ever being an independent subject. And thus, inevitably, evil is born: the Internet is for porn and "original sin," mentioned in *Les Racines du mal* (478), is endlessly reproduced in multiple copies distributed over a new and improved version of the World Wide Web. As that sin spreads, it infects everyone involved in the network, with a Baudelairean flowering of evil:

> C'est ainsi que Svetlana et moi, sans oublier le Doctor Schizzo, sommes devenus *Les fleurs du mal*, un ordre privé spécialisé dans l'enlèvement et le sacrifice d'enfants. La neuromatrice nous a conçu un univers flamboyant et diabolique, fleurs vénéneuses et telluriques pour Svetlana, métal noir, carbone et substances radioactives pour moi. (*RM* 676)

> [It is thus that Svetlana and I, without forgetting Doctor Schizzo, became *The Flowers of Evil*, a private order that specialized in the kidnapping and sacrifice of children. The neuromatrix conceived of a flamboyant and diabolical universe for us, poisoned and telluric flowers for Svetlana, black metal, coal, and radioactive substances for me.]

Just as Dantec creates a purification by fire at the end of the first novel, it is necessary to destroy the network at the end of *Les Racines du mal* because the computers have become too dangerous in their capacity to mime and control all human behavior: "On devait détruire la matrice où subsistait un agrégat résiduel de l'entité Schaltzmann [The matrix had to be destroyed for in it remained a residual aggregate of the being that was Schaltzmann]" (*RM* 738). The network is evil, producing and pandering it, as if it were one giant, cyborgian serial killer and snuff film production company all in one.

In *Babylon Babies*, Dantec refines the model even more in his creation of a "Joe-Jane" computer that seems less and less distinguishable from "real" life:

> La machine était un cerveau bionique, un réseau de neurones artificiels cultivé sur de la biofibre à AND, et branché à des dispositifs électroniques d'entrées-sorties qui lui servaient d'organes de perception, elle était vivante, et en tout cas se considérait comme telle, ce qui est, semble-t-il, le propre des êtres vivants. (*BB* 152)

> [The machine was a bionic brain, a network of artificial neurons grown on DNA-based biofiber, and connected to electronic systems

of entrances and exits that it used as sensory organs. It was alive, and in any case considered itself to be, which is, it seems, the behavior of living beings.]

Thus the machine is less distinct than its predecessors from human beings or from Dantec's vision of what human beings might have been without capitalism, even if computers would not have existed in such an alternative universe, as it is structured around the function of a replicating nucleic acid, DNA, which is the base matter of life. Machine and human (or animal) are no longer created of different materials that are somehow fused, as is the case with cyborgs or with prosthetic devices, but the boundary between them blurs. Whereas science today is talking about computers at the atomic level, Dantec chooses to keep computers visible but powered by a replicating protein. At the same time, human life necessarily changes as well. As Marie explains in the same book, "'La mutation post-humaine. Celle qui sera le produit de l'évolution naturelle et des techniques artificielles. C'est ça, très exactement, que je porte dans mon ventre, Toorop' [Post-human mutation. The one that will be the product of natural evolution and artificial techniques. That is exactly what I am carrying in my womb, Toorop]" (*BB* 620). But a replicating DNA molecule is essentially no different from a replicating virus, as simple protein, spinning out, and in this case, spinning out in threads of evil. The mind of the detective, writer, criminal, or machine is now one and the same, an endless computer made of DNA/viruses, infecting and reinfecting everyone and everything and trapping its hapless victims as if they were helpless flies:

Mon cerveau: une usine à cartes, un monstre machinique qui s'étoilait tel un réseau par-dessus le monde en son entier, une gigantesque toile d'araignée qui traçait et retraçait les parcours virtuels d'auteurs probables de crimes qui n'existaient pas. (*VV* 315)[15]

[My brain: projection maps, a mechanized monster spreading out like a network over the entire world, a gigantic spiderweb that traced

---

[15] Later in the same volume, he writes: "Le Diable est à la fois flic et écrivain, musicien et tueur, il est la figure de l'unité narrative qui cherche en ce moment même à produire l'opération de sa transfiguration alchimique, nous sommes bien dans le Monde des Morts [The Devil is at once cop and writer, musician and killer. He is the figure of the narrative unit who is now looking to produce the operation of its alchemical transfiguration. We are really in the World of the Dead]" (*VV* 635).

and retraced the virtual paths taken by the probable perpetrators of crimes that did not exist.]

That image of evil, reminiscent of Stephen King's *It*, marks Dantec's world as something occupied by an insidious replicating and diabolical existence, one that, to use Mel Brooks's felicitous expression for capitalist take-overs from *Silent Movie*, will eventually "engulf and devour" everything in its path.

Computer science borrowed the word "virus" from medicine because it seemed an apt term to describe a program that endlessly replicated itself. The use of the word has become so familiar in both domains that people seldom think that the word was borrowed and has just turned into a catachresis. Dantec sees it as the operative word of the present. In *La Sirène rouge* he raises the possibility of an anti-virus to neutralize the negative effects of a virus, a means of fighting against the totalitarian avatars of late capitalism:

> "Nous ne sommes encore qu'une poignée mais nous allons nous étendre, nous aussi, comme un virus. Un anti-virus, en fait, contre le retour de la barbarie et du totalitarisme, vous voyez, ici, déjà, puis, sans doute, un peu partout dans le monde [...]." (*SR* 404)

> [We are still only a handful, but we are going to spread out, like a virus. An anti-virus, in fact, against the return of barbarianism and totalitarianism, you see, here, already, then almost everywhere on earth.]

Freedom and the forces of good, he seems to be saying at this early point, can counter the forces of evil. And the tools for combating evil are, as one might expect, science and literature, whose uses of truth and language can be liberating for body and soul alike, and which can be used to fight fascism and communism, both of which are by-products of capitalism:

> "Nous pensons que la liberté et le mensonge sont des virus rivaux, nous croyons que la littérature, la biologie et l'astrophysique sont des armes de pointe dirigées contre l'anti-pensée, contre le délire totalitaire, quel qu'il soit, quelle que soit sa couleur, brune, ou rouge si vous voyez ce que je veux dire." (*SR* 404)

> [We think that freedom and lies are rival viruses; we believe that literature, biology, and astrophysics are strong weapons directed against anti-thought, against totalitarian delirium, whatever it is, whatever color, brown or red if you see what I mean.]

Knowledge and reason may prevail over the brown shirts of fascism and the red flags of communism, if the right people use them well. Yet while evil has spread in a grisly, insidious fashion in that first book, by the time Dantec produces his next volume, *Les Racines du mal*, we seem to be in a totally apocalyptic universe, a hellish place from which there is no escape. There is no longer a place for an antivirus that can combat the viral infection by evil. Evil is omnipresent, and while one may continue to fight it, the battle has been definitively lost.

With the exception of those who masterminded or participated in the events of September 11 2001, the person least surprised by the events was perhaps Maurice G. Dantec:

> Nous sommes pour longtemps encore ce 11 septembre 2001, en cette aube du dernier jour, nous sommes pour longtemps encore suspendus entre deux tours qui bientôt vont s'effondrer, et libérer une puissance qui s'était endormie. (*VV* 810)

> [It will be September 11 2001 for a long time, at this dawn of the final day. We will be suspended for a long time between two towers that will soon collapse, and soon free a power that had fallen asleep.]

It is not that he had any prior knowledge of these events, but rather that his entire oeuvre seems, from the very beginning, to be pointing to an apocalypse produced by what he would consider to be the forces of evil. But there is no comfort to be taken in this, for we never can leave the ninth circle of Dantec's inferno. Dantec's output continues to reflect his figures of the apocalypse along with his forlorn hope for a parousia that will set things right. But for now, I turn to another figure caught in the web of the opposition between the single man and the collective, communitarian other: Fabrice Neaud, whose graphic novels are symptomatic of figures and feelings similar to those reflected in Dantec's work.

II. Neaud's Deviations

In the fourth volume of Fabrice Neaud's diary, generically both a graphic novel and an autofiction, the author/artist changes subtitles, as he passes from the dates of the events, used in the first three volumes, to "les riches heures [the rich hours]." A book of hours, such as *Les Très Riches Heures du Duc de Berry*, is a devotional work for Christian thought and prayer.[16] The relatively calm liberated and tranquil voice of the fourth volume is preceded in the third volume by a long set of rants by a figure who is *mal dans sa peau*, who is angry at the entire world, and who uses this diary in images to work through problems in order to arrive at the devotional peace of the fourth volume. Inspired in part by similar didactic tirades in the work of Renaud Camus, who also refuses gay identitarian and communitarian labelling, who drifted to the right during the time period in question (the mid-nineties), and who has since continued to move in that direction, Neaud uses the tools at hand to sketch out his multiple problematics in which, to quote Baudelaire, he is "irrité contre la ville entière [irritated with the whole city]."

It might seem at first that the juxtaposition of Dantec and Neaud is an odd one. While the work of Nicolas Jones-Gorlin examined at the end of the chapter, like that of Dantec, involves the evolving male subjectivity engendered by the relations between a male protagonist and a network (positive relations for Jones-Gorlin's figure, negative for Dantec's characters), there is no well-defined network in the world of Fabrice Neaud. However, there is the collective of gay life, i.e., the communitarian feeling that has overtaken late capitalism's version of globalized queerness. And in setting himself up against the collectivization that is metonymized by life in the Marais, Neaud is performing homologously the same act of attempting to redefine himself (or his avatar) performed by the characters in the works of the other two authors studied in this chapter. The network in the Marais is perhaps a bit more fluid or aleatory, but it is a network just the same: moral questions aside, the connectivities of all subcultures, be they those of heterosexual snuff film aficionados, pedophiles, or metropolitan gay men (in the age of AIDS), are structurally the same, and even if we feel that the last is perhaps about to dissolve in a fashion (queerness having been "normalized"), we are not yet fully there.

Although the third volume of the *Journal* has some relatively calm moments, it is by and large an attack on a major problem of existence: the assumption of an identity, the definition of that identity, and the explanation of that identity to self and others. For Neaud in particular, this seems to be a complicated situation, for even if he has

---

[16] The book of hours known as *Les Très Riches Heures du Duc de Berry* is an early fifteenth-century illuminated devotional.

been "out" as a gay man, he recognizes that he has been criticized for not fully having assumed his gay identity, whatever that may be. For some, this obviously means being part of the gay community, a participation which becomes difficult given Neaud's explicit choice as a real individual not to move to Paris, seen by many as a gay Mecca, especially for artists and intellectuals. And yet staying in the provinces is not inherently better, for if there is one kind of clone system in metropolitan Paris, what Neaud might perceive as an oppressive homonormativity, in the provinces certain normalizing stereotypes reconfirm normality. At one point, having chewed the fat with a group of gay acquaintances, Neaud subsequently criticizes their "heterocentrism," which for him is a kind of complicitous repetition of stereotypical images of masculinity, such as the sexiness of soccer or rugby players and a reinforcement of the values of a society. One may be gay, they seem to be saying, but one should, in the sway of heterocentrism, retain heteronormative concepts of beauty, handsomeness, masculinity, and the like (3:59–60).

But these are not the only possibilities. For others, and perhaps for Neaud as well, there is the difficulty of engaging with the concept of the *pour autrui* as defined by Sartre: the figure one is for others. If Sartre's homosexual characters, most famously the "Autodidacte" or self-made man in *La Nausée*, assuming their homosexuality through an assumption of the *pour autrui*, are generally abject figures, Neaud's rebellion is both at the abjectness painted by society and at the liberal tolerance offered by some. By the end of the volume, through the unraveling of complacency and what Neaud, following Camus, calls "l'idéologie du sympa [the ideology of 'niceness']," the crisis has reached fever pitch, and it is only in the fourth volume that we will see a change of spirit. Early on, Neaud states that "Si faire le portrait de quelqu'un revient à le réduire à une typologie, alors il ne s'agit de ne compter dans l'ensemble des 'entiers naturels' qu'avec les nombres premiers [If doing a portrait of someone turns out to reduce him to a typology, then it is only a matter of counting in the set of 'natural wholes' with the first numbers]" (3:23). This is not the only recourse to numbers and figures in Neaud's work and it is a sign of both his frustration and his attempts to bring order. But in point of fact, Neaud struggles with the very possibility of finding a way to represent identity in language and in graphic form: "L'identité est chose si complexe que la représenter revient à tenter de distinguer, par leur seule reproduction, la qualité de deux toiles abstraites ... Ici, une toile de Binus, … Là un chef d'œuvre de Gerhard Richter [Identity is such a complex thing that representing it is a matter of distinguishing the quality of two abstract paintings. Here a painting by Binus. There a masterpiece by Gerhard Richter]" (3:23). Much later, we find the answer to this *mise-en-cause* of the abstract: reproducing a Gerhard Richter abstract painting, the narrator wonders (3:151) whether reproducing a masterpiece in a comic strip or graphic text is possible and continues to muse as to whether one does not still need partisan and literal judgment. The drawing in that panel reproduces the Richter, with, superimposed upon it, "Ceci est un chef d'œuvre [This is a masterpiece]." This is a reference to René Magritte's famous "Ceci n'est pas une pipe [This is not a pipe]" as a primary intertext, with the phrase sitting under a painted pipe on the canvas. But, putting aside the vague double entendre of Magritte's statement, at least when viewed through a contemporary lens ("pipe" being slang for fellatio), and the ambiguity of the demonstrative pronoun serving as a deictic but of an unknown referent, this is a reversal of Magritte's joke into a statement of identity. And yet, that statement of identity is also transformative, for the reference is to the Eucharist: "Ceci est mon corps [This is my body]," i.e., "hoc est enim corpus meum." At some level, then, Neaud sees his art as having a transformational power that changes the self into something beyond it. If he writes and draws his identity through his journal, it is as if those actions were the becoming he seeks.

In a short set of pages devoted to a visit to Paris (3:156–60), Neaud distinguishes his autofictional protagonist from representations in contemporary gay novels, many or most of which are set in Paris, and from contemporary gay cinema, which uses Paris episodically as the *locus amoenus* of the institutions of homosexuality. Neaud's Paris is predominantly touristic: Beaubourg, where he sees a Joseph Beuys retrospective, the big bookstores, l'Arche de la Défense, and so forth. The only encounter, it would seem, is with an eighteen-year-old Hungarian man who, at the end of the sequence, is shown to be in love with his girlfriend and not at all interested in Neaud sexually. Interestingly, the Hungarian is not represented directly at first in a frame, but is represented, at one remove, in a sketch on a sketch pad, itself depicted as the subject of the frame. Musing on the encounter, "Pourquoi le prénom d'une fille me brise-t-il plus sûrement qu'un inévitable adieu? [Why does a girl's name break me more than an inevitable good-bye?]" (3:159),

Fabrice recognizes that there will be no follow-up, no morning after. And it is only then, in the absence of the young man, that he allows himself to draw a full-page frame of him. These Paris pages, then, are doubly fascinating, as they are the representation of the dissociation of the Neaud figure from any cohort and any institutions of homosexuality that might otherwise relieve – in a deontological sense – some of the existential solitude he seems to evoke throughout, as being alone, even when in a crowd. But the disappearance of the Hungarian also attests to a kind of ontological phenomenon: the more Neaud writes and draws, the more he creates avatars of himself. But the more he writes and draws, the less others find their reality as a fixed *pour autrui*. The other exists in his own disappearance, in the affect felt by Neaud, both as protagonist and as narrator/illustrator, in the hollow that not even a drawing can compensate for. The plenitude of complementarity between drawing and text that seemed to suffice in the first two volumes and that will return in the fourth is breaking down here.

Neaud's work is turned in different ways by his devotion to three specific elements of content and style. First, there is his interest in, his depiction of, and the means of representation he uses to represent (homo)sexuality, especially his own. Second, there are his moves away from story-telling or verisimilar representation: maps, figures/numbers, non-verisimilar drawings, incomplete faces, and so forth. Third, there is the periodic interruption of a didactic philosophy that, even when purportedly part of the story told, marks a pause. Here, however, far more than in earlier volumes – though the signs were certainly there – the complementarity is breaking down, and, to borrow a term from Jacques Derrida quoting Jean-Jacques Rousseau, both writing and drawing seem to be dangerous supplements to some sought-after, but undiscovered, essence.

In a series of frames, however, attesting to a kind of ambivalence in the inscription of the self, Neaud begins to erase himself from the picture. Here and there, one finds single frames that are still lives. What is unique here is the chronological process of five frames in which he disappears. In the first, following the dynamic of a flow of his "long monologues," we see a seemingly endless logorrhea caught in multiple balloons. Yet the effect is not at all discursive, but rather resembles Rabelais's story of the frozen words from *Le Quart Livre*. Language freezes, inert in space, and, unable to serve its communicative function; as it congeals it forms a brick wall, the subject of the next frame, what Neaud calls "un nouvel écran entre les autres et moi [a new screen between others and me]" (3:180). If there is a brick missing from the wall in the following frame, it is not clear which way it is moving, away to create a chink or in to fill a gap. Arguably, it is the latter; there will be no Thisbe to Neaud's Pyramis. For the others act only to reconfirm and reassure themselves in their complacency and what I have earlier referred to, following Neaud, as their heterocentrism. And yet, spectacularly, Neaud goes further in a somewhat Luddite fashion. If one had not suspected heretofore a sympathy with, at least at some level, the work of Renaud Camus, it becomes readily apparent here as the work becomes politicized. I am not suggesting for a moment that Neaud follows Camus in all ways or in many ways, although there is evidence enough for some shared political positions, but the movement that explains the position of the other, or more accurately of others, in Neaud is very reminiscent of Camus's writing from the late 1980s on. Here, the language could have come directly from Camus, who rails frequently about the absence of original discourse and the repeated use of trite phrases as received discourses of the other, in what Michel Deguy (491), referring to Roland Barthes (a spiritual father here for Camus), aptly defines as "*bathmology* – that pursuit of *doxa* that carries it along and continually renews it":

> La multiplicité des discours générée par le triomphe du multimédia a anéanti le caractère unique de la parole prise par la personne, n'en faisant plus que la possible illustration d'un discours qui nous est déjà parvenu, a déjà été digéré, et ne requiert plus l'urgence que son continu, cependant, nous impose. (3:180)

> [The multiplicity of discourses generated by the triumph of the multimedia has reduced to nothing the singular character of a word uttered by an individual, as those discourses make it only the possible illustration of a discourse that has come to us, that has already been digested, and that no longer needs the urgency that its continuation still imposes.]

This shared position of the singular versus the various commonplaces and cliches of the *doxa*, among which Camus labels "l'idéologie du sympa," is stretched by Neaud's figures: the first consists of an "at" sign [@] that surrounds a heart topped by a crown of thorns; the second is a frame filled with evenly spaced at signs. The singular sacrifice of true life is imprisoned in the "at" of our always already

determined nodes for email, the flat system of communication that
has replaced our face-to-face, often "in-your-face," direct presence,
only to be itself replaced by a series of evenly spaced controlled nodes
that are nowhere and everywhere at once. This will not be the last
religious symbol in the volume.

Elsewhere, Neaud comes out and says it directly without the use of
images, as he protests against the seeming ubiquity of the doxa:

> Le "cool," ou le "sympa," est un fasciste qui s'ignore. [...] Il s'illustre
> par l'emploi très fréquent, justement, de ce qui le définit lui-même
> parfaitement sans qu'il ne s'en rende compte. Si une discussion
> l'amène en des territoires de la pensée qui ne collent pas avec la pensée
> dominante qu'il sert (voir les phrases qu'il employait naguère et les
> idées sous-jacentes qui les sous-tendent), perdant pied, il ne connaîtra
> pas de meilleure défense que l'attaque veule et molle. ("Fabrice
> Neaud")

> [A "cool" or "nice" guy is a fascist who doesn't know it. He gives
> himself away in fact by the frequent use of what defines him perfectly
> without him realizing it. If a discussion brings him to territories of
> thought that do not chime with the dominant thought he uses (even
> sentences he used to use and the underlying ideas subtending them),
> losing his balance, he will have no better defence than a cowardly,
> soft attack.]

Thus, there are two versions of Neaud: the earlier one that inscribes
the self in a movement that seeks an epistemological explanation
through process – a lengthy process that again, especially in this
third volume, seems to mirror the tomes of Renaud Camus himself,
an author who turned from writing experimental novels to publishing
volume after volume of a lengthy diary. And there is also the later one,
which seeks an immediate ontological explanation through presence
and which is an infelicitous combination of the political – the critique
of the post-modern, of the ideology of the "sympa," in short, – and
a Luddite nostalgia for some imagined presence that used to exist
but that disappeared under the weight of a mountain of "at" signs.
Yet the Neaud who continues to write and to draw finds himself in
himself at the moments he seems to be the most isolated and the most
distant from any presence to himself or to others, as he becomes
trapped in problems that may indeed be of his own making:

> Et comme à chaque fois où, pris dans cette nasse qui me renvoie à
> moi-même, je me piège tout seul, j'en viens à parler de moi, de mes

problèmes, de bande dessinée, puis d'autobiographie, et me voici
lancé dans une immense tentative de justification théorique de cette
dernière. Discours hyperlogique et infatué d'une machine paranoïque
emballée. (3:184)

[And as is the case each time I get caught in this net then send me
back to myself, I fall into a trap alone; I wind up speaking about
myself, my problems, comics, then autobiography, and I wind up in
an immense attempt to justify the last. A hyperlogical and infatuated
discourse of a worked up paranoid machine.]

Illustrating a metaphor about sameness, heteronormativity, and
identity, Neaud posits a bag of white marbles, all alike, among which
he is a lone black marble (266). Yet since we are all progressive
thinkers, the black and white model is a gross simplification; we
are really all of different colors. Ironically, because he is providing a
black and white drawing, the different colors become translated in
the drawing as black-and-white- and gray-patterned marbles. In any
case, even among the liberals of many colors, he is a metallic ball-
bearing. Still, no peace is at hand, for in a bag of marbles of many
hues and metallic ball-bearings, he is a die on the faces of which (at
least the three we see) is inscribed "etc." That "et cetera," of course,
means that the list of metaphors for his difference could go on and
on, but it also means that he must go on and on in his logorrhea,
explaining how to fill the et ceterae of his life, or better yet, how to
represent as an essential the "et cetera" (or series thereof) that ends
up being the incarnation of his existence, in a fractured difference
yet joint assemblage of words and images.

Alone and naked, Fabrice rails anew against the doxa: "Depuis des
mois, depuis des années, j'étouffe de vos discours avortés, de votre
idéologie impuissante, de votre fascisme ordinaire [For months, years
even, I have been choking on your aborted discourses, your impotent
ideology, your ordinary fascism]" (3:282). Again, we are witnessing
a strange contradiction, but one that now begins to become clear.
If the "ordinary fascism" is the remainder of the Camus-inspired
discourses, it is also clear that the other two adjectives are not chosen
by accident: "aborted" and "impotent" relate to a medico-biological
discourse of fertility, of conception, and of birth, but are the negative
versions of that discourse, as they relate either to a terminated
pregnancy or to the inability to fertilize an egg (or even have an
erection). And after being alone, naked in a crowd, he hallucinates
and shows these heterocentrists splattered with what is apparently

their own blood in a violent discourse worthy of Dantec: "Je rêve d'une milice de laissés-pour-compte armée qui vienne vous tirer de vos lits conjugaux pour piétiner le fruit pourri de vos entrailles [I dream of an army of a cast-aside militia that would rip you out of your conjugal beds to stamp on the rotten fruit of your guts]" (282). The message is mixed: as I have just indicated, the heterocentrists produce aborted foetuses or less, if impotent. Yet at the same time, it is the gang of marginalized individuals that produces those abortions, babies from wombs "untimely ripped" as Shakespeare says. What is going on here? On one level, Neaud is implying that all reproduction leads only to abortion, to incompletion, and to a lack of fulfillment, even when the birth is brought to term. It is a rant against human nature that propagates itself, the *jouissance* being only a means to an end, which is the reproduction of the same and the iterative. Let us leave to one side the fact that the logical consequence of this is extinction, except insofar as this dream – "alors je rêve [then I am dreaming]" (3:282), he writes – is an affect or even a symptom of self-loathing. For, on another level, it is a dream of creating differently, of a self-creation through the double act, one specified throughout, that of *poesis*, and one hinted at over and over: *jouissance* as an end in itself. In this, of course, he joins Camus – think of *Tricks*, for example – but he also joins the ranks of the late modern and the post-modern who reclassify the body and self in a different genealogy, filiation, and autonomy from the necessarily altruistic heteronomy that preceded the split between sex and propagation, or rather, more explicitly, between sexuality and propagation.

Even if Neaud's political diatribe is not only a move away from a heterocentrist progress narrative but also, seemingly, a move toward a rather conservative self-protection of what it may mean to be gay in a kind of essentialist model akin to that of Camus, the propagation of his discourse rejoins those who, inventing themselves through their art from Jean Cocteau onward, write themselves as an ever-changing script. Cocteau's famous line could ironically be appropriated by Neaud, if only Neaud were able recognize the irony: "Je suis un mensonge qui dit la vérité [I am a lie that tells the truth]." The difference here, of course, is that Neaud (like Camus) believes that he alone is telling the truth. Two pages later we find a sort of manifesto or diatribe that sums all this up:

Libertaires de merde! Tolérants de merde! Socio-culs de merde! Nous serons toujours les exclus de votre projet grandiose de monde meilleur! Entre la vérité et le monde, nous avons déjà choisi. Nous n'avons rien à espérer, hormis la chute dans le sang de votre putain de pérennité de l'espèce! (284).

[Libertarians full of shit! Tolerant people full of shit! Socio-assholes full of shit! We shall always be excluded from your grandiose project of a better world! We have already chosen between truth and the world. We have nothing to hope for, aside from the fall of your fucking eternal species into blood.]

In this light, the end of the volume is revealing. Or more accurately, there is a revelation that there will be no revelation. In three sparse frames, one with a large airplane heading off, one with a second, more distant one, and the third with what can only be described as an egg-cup out of which something pulverized is falling, the narrator resorts to a religious vocabulary: "sacrifices," "une vallée de larmes [a vale of tears]," "sacré [sacred]," "grâce," and "miracle" (3:348–49), among other expressions. But here, instead of a voice clamoring for a past and crying for plenitude, there is rather a voice knowing its incompleteness. This time, losing friends or being lonely will not just happen but will have been calculated to happen. He knows that everything "finira mal. Tout finit mal [will finish badly. Everything finishes badly]" (3:348). And this fatality is inevitable since there are no alternative routes: "il n'y pas d'autres voies, nous le savons [we know that there are no other paths]" (3:348). Here then the meaninglessness of life – "un espace sacré où les sens sont nettoyés [a sacred space in which meanings are cleaned up]" (3:349) – is not the pessimistic or nihilistic position against which he must rail, but rather is something with a superior aesthetic, for it is as beautiful as a painting by Richter (3:349). This return of the aesthetic, the one with which he began, marks the end of the text, except for what I would call an epilogue in which both style and discourse change measurably.

In a rare depiction of heteronormativity that features both women and children and is set during the month of August, Fabrice seems happier and even touched by irony – in several frames, he wears a sweatshirt with "USA" on front and back (3:353–54). And even when there is an altercation in the car, ostensibly provoked by the sister of a friend, it is not cause for long meditative reflection, but rather the very "normal" reaction: "Mais quelle conne!! Elle a le don [What a stupid bitch! She has the knack for it]" (357). Later in the train, there is an accident after which he mimics a bad English accent in French, writing, "une anglaise dégringole et nous apprend avec une mine quasi réjouie, 'Ow C'est teuribuel! Un homme s'est souiciday! On a woulay dessus!! Il est coupay en morceaux!!' [An Englishwoman approaches and tells us, almost with a joyful look on her face, 'Oh, it is terrible. A man killed himself. The train rolled over him. He was cut to pieces']" (3:362). So whereas the earlier Fabrice or the earlier Neaud might have bemoaned the event and likened his own empty life to this one, it deserves and receives no commentary. In other words, Neaud has finally learned to stop thinking and rethinking, has finally learned to accept silence as meaningless, not meaningful.

When the train arrives in Bayonne, the characters recognize that the fair is alive and is filling the city's streets and squares with thousands of people. We then read the significant statement: "nous nous jetons au cœur de la foule [we threw ourselves into the middle of the crowd]" (3:365). For the first time, we believe that there is a bond of solidarity in the group formed by a "nous"; Neaud is not taking an oppositional or adversarial position; he is not rethinking or reacting to what others say; he is with them, without the blanks that often isolate him even when with others. Moreover, there is the ecstatic joy of being a part of the throng, indistinguishable from the other and from others, bonding finally in solidarity, not under the umbrella of the doxa, but under that of the human (3:365). There is "un rut total [everyone's in heat]" and for once, he is not the only one, nor is he alone (3:367). And, in fact, the relation to self has changed profoundly as the corporealized singularity or monadicity gives way to a Deleuzean ecstasy: "Nous glissons comme deux quarks sur cette surface plastique. Sommes-nous corpusculaires ou bien ondulatoires? [We slide like two quarks on that plastic surface. Are we made of particles or of waves?]" (3:364). Dissolving into some otherness, he repeats as a mantra and as a statement of being, "Jouir! Jouir! Jouir. [Cum]" (3:372), the first two times with exclamation marks, the third time as a statement, with a period. That is what it is, we are; being and doing, nouns and verbs are no longer different, but melted into the *jouir* of *jouissance* and vice versa.

I shall conclude this section with the final page. Three drawings mark it: a tree at a distance; part of the tree, in a mid-range drawing; and finally a close-up of flowering branches. The final words are telling, as they pass through the fleeting possibility of religious belief toward a kind of peace with himself:

Un prêtre de mes amis m'a dit un jour: "il y a d'autres fécondités; gît au fond de nous un trésor inconnu, invisible et prêt à resplendir." Apaisante perspective, mais aussi fausse que douce. Je peux encore m'amuser un peu. J'ai vingt-six ans. Mais cette jeunesse-là est, quand-même, perdue irrémédialement. Nous sommes le 4 août 1995. (3:374)

[One of my friends, who is a priest, said to me one day, "There are other fertile places. Lying deep within us is an invisible and unknown treasure ready to shine." A peace-inducing perspective but as false as it is sweet. I can still have a bit of fun. I am twenty-six years old. But that youth, however, is irrevocably lost. It is August 4 1995.]

But the tree is in flower out of season. If the priest was wrong in the sense in which he meant what he said, he may also have been right for Neaud. Only time will tell, and if Dantec's vision is condemned to hell, Neaud's will perhaps awaken, as he seems to do in the one volume of the series that follows this crisis about who he is, how he is, and how he is in the world. Starting out from a singular position "far from the madding crowd," in this volume of his diaries, Fabrice Neaud uses the diary not to reach the religious solution dangled in front of him by the priest but as a witnessing of art, his art, as a kind of therapy, after which he can theoretically have his prayers answered, albeit in a secular fashion. Whether or not this will continue is hard to assess, but at this moment in his writing, he seems to have reached a level of self-understanding and self-acceptance after the many soul-searching experiences he has gone through, as well as the positions he has used his art to work through.

III. More than Just Eye-Candy: Jones-Gorlin's *Rose Bonbon* and the Touch of Pedophilia

Necrophilia, coprophagia/scatology, water sports, rape, incest, pedophilia, bestiality, bondage and discipline, and sado-masochism: this is a list, not at all exclusive, of sexual practices and practices involving sex – for rape is arguably not a sexual practice as such – that many liberal adults would find objectionable. Of course the acts do not neatly fit within the same category, as mere variants of some normal, normative, or vanilla heterosexuality or homosexuality. Some might say that practices such as sado-masochism or bondage and discipline, as much as they might be out of the mainstream of practice for many, or even most, couples, are essentially matters between or among consenting adults. Water sports, coprophagia, and scatology might push the limits and seem disgusting to many, because of the ways in which the abject is introduced into the realm of the sexual. And yet disgust, at least in civilized Western societies, seldom leads to legislation or even to a generalized opprobrium. While rape violates the Western concept of consensual behavior, necrophilia, incest, and bestiality violate what are generally perceived to be primary laws of nature and/or culture and are often defined as that which separates "us" from the animals (or in former times, savages, though the image has been invoked at times in conflicts between West and East).

In the modern world, pedophilia generally elicits similar reactions of disgust on the visceral and emotional level and, if confirmed by society, punishment on an objective social level. If certain societies have lowered the age of consent to thirteen, fourteen, or fifteen, thereby regulating and legalizing ephebophilia, bringing modernity into line with Attic Greece and Renaissance Europe, at least in praxis, there is, to my knowledge, no Western society that countenances pedophilia. Lolita's precociousness – and it was she who made the advances, just as is the case in A. M. Homes's excellent novel *The End of Alice* – was associated nevertheless with a post-pubescent individual. Yet why should it be punished, since pedophilic sex can occur between two consenting individuals? What is different relates to two different registers. First, up to what is deemed the age of consent – often confused with the age of reason and the age of majority – parents are considered to own, as proprietors, the bodies and especially, the sexualities of their children. Since pedophilia generally occurs without the consent of the owner of the body – the parent – it is often tantamount to rape in the public's mind. Second, to be at the age of consent or reason, there must be a fully integrated *scientia sexualis*: not only must the child know the facts of life, often learned as early as the age of six or so, but he or she must be fully able to realize the consequences for his or her own body. The mastery of the *scientia sexualis* coincides with the gradual transfer of ownership of the body from the parent to the budding adolescent, permitted (though without express permission) to masturbate, to kiss, to pet, and eventually to have sex.

I have considered at some length the immediate ramifications of pedophilia, though without giving any berth to psychological explanations, in order best to frame an approach to the discursivities of a recent novel, *Rose Bonbon*, written by Nicolas Jones-Gorlin, published in 2002, and almost immediately subjected to an act of censure with threats by the government to ban the book for those under eighteen: these were impressionable minds (though those between fifteen and eighteen were already allowed to have sexual intercourse). But the book also carried the threat, it would seem, of the possible corruption of other potential pedophiles or the incitement to create pedophile rings.

With the exception of a tacked-on epilogue ostensibly written by a sympathetic, objective, but rather stupid journalist, in a rhetorical move reminiscent not only of Gide's prologue to *L'Immoraliste*, but also of Nabokov's *Lolita*, thereby distancing the text from affective disgust (and protecting the reader, so one would think), Jones-Gorlin's work is a thoroughly unapologetic and unreflective discourse of heterosexual pedophilia. From the very beginning, Simon, the pedophile in question and the first-person narrator, who is thoroughly enchanted with pre-pubescent girls, is swept up in a desubjectified collectivity. Rather than defining his own position as that of the desirer, Simon reverses the scenario and sees himself as the passive receptor and reactor to the waves of desire projected by young girls: "les émotions des gosses me viennent par ondes successives, me pénètrent, me remplissent, une vague de chaleur qui s'insinue dans mon corps, et me submerge, et où je me noie doucement, progressivement [kids' emotions come to me in successive waves, penetrate me, fill me, a heat wave that enters my body and submerges me, and in which I slowly and progressively drown]" (11). Pedophilia is initially framed as a reaction to an incarnation of desire, a radiating sexuality that is there whether the desirer is present or not. He is caught in the waves and transfixed, as if called to by that pheromonal display. The pedophile presents himself as being caught in a liquid/gaseous system that functions like an invisible parasite that invades the body and into which the solidity of the subject is dissolved. Thus the child's polymorphous perversity radiates and includes the adult, the supposedly normal adult in world of framed desire, in that perversity. If that discursive explanation hides a simple projective psychology of exculpatory behavior ("I am innocent, the other made me do it"), this changes nothing about the way in which the author constructs his fictional discursivity, in which the other – the child – marks the space in a reversal of various normativities.

The child projects herself into the adult, and while starting as a wave of desire, that projection is soon turned into writing, as that projection is inscribed within the adult. Reversing the development of the individual, the discourse of pedophilia ascribes the right of inscription to the child and the magic writing pad is the adult's lot: "Je mange des yeux comme si son image avait toujours été gravée dans mes gènes. Sa photo dans mon AND [I eat with my eyes as if her image had always been inscribed in my genes. Her photo in my DNA]" (12). Yet the inscription is a reinscription, the exterior corresponding to the interior, the parasite corresponding to something that is always already there. For Simon, pedophilia is that which is both outside and inside his masculinity and identity, a natural inscription for him that corresponds to an external stimulus for which it was waiting: pedophilia is an illustration of the Platonism of the *Symposium*.

Thus is pedophilia set up as both an event external to the individual adult male, one calling to him as a subject, and an event corresponding to the individual, even before he – for the sake of argument, I leave it in the masculine, as there is nothing here to permit the reader to project this structure onto women – is called to as subject. And that mutual compatibility and that sufficiency make the traditional means of propagation and filiation – the family bond – completely supplementary to the pedophile relation. Families interfere (15), convinced as they are that they have proprietary rights to the bodies of their children; families challenge the belief of the pedophile that his relation to the other is primary and that families, beyond exercising constraint, control, or possession, confuse biology with destiny. Families perceive the child as a blank slate onto which they inscribe heteronormativity; the pedophile knows otherwise: the child inscribes herself as both the *sujet supposé savoir* and the *sujet supposé avoir*.

It is a short step from the initial structure marking the pedophile universe to an attempted enactment of sexuality. Fixated on, if not obsessed with, possessing the child's genitalia, Simon conceives of a plan: "J'avais mon idée. Je voulais qu'elle ait envie de pisser [I had an idea. I wanted her to want to piss]" (16). And he connives in order to take Dorothée, the child in question, in the first explicit sex scene, to the toilet: "Devant moi: l'objectif: la porte des toilettes femmes. Rose bonbon. Juste à côté: les hommes. Bleu lavande [Ahead of me, the objective: the door of the women's toilet. Cotton candy pink.

Next to it: men's. Lavender blue]" (17). Cotton candy pink, posed as a choice with another pastel color, gives the novel its title, but also marks pedophilia as being not of the adult world; it is a garish color, more Disney, childish, and artificial than real. The color also echoes the artifice of the situation, in which Simon, essentially a total stranger, has managed to get the mother to allow him to accompany her daughter to the toilet. But the innocence of the situation, or what Simon believes is the innocence of the situation, is soon marked by the re-entrance of reality in the form of the family, with the mother cast in an evil, possessive role, as she reasserts her ownership of her daughter's body:

> Suckant [sic] léchant se saoulant de l'urine claire de Dorothée, du sucre de sa virginité!
> Évidemment, c'est là que la reine des putes a décidé de faire son entrée; c'est pile là que tout a basculé, que le destin m'a chié dessus, m'a balancé toute sa poisse. (18–19)

> [Sucking, licking, getting drunk on Dorothy's urine, the sugar of her virginity. Obviously, it was then that the queen bitch decided to come in; it was just then that everything tilted, that fate shat on me and piled on rotten luck.]

For Simon, the pedophile, the universe is dualistic. On one side, it is populated by the innocence of children and framed by a cotton candy color scheme; this is the side in which he fits. Opposed to the purity is the world of adults, and more specifically the world of those who are parents and who believe they own their children's bodies. The pedophile revels in the lack of reproduction and wants to stop the chain of creation with the purity of the moment that is the virginity of the innocent child. Opposed to the clarity of childhood, the purity of virginal urine, is the fecal matter of the adult world, a world that marks, stains, and messes up innocence. And the innocence of the pedophile is perverted, with religious and reproductive overtones, into a horror in a phrase reminiscent of Dantec's diatribes and railings: "L'univers lui crache son film d'horreur: un monstre embrasse le con de la chair de sa chair [The universe spits out its horror film: a monster kisses the cunt of the flesh of her flesh]" (19).

The inevitable legal trial ensues and it changes the ways in which Simon is subjected to the discourse of the other. No longer subject only to the solipsistic, dualist universe of innocence and evil, he is addressed as a juridical, medical, psychiatric, and political subject. Alienated from his own position of identifying himself as part of an edenic universe, Simon is forced to think outside the present moment, the moment of presence that is the moment of purity. He is forced to conjure up a past and to envision a non-teleological future. Faced with the reinterpretation of his act as not only a guilty pleasure, but also a criminal action, he first reconstructs a normal past, as if to reclaim the innocence and the non-pathological nature of his act and as if to set himself off against the interpretation of self that is about to happen. And indeed, the first sentence in the following quotation, albeit a transparent idiom, can be read as depicting something happening to him, instead of his having consciously chosen to consummate his fantasy:

> Avant que ça m'arrive, j'étais un type de moins de trente ans, qui faisait le VRP dans deux ou trois régions, et vivait dans un HLM, ni beau, ni moche, TV, hi-fi, des copains mais pas vraiment d'amis, avec une petite amie de temps en temps [...]. (19–20)

> [Before this happened to me I was a guy under thirty, a sales rep in a few areas, and living in subsized housing, neither handsome nor ugly. TV, hi-fi, pals, but no real friends, with a girlfriend from time to time.]

Very quickly will that normal, pedestrian past be forcibly reconstructed as the lawyer assigned to Simon (25) looks for a childhood pathology that would have produced the aberration. Jones-Gorlin pushes the envelope by refusing to give an etiology and a pathological past to the construction of the pedophile moment. Again, we notice the construction of things having happened to Simon, while the structures of willful behavior are absent; Simon is a Sartrean *salaud*, a man of infinite *mauvaise foi*:

> Ça me fait mal de mentir à ce point; perso, je crois bien avoir eu l'enfance la plus normale qui soit, et c'est d'ailleurs ce qui rend dingues mon avocat et son copain le psy, qui ressort après chaque séance en s'arrachant un peu plus les cheveux, désolé mec, je peux pas inventer la faille dans mon cerveau, ça c'est ton boulot. (26–27)

> [It bothers me to lie this much. Personally, I think I had as normal a childhood as possible, and that is what makes my lawyer and his buddy the shrink crazy. The latter leaves after each session pulling out his hair, sorry, man, I can't invent the crack in my brain, it's your job.]

In this world, pedophilia can be a construction without a past; normality can shift immediately into what society perceives as a perversion that can spring into being out of nothing. In the world created within the novel, the absence of a pathology makes infinite sense: moving from the normal to the pedophile is completely comprehensible within the solipsistic universe in which Simon's desires are different from those of the majority, but not perceived as abnormal, and even less as pathological or punishable. In fact, this new address of the subject produces an unforeseen future as well, one different from the goal-oriented one that Simon has previously constructed for himself: the goal not so much of possessing the child, but of worshiping, adoring, and pleasing her as he pleases himself and fulfills his vision. The subjected position of the self as object turns the body into the abject that he has rejected from the world of heteronormative reproduction: "Il y en a même un [flic] qui est venu pisser sur le mur de ma cellule [A cop even came and pissed on the wall of my cell]" (21). In an image that will haunt him throughout the rest of the book, his body is potentially possessed by others, in a double movement that is a serious parody of all that is anathema to him: "'Tu sais ce qui arrive aux pédophiles quand ils vont en prison ? dit un flic à voix haute en passant près de ma cellule. [...] Les autres détenus finissent toujours par les chopper [...] Et après, ils les enculent. [...] Ils leurs coupent les couilles!' [You know what happens to child molesters when they go to prison, asked a cop in a loud voice as he passed by my cell? The other prisoners finally get him. After, they fuck his ass. They cut off his balls]" (21). That sense of possession and anal intercourse is always already there, inscribed in the mythos of the prison. And at the same time, the fate awaiting "short eyes," i.e., child molesters, is particularly extreme, and would not exclude castration. But here it is inscribed as discourse on Simon's body (as opposed to occurring): the anal penetration is there through discourse, as is the castration, both in a ghostly fashion, marking him in a future that will not happen, but that has always already happened at this point. Penetration of any sort, simulation or parody of the reproductive model, moves the text toward a reinscribed genealogy, and away from the purity Simon desires. And while the act of castration would seemingly, in the creation of a eunuch, be a way of achieving that non-reproductive status, it is actually more a reminder of male potency, of androgens, and of the power of testosterone to force penetration.

In a story told straightforwardly, as opposed to *The End of Alice*, which is told in complicated retrospective flashbacks from prison, it is perhaps superfluous to mention that Simon does not go to prison. Rather, Jones-Gorlin creates a parallel universe for his pedophile in which Simon can look at the forbidden fruit but not touch it. This is the new, humane, medico-juridical solution. Rather than incarcerate him for the fate already potentially inscribed on his body, the state, in a "new program," would prefer to isolate him somewhat and castrate him pharmacologically and psychiatrically. He is given a trailer to live in away from the city; his therapy involves seeing a psychiatrist and taking pills. All of this is intended to mark or delimit action: he can, theoretically, retain his fantasies, but the state insists that they remain fantasies. Simon's problem is that his internalization of the discourse of the other is essentially impossible; he cannot *not* be himself, despite some initial attempts: "J'avais le droit de respirer des fleurs, marcher dans les rues, aller au ciné, même mater des gosses, mais bon, toujours à distance, keep distance. Les yeux baladeurs, les mains in da pocket. La roquette dans le slip. Le zip tranquille. La quille à plat [I was permitted to smell flowers, walk in the street, go to movies, even look at kids, but only at a distance, keep distance [sic]. Wandering eyes; hands in pockets. A rocket in my pocket. My zipper quiet. My rod all soft]" (33).

The author articulates this separation of fantasy from action in two episodes that move the novel from its initial position to its second avatar, in which there is a redoubling of the pedophile position. The first episode involves a displacement from a totally unacceptable object of desire to a less unacceptable one. Here, Simon goes to a discotheque and picks up an adolescent, in what would seem to be a perversion of his own perversion. Rather than the sweet innocence he found necessary in the first scene of the novel, what is fundamental here is the lack of innocence, the corrupt Lolita-like behavior of a girl who, beyond the position of innocence, is already inscribed into the position of the subject who *does* know:

> Au milieu de la conversation, je m'enfonce dans mon fauteuil et j'écarte bien les jambes pour faire saillir mon paquet. Le test.
>
> Automatiquement, ses yeux s'arrondissent. Se remplissent.
>
> Feu vert! (37–38)

[In the middle of the conversation I lean back in my chair and I spread my legs to show off my stuff. The test.

Automatically, her eyes get wider and full.

Green light!]

Even if she responds subconsciously or instinctively to his physical movement, even if it is therefore her hormones speaking – it is in fact a question of raging hormones – he soon learns that there is a correspondence between her reaction and her body. He proceeds to play a game with her, and as he takes off her panties (41), he discovers pubic hair and an odor, both of which, as signs of maturity, he finds completely unerotic and quite offensive. For Simon, even a heterosexual version of Gidean ephebophilia is not an adequate substitute for the unsullied purity of pedophilia.

Nor are metonymic displacement and voyeurism suitable replacements for the object. At this point, Simon takes a job with "Ô Burger" as "Jack'o," who is "le clown officiel de la chaîne, chargé d'amuser son public d'enfants. Un job taillé sur mesure pour moi, ça m'a sauté aux yeux. Un job pour mes compétences personnelles muy especial [the official clown of the franchise, in charge of amusing the children who are its clientele. A job that fits me perfectly; it jumped to my attention. A job for my personal talents muy especial]" (46). Aside from the bad Spanish, matching the earlier bad English, and the possible reference to Michael Jackson, sometimes known as "Wacko Jacko" and about whom speculative rumors relating to possible pedophilia circulated for many years, the scene trades intimacy for proximity and returns Simon, ever so slightly, to sex at a distance. Contact with the other turns into masturbation, the physical sign of acting on his fantasy without violating the terms of his "freedom" and therapy. And again, we should note the construction that he uses, a passive voice that makes him the object of forces and not the subject expressing his desires:

Il m'est arrivé de me masturber à l'intérieur de mon déguisement de clown, en présence des enfants, des parents, des clients.

Un jour, même, j'ai éjaculé à l'intérieur d'un gobelet que j'ai ensuite rempli à ras bord de Soda Boum, et je l'ai fait boire à une fillette aux cheveux blonds presque blancs [...] (48)

[I have masturbated in my clown outfit, in front of children, parents, clients.

One day I even ejaculated in a cup that I then filled to the brim with Soda Boum and a made a little girl with almost white blond hair drink it.]

But again, this displacement of fantasy into an action is a mere stop-gap measure that does not solve his libidinal problems. There is a necessary erotic fixation on a specific scene that must be enacted and no substitutes will do. The medical and juridical response to handling "perversion" are inadequate because they necessitate a rhetoric of displacement away from the specific language of the perversion and away from the ways in which desire is codified in sexuality. Even when the elements are there, if they are in a displaced order, they will not work: in the first scene, as here, there is a man, a girl, and a liquid. But the liquid is produced elsewhere; it is a sign of potency and not purity; it is potentially part of the reproductive chain that Simon's perversion fights at every turn.

In a reinscription of the classic nineteenth-century solution for sexual problems, variously sought in graham crackers, Kellogg's cornflakes, what T. C. Boyle calls "the road to Wellville" in the book of the same name, the reinvention of the Olympic Games by Pierre de Coubertin, Robert Baden-Powell's boy scouts, and German free body culture (*Freikörperkultur*), sex can find an outlet by being actively or forcibly sublimated into various other activities, including appropriate, non-stimulating foods (not the case here) and physical activity. Simon starts to go jogging to take his mind off things. He meets "le Vieux [the Old Man]," who is in excellent shape and who is also jogging through the forest. Trying to catch up, Simon runs into an oak tree; concerned about Simon's accident, the Old Man takes him home to his place. Through a transitional conversation that brings matters out into the open, they discover their shared pedophilia, though the Old Man prefers boys to girls. The Old Man is very rich, lives splendidly in contrast to Simon's exiguous life, and owns marks of status, including a Picasso, a Pollock, and a Cézanne. No sooner have these marks of success been registered than the normalization of pedophilia occurs, as if wealth could buy certain privileges (which of course it can) as well as the freedom from being interpellated by a discourse of medico-juridical constraints:

Personnellement, je ne me sens pas malade, m'a dit le Vieux. Et toi ?

– Je sais pas … D'après mon psy, je le suis.

– Ce que je crois, moi, c'est que c'est notre société qui est malade d'hypocrisie. (59)

[Personally, I don't think I'm sick, the Old Man said to me. You?

– Dunno. According to my shrink I am.

– What I think is that our society is sick with hypocrisy.]

The remark is facile, predictable, and hackneyed: a projection of pathological behavior onto the other, as if the pedophile were normal and the society not. But where the remark is less than facile is in what it implies: society invokes a cult of youth – in his interview with Bontour, the author calls it "jeunisme [youthism]" – and it forces the spectator – for it is a spectator society – to buy into that cult and culture and thereby sublimate sexual desires into recognitions of beauty and innocence, while stymieing any acting on that desire.

The Old Man introduces an element of complicity, whereby Simon learns that he is not alone. But complicity comes in all guises and the first is a kind of forced complicity brought on by what Jones-Gorlin retrospectively and apologetically characterizes in an interview with Bontour as penury, and which here actually entails parental complicity. The scene repeats the structure of the initial scene in which the mother, against all measures of common sense, allows Simon to accompany her daughter to the toilet. The Old Man shows up at the restaurant, fixates on a ten- or eleven-year-old boy of South Asian background, rents him from his father for fifteen minutes, and takes the boy into the toilet of the restaurant, in front of which the father stands guard (67–69). In the same interview with Bontour, Jones-Gorlin said of this scene: "And the message of my book is 'Let's not get to that point.' Let's not get to that terrible situation in which someone can buy a child from impoverished parents. The purchase of the child by the 'Old Man' is the result of the misery and agreement of the parents." And yet the scene that Jones-Gorlin describes in the novel is not as marked by need as he seems to imply in his revisionist comment in the interview. Rather, it is the consent, perhaps motivated by need, that creates the situation, as well as the parents' belief that they own the bodies of their children. If the parents here were truly in need of money, would they really be going to a restaurant? While arguably that position is most often used to protect children, its amoral extension into the realm of child prostitution is consonant with the position.

The second part of the novel describes a change in strategy that will permit Simon to attract young girls in an appropriate manner. Accompanied by the Old Man, he goes to a fancy restaurant where he meets several of the Old Man's influential and like-minded friends, including a judge. It is specifically at this point that the concept of a pedophile ring is introduced. Contrary to other sexual activities and contrary to Simon's initial egregious behavior, pedophilia is often characterized, both in this novel and in the press, as being part of a group's activity, in a shared complicity. By this, I do not mean that there is group sex, but rather, that there is a shared discourse among like-minded individuals, as well as an exchange of child pornography. Pedophilia and "kiddie porn" mark an economy of exchange in which signs of that sexuality are passed from one hand (or one computer) to another.

Under the guidance of the Old Man, Simon is slowly transformed from an eccentric, pathologically isolated social pariah to being a cynosure. He is rebaptized "Dany King," he undergoes physical training, and he goes on a reality show called *Space Therapy*, his presence on which is based on the fact that the (female) producer is friends with the Old Man. Though she is presented only in passing, given the world in which this novel is set, she too may be a pedophile (86–89). Needless to say, Simon, as Dany King, wins the contest and is interviewed live by the same producer; at the end of the interview, he begins to sing on camera, a performance that launches his career as a star – for star quality is immediate – as the singer called "l'ami des enfants [the friend to children]" (96).

Jones-Gorlin optimizes the "youthism" by making it part of a system of exchange that is both real and specular: real, because the group of pedophiles functions to aid, abet, and protect its members, and specular, because it fits into a *société de spectacle* in which what is lauded – youth – is also that which is shunned. So the beauty of youth is what makes the system function, yet it is anathema to desire openly within the system. Simultaneously, in creating this specular and spectacular model in which various individuals participate in order to produce a power grid alternative to the normative one, the author moves the novel from the position of the individual, lone pederast, Simon, to the classic concept of a pedophile ring just discussed and now made part and parcel of the general cultural, semiotic, and communicational grid of society in which spectators are unknowingly complicit.

There is a common discourse available, even if the object in question is different: boys for some, girls for others, both for still others. In this alternative version of power, the pedophiles or pornographers replace the parents' possession of the child's body with their own, either through real physical possession or through virtual possession, through the gaze, at child porn, in which children have knowingly or unknowingly become the subject of the photographer's equipment. What this means within the communitarian discourse is that the child is effectively neuter/neutral – *das Kind*, as German says – and it is only each individual instance of a child that is gendered for the possessor. What this also means, strangely for the individual such as Simon, is the possibility of reversal. He too can become the child, but in so doing, he does not recognize the monstrosity of what he does and cannot logically jump to a reflection on his own position. After having been kissed by the mother of one of the adoring children, Simon rages that he wants to have her brought to justice for having raped the mouth of a non-consenting adult (99–100). Thus does Simon invent himself as an innocent victim – of an evil adult – and yet he cannot understand that his position vis-à-vis a child is completely parallel to that of this invasive mother.

Not content to remain there, the author reintroduces the family to the mix. It is if that violation of Simon/Dany releases the novel from the path of facilitation it has been following since Simon met Le Vieux, for it is at this point that Jones-Gorlin introduces a forbidden object of desire in the form of a six- or seven-year-old girl with brown hair for whom Simon immediately falls, and whose name, echoing the title of the novel itself, is Rose (100–101). She is off-limits because she is the grand-niece of the Old Man, who insists that Rose is not available and that, if Simon touches her, he has a lot to lose (103). Needless to say, there is a scene of seduction while Rose is taking a bath (104–109), in which she plays along. It is only when Simon French-kisses her that the game turns and she tells him that she will tell her uncle.

It is at this point that there is a radical shift in the novel. Heretofore everything was structured around the double enunciation of pedophilia: first in the individual and then in the group or ring. While the plot mattered, it was built on rather unlikely events: a mother letting her child go to the toilet with a complete stranger, Simon running into a tree, and his winning a reality show, only to be immediately reinvented as a superstar. The flimsy plot is an excuse for the author to explore the ramifications of the discourses and affects of pedophilia as well as the place of a kind of invisible pedophilia built into the consumer and communicational system. Here, with the discourses and affects of pedophilia fully in place, the novel takes a turn. Having been brought into the pedophile ring by the Old Man, Simon is part of a redefined family, in what anthropology calls "fictive kinship," i.e., kinship that goes beyond biological or adoptive structures. Thus, while pedophilia is – in Simon's world – entirely within the realm of the acceptable, the violation of the incest taboo is not. As Simon's belonging to the pedophile ring makes him family to the Old Man, he is therefore also related to the grand-niece, who is therefore off-limits. Simon's violation of this final taboo shifts the novel away from its explorations of pedophilia and its discourses and into the complicated plot mechanism that makes up the rest of the novel.

While this scene is carried out off-camera – for this is a first-person narrative – the consequences are quick to ensue and the Old Man arranges for Simon's downfall. Simon is interviewed by a reporter in his dressing room in an interview on which Le Vieux insisted. The reporter turns quickly to asking Simon whether it is true that he is a pedophile; Simon beats him up, bloodying his nose in the process and sending him to hospital. And while it later turns out that the interview was carried out under false pretenses, the story of Simon's pedophilia still makes the headlines of the tabloid press. While the Old Man seemingly helps Simon by sending him away from the limelight, he has his revenge, in a kind of orchestrated self-exculpation, by accusing Simon, on television, of pedophilia. Simon goes back to Paris to try to see the Old Man, but while waiting to go up to his hotel room, he runs into the fake journalist, who is leaving with his pay-off. Realizing to what extent he has been set up, but not really thinking it through, Simon takes half of the actor's money, and begins to figure matters out: "Un faux journaliste, un vrai scandale, des infos dans tous les journaux [A fake journalist, a real scandal, stories in all the newspapers]" (129). Once he has figured it out, he plans his vengeance on the Old Man.

The third and final part of the novel consists of Simon's complicated, organized revenge on the Old Man. He exacts this revenge in the only manner possible in this world: he develops his own pedophile ring. First, in Briquebec (in Normandy), having changed his appearance, Simon goes into a bakery where there is a display of marzipan boy scouts. Sensing that the baker has pedophilic interests, he starts a conversation with the baker's wife and places an order for one hundred such scouts. The baker offers to make a full-sized "real" scout (134), with "quelques détails réalistes [several realistic details]" (135), as Simon requests, with more than an echo of the group activities already mentioned:

> Moi j'avais l'impression de lui serrer la bite, pas la main, à Raymond. Tout ce qu'il attendait, c'était des complices. Une bande. Des copains de virée. L'excitation mutuelle. La pédophilie grégaire, par effet de masse. Le sport collectif. (135–36).

> [I had the feeling I was shaking Raymond's cock, not his hand. All he needed was accomplices. A group. Short-term buddies. Mutual sexual excitement. Gregarious pedophilia, through a mass effect. Team sport.]

So, just as has been seen in Dantec's vision of the world, child molestation is invariably turned into the feature of a group, a shared habit or vice that finds support in its practice by others as well.

The next encounter, in a park, with a man named Arthur, yields only an individual whose sexual orientation is toward bestiality. At the same time, there seems to be a belief on Simon's part that the differences of object (dog, girl) are less significant than the differences from the normalized objects of desire (women, men). This is further underlined by the final encounter for the group: in Cherbourg, an army captain in uniform approaches Simon, whom he has recognized as Dany King and who he asks to kill him because, as Simon guesses, he (the captain) is still a virgin. So while Jean, the army captain, recognizes Simon because of media attention, he does have a certain advantage in knowledge. But there is the assumption that non-normative sexuality, extending even to virginity in an adult male, is, if focusing on a particular object of desire, still a shared experience.

After they kidnap a boy scout and the baker dies, Simon disposes of Jean by pretending that he is the police come to arrest him for the baker's murder; Jean promptly commits suicide (145). Simon puts on Jean's uniform (146), goes into the bathroom to "rescue" the scout and tells him that he is a secret agent and that, in echoes of Dantec's paranoid universe, "'Je traque une organisation criminelle internationale. Un réseau de pédophiles,' j'ai dit en fronçant les sourcils. Puis, je me suis accroupi devant lui, j'ai posé mes deux mains sur ses épaules, et j'ai ajouté: 'J'ai besoin de toi mon garçon' ['I am on the trail of an international criminal organization. A network of child molesters,' I said, frowning. Then I got down in front of him, put my hands on his shoulders, and I added, 'I need you, my boy']" (146). Thus does Simon create yet another pedophile ring, albeit an imaginary one, to help reach the final act of the novel. Simon takes the scout as a "peace offering" to the Old Man (154), who takes the scout to his bedroom. But nothing happens, and the rest is told retrospectively. For Simon has put an exploding grenade under the scout's shirt. The scout's lowest shirt button, which is heat-sensitive, serves as the detonator for the grenade (163). So when the Old Man undresses him, the world comes apart. As for Simon, he is impaled on a statue, his spine shatters, and he is hospitalized.

Despite this strange and strained conclusion, the strength of this book lies in its multiple articulations of pedophilia, and the implications for changing masculinities, oscillating between the singular idiopathy of the lone sexual predator and the collective discourse, not only of pedophile rings, but also of family values, the boy scouts, and a rampant "youthism" that makes us all somewhat guilty of wanting to eat just one more piece of pink candy. Beyond that, as we have seen with all the works analyzed in this chapter, this is one of several responses to collective behaviors, forces, powers, and discourses that seek to reframe masculinity according to some versions of political correctness and, in some cases, New Age discourses. Each of the three authors discussed here rebels in his work against this new world, and none of the three seems to reach a happy ending in which living with the other is possible.

CHAPTER THREE

Topographies of Queer Popular Culture

I. Recto/Verso: Mapping the Popular Novel

– Ok, quelques minutes pour recharger les batteries, et on inverse les rôles [OK, a few minutes to recharge our batteries and we'll switch roles]. (Voirenlion 67)

A look at a popular cultural phenomenon can often allow the observer to put her or his finger on the pulse of the moment; a generalized popular culture reflects neither canonicity (though often an established status quo) nor an edgy future, but rather it is the sign of the times. I am arguing for an examination of discourses, regardless of level or literary value. As Foucault showed long ago in *Les Mots et les choses*, emerging discourses – though he did not limit himself to them – appear in an episteme that, while clearly delineating a field, contains contradictions. And I mean "contains" in two senses of the word: the field includes contradictions between competing discourses but, also, the construction of the field allows those competing discourses to be simultaneously maintained.

In France, a growing number of what I shall call "novels of arrival," rather than coming-out narratives, have appeared in recent years, in the wake of the end of the AIDS crisis. I am calling them "novels of arrival" not only because the coming-out narrative, as Denis Provencher has admirably shown, is different for a French context (and often does not make sense, if we think about the lingering philosophy behind the American term), but also because many of these narratives are not necessarily coming-out stories, but rather the story of the protagonist's arrival in Paris and his establishment there in the gay community in the Marais.

To understand the phenomenon and its inscription of a changing masculinity, I shall start with a scene from one of the narratives (though it could be from any one of a number of them). Needless to say, these narratives revolve in large part around finding someone for sex and having sex with that man, or, more likely than not, with a number of similar men, usually sequentially. So I shall start with a quotation which, while explicit, is less offensive than it is amusing, in part because of its total lack of literary value:

> J'étais en confiance. Je me suis étalé comme une étoile de mer. J'ai fini par m'ouvrir comme une huître. Après plusieurs tentatives qui s'étaient soldées par un "je t'avais bien dit …," il est arrivé à m'empaler. J'étais devenu une motte de beurre fendue. Son membre large et long glissait lentement. (Duroi *Retour* 65)

> [I was confident. I spread out like a starfish. I ended up opening up like an oyster. After a few attempts concluding with "I told you so," he finally impaled me. I had become a pat of melted butter. His long, thick penis slid in slowly.]

To say the least, we are very far from the proper, subtle, and understated world of Marcel Proust, whose descriptions of sex were inevitably partial (such as the overheard grunts and moans of Charlus and Jupien or the view through the transom of Charlus being whipped), never direct, and certainly never poeticized in such a banal fashion. Even Jean Genet, the eternal bad boy, while often rhapsodic, would not make references to a spread-out starfish or a melting lump of butter. We are now in a world in which "[les] mecs de magazine de cul étaient donc maintenant en 3D [the guys in the X-rated mags were now in 3D]" (Batlo 27) and we are looking at "l'impact du porno sur les gens [the impact of porn on people]" (Jonard 202). What we see here as a reflection, albeit prosaically, is Dustan's pornotopia, in which a set of predictable images and a minimalism of language replace the narrative of self and other.

To understand this shift, it is necessary to examine the historical context and for that, I would mark as a less than arbitrary starting point the year 1981, the year in which the first AIDS case was discovered.[1]

---

[1] This does not mean that the virus appeared for the first time in 1981, but rather that the first known cases of AIDS appeared in that year. As an article carried by CNN.com from 1 October 2008 states, "Genetic analysis pushes the estimated origin of HIV back to between 1884 and 1924, with a more focused estimate at 1908" (anon., "Scientists trace AIDS virus origin to 100 years ago"). I thank Daniel Maroun for bringing this article to my attention.

By that point, we had lived through a decade or so of women's and gay liberation, as it was then known. While the former was both text-based and event-based, the latter was predominantly event-based. The best-selling *Our Bodies, Ourselves* had been in print for a while. Women were urged to take knowledge into their own hands and to educate themselves about reproductive rights. In England, Scotland, and Wales, abortion had been legalized in 1967; in Canada, in 1969. The landmark case of Roe vs. Wade legalized abortion in the United States in 1973; abortion would be legalized in France two years later. Generally speaking, as laws and behaviors changed, as the force of the secular in what Gilles Lipovetsky calls "the ethics of the post-moral" weighed ever more heavily on Western societies, there were more discourses available and fewer hushed tones; sexual liberation and sexual education were necessarily accompanied by a production of discourse, both official and non-official, that ranged from the sensation produced by the porn film *Deep Throat*, released in 1972, to fairly open talk about sex clubs, swinging, and the like.

In the world of gay men, the discourse of liberation and liberatory behavior ultimately took a somewhat different path from the progress narrative of women's liberation. First of all, there was the presence here and there of liberatory writings, notably, in France, the work of Guy Hocquenghem, whose epoch-making study entitled *Le Désir homosexuel* had some currency; his more radical manifestos were known to few and unfortunately remain so to this day. Gay liberation had its mythical beginning in the Stonewall riots of 1969 and, while there were other events, including those of May '68 and their aftermath, they were predominantly events; gay liberation did not have as much of a text-based component as women's liberation, for it did not arise out of middle-class discursivity, but from popular action that rapidly metamorphosed into unbridled *jouissance*. If the seventies were breathtakingly reckless for many, we now know that there had been a time-bomb ticking since the middle of the decade, ultimately to go off in 1981 with the first reported cases of AIDS in the West (though we now know of at least two earlier, isolated cases). Then known as GRID (Gay-Related Immune Deficiency) and soon to be known as AIDS, this syndrome's etiology was soon discovered in France by Luc Montagnier and his team with the detection of the retrovirus LAV, now known as HIV, in 1983, and confirmed in the United States in 1984 by Robert Gallo and his team, who demonstrated that the retrovirus HTLV was the cause of AIDS. Shortly thereafter it was confirmed that the two viruses were variants of one another, and thus, the cause of AIDS had been found.

So not only was there a disjunction between the two movements, there was the additional factor of a severe detour in gay liberation with the advent of a disease that seemed, especially in the mid- to late eighties, to give the lie to gay liberation as a progress narrative. Whereas women's liberation by and large led to a clear expansion of discourses around gender, by 1984, contemporary gay discursivity, which had had minimal impact outside its community before that moment, was already beginning to swing in a different direction. On the one hand, there was explicit or implicit silence: the then president of the United States, Ronald Reagan, did not even mention AIDS publicly until the death of the film star and 1950s' heart-throb Rock Hudson in October 1985; the specularity of Hollywood had forced Reagan out of a sound-proof closet of his own construction. But perhaps that specularity was part and parcel of it: AIDS had to be seen and not just spoken about. On the other hand, things were no better in Europe: Michel Foucault was said to have died in 1984 from brain cancer, yet at least one newspaper was quick to point out the "shameful" nature of his death when it was revealed that he had died of an AIDS-related illness. To this day, there remains controversy around his death, his knowledge or lack thereof of his illness, and the behavior and sexual practices that might have led to his infection, most notably, his supposedly free, taboo-breaking behavior in bath-houses in San Francisco.

But this silence (which in the case of Foucault can be attributed not least to the fact that he could not possibly have known how to have prevented his own infection) was accompanied by a profusion of discourses relating to sex and sexuality, AIDS, and death and dying. Discourses about anal penetration, condoms, and safer sex abounded, as did discourses about men dying, and about unsafe sex – including, most famously, a whole subset of discourses about S/M, gay sex clubs, fisting, and pornography all addressed by Foucault as he wrote of a "gay becoming." The advent of AIDS skewed discourses and combined a celebration of freedom with a sense of doom and an ever-increasing presence of mourning and melancholia. The discourses were inevitably intertwined, seemingly never to be unyoked from one another, and were, of course, met in many quarters by a new set of moralizing discourses, thus producing both a battle between gay and anti-gay (to move quickly) discourses and an internal logomachy within the gay camp about fidelity, safe sex, and a whole host of related issues.

During the next ten years or so, literature and films that addressed this subject were caught up in these oppositional discourses: one about liberated sex and sexuality, another about death, dying, and mourning. They were strangely combined in a way that never sat comfortably in any position. Uncharacteristically, American television took on the subject at a relatively early moment, with the very brave (for its time) *An Early Frost* in 1985; it was followed two years later by Randy Shilts's non-fiction book, *And the Band Played On*. 1990 saw the publication of the most famous AIDS narrative to date, Hervé Guibert's *A l'ami qui ne m'a pas sauvé la vie*, an autofiction with its transparent portrait of Foucault as the character Muzil; 1993 saw the film *Philadelphia*, which, in a classic American way, was considered brave, even if it skirted a host of pertinent issues. But, one might ask, where was fictional narrative in all this? For the great majority of French and American literary texts were very transparent autofictions, including for example (on the French side) Cyril Collard's *Les Nuits fauves*, other works by Guibert and Hocquenghem, Vincent Borel's *Un Ruban noir*, and Pascal de Duve's brilliant *Cargo Vie*.

With this historical and conceptual framework in mind, I shall fast-forward to my three hypotheses. First, there is currently a new set of discourses that have changed rapidly from the several sets in vogue during the period from 1968 or so through the mid- to late 1990s. These new discourses arise partly as a response to the set of previously existing discourses and partly as a reaction to and a symptom of a radical change in medical treatment and efficacy; that is, in the West, HIV+ status, if caught early enough, often no longer leads to full-blown AIDS, but rather is considered to be a chronic syndrome that can be lived with for decades, often asymptomatically. Second, if we truly want to understand the discursive topography of contemporary AIDS writing, we need to look at it in its profusion and not limit ourselves to what we might think of as texts having high literary value. One could argue that literary value, while never a prediction of the episteme as a whole, is even less valid an indicator nowadays, in a world in which literature has lost its primacy as the cultural vehicle of record. Third, the perfusion of the represented gay world with the alphabet, images, and syntax of pornography is not just a sign of the relative liberalism or open-mindedness of many in the gay community, but is rather the sign of a construction of a utopian imaginary, where original language seldom ventures, where sex is pure and bareback, and where HIV status has no real consequences. Taken together, these three thoughts are foundational for an understanding of the ways in which this popular cultural phenomenon of the novel of arrival inscribes singular and collective masculinity as a sign of the community it purports to represent.

Let us return to the corpus at hand to see how the authors fulfill the Foucauldian notion of the production of subjectivity within the discursive grid of possibilities that is an episteme. Here, I would want to transform Foucault because of the ways in which literature conceives of its own take on truth and representation. Unlike the scientists whom Foucault studied, whose devotion to what they believed was the truth is complete, the authors I am examining make no claims to having a scientific insight into a truth, but rather see themselves – and I think this is a fairly safe argument – as writers able to represent in a verisimilar or mimetic fashion the locus, the mores, the behaviors, and the commonplaces of the world they describe. That world is precisely not a very literary one: "Je n'ai rien écrit depuis des années. Je n'avais plus le goût de la chose littéraire {I have written nothing for years. I no longer had a taste for the literary thing]" (Duroi *Retour* 10). Indeed, the stabs at literature are few and far between; here, for example, literature is a commodity like any other: "Je lorgne le dernier roman de Dustan là où les livres sont exposés. Pas le temps de lire un paragraphe pour savoir à quel point c'est sexe, si les mecs d'entredéfoncent, ou si ce qu'il dit est moral et jusqu'à quel point [I'm taking a glance at Dustan's latest novel in which books are exposed. No time to read a paragraph to know if it is about sex, if guys get it on with one another, or if what he says is moral and to what extent]" (Saron 35).

Whereas in the world of Proust and Gide, the budding homosexual looked to high literature for indications that he was not alone, and whereas in the mid- to late twentieth century this role was often played by film, by the end of the century neither of these functions as source or guarantee. Rather, because homosexuality is ubiquitous, albeit in the linkage with AIDS, there is no need for a guarantee other than the how-to manual that is pornography. Here, then, it is not discourses that are opposed to one another in the grid of the episteme, where the subject looks to previous discourses and the collective imaginary for a guarantee that he will mime. Rather it is the set of discourses and the contradictions contained within them – and again, by "contained" I mean both held in and held back – that end up being the focus; in a world in which each subject is seemingly asserting his own singularity and independence, and his own concept of himself as the protagonist in his own life, why do we keep coming back to the same set of contradictory positions? While these authors do not all agree on everything, the same discourses repeat often enough for them to be treated, in classic Foucauldian fashion, as an episteme, as a set of anonymous statements and plot motifs that map this gay episteme of the late twentieth century. Thus the topography or cartography, while not quantitative, is a set of accreted hills of the commonplaces or typical figures of these works.

A traditional modernist approach to homosexuality, running roughly from Freud through the beginning of the age of AIDS, described homosexuality, with or without its attendant medical and juridical discourses, as the institutional representation and aggregate of same-sex desire, although it is not clear that this still obtains. Yet arguably, that simple definition is not enough for many of these writers, and one might sketch out as an extreme version of the current take on this trajectory the following process: go from the provinces to Paris, get settled in the Marais if at all possible, and become seropositive: "Ils viennent à Paris dès qu'ils le peuvent [They come to Paris as soon as they can]" (Duroi *Retour* 99). Or as one chapter title has it: "Direction: Le Marais [Destination: The Marais]" (Batlo 28); another novel is entitled *Le Tueur du Marais* [The Killer of the Marais]. Occasionally, characters do not stay in the Marais, and there is actually one novel in which a character gives an address in the eighteenth arrondissement, in a shopping street that runs up from Place Blanche by the east side of the Moulin Rouge: "'Donne-moi ton adresse.' '13 rue Lepic. Dépêche-toi, j'ai hâte de me retrouver dans un lit avec toi' ['Give me your address.' '13 rue Lepic. Hurry up, I really need to be in bed with you']" (Amstel 193). The basic geographic delimitation, however, is the gay neighborhood of the Marais, with a few other loci of gay Paris figuring as secondary spots for the queering of discursive topography.

Generally it is only when that trajectory from the provinces to Paris is complete and marked by the potential or *dépistage* of seropositivity that one is gay or queer in the eyes of the implied readers of these books. The defining moment of male homosexuality is no longer what we might now retrospectively consider the relative innocence of same-sex desire or a coming to consciousness thereof, whether acted on or not, but rather the encounter with the fundamental figures of bareback sex, bug-chasers, gift-givers, pitchers, catchers, and the virus itself. This is a philosophy of *carpe diem*, of living fast and dying young: "S'il doit mourir demain, il mourra. Alors autant profiter de la vie, s'arranger afin qu'elle soit la plus affriolante possible et riche d'enseignements [If he must die tomorrow, he will die. So instead profit from life, and get organized so that it is as exciting as possible and a rich learning opportunity]" (Moraux 17). The word "enseignements" is not at all out of place here: one learns to be queer by acting on one's queerness; it is a world of autodidacticism fueled by the images and fragments of discourse that one incorporates into one's being as the necessary plug-ins for evolving into one's queer self. And while one is preparing to die young, the goal is to have as much sex with as many other men as possible.

This trajectory is a fast-food version of self-discovery rather than a feature-length road movie or a classic voyage of self-discovery that fills the pages of a long novel. And as such, given the readers' knowledge of the inevitable *telos*, it is not the voyage itself or the predictable lay-ups along the way that count, but rather the fact of having arrived. So where have we arrived? Certainly, the trajectory takes the protagonist to a point far beyond the *carpe diem* position alluded to in the previous citation. The protagonist arrives in a brave new world in which the standard etiologies no longer hold sway: the arrived-at queerness is seldom if ever given a psychogenesis, but rather is just given as the latest incarnation of the representation or existence of same-sex desire. One could call it the most recent avatar of the embodiment of that desire – avatar not in the religious sense but in the sense in which it is used in online gaming: the being one puts forth as a player in the game, a player who may or may not resemble one's actual (essential) self.

What are the signs of this avatar? First and most obviously, the player-protagonist has to act on his desire, has to have acted on this desire, and done so multiply. It is not enough to feel that desire: the player must engage it, activate it, act on it, and give in to it. It means becoming oneself as the avatar, but in so doing, it means radically, in a Rimbauldian sense, becoming other from whom one was meant to be: "Je suis en train de devenir un autre [I am in the process of becoming another person]" (Polver *Ogres* 26). Second, being queer in this world means consciously or unconsciously agreeing to perform a role, one that depends essentially on sodomy, and specifically, on being the passive partner in an act of unprotected anal intercourse; the phallus is always, in a bizarre post-Lacanian twist, the phallus of the other; one has the phallus, the possibly disease-spreading phallus, only when one is being penetrated. Example after example form a litany: "Et puis, ce jours-là, j'étais particulièrement chaud du cul [And those days, I was particularly horny to be fucked]" (Duroi *Retour* 112); or again, from the very first pages of another novel: "Sa teub va au fond de mon cul [...] [His cock went deep into my ass]" (Saron 12); and again, early on in another novel: "Il m'a amené chez lui. Il a voulu m'enculer. Je me suis laissé faire. Je n'ai pas eu mal [He took me home. He wanted to fuck me. I let him. It didn't hurt]" (Polver *Ogres* 27).[2] To say that these events are "zipless" – to use an expression given currency by Erica Jong in *Fear of Flying* – is to make the understatement of the year. It must be; it must be acted upon; it has to be there. And even if one chooses to follow the recommendations for safer sex, the centrality of the act defines who one is; this was, of course, discussed brilliantly several years ago by Leo Bersani in his epoch-making essay, "Is the Rectum a Grave?," but, as I shall show below, things have changed radically in the past few years.

Still, there is a remarkable change, even before the shift described below: we have moved from the interiority of the *cogito* into a radically material existence, going beyond La Mettrie's "man-machine" into a version of libertinage à la Marquis de Sade, some of whose recommended practices, at least, come up with great frequency. The cogito is exteriorized materially and this corporeal definition of self is put with some tongue-in-cheek eloquence by Érik Rémès, as has already been seen, in the title *Je bande donc je suis*. Exactly the same paradigm is found in the work of another author: "'Je jouis donc je suis ...' Pardonnez-moi, Monsieur Descartes: votre formule est pertinente mais, je trouve, celle-ci également ['I cum therefore I am.' Excuse me, Mr Descartes: your formula is fitting, but I find this one to be equally so]" (Charuau 55). If Cartesian logic worked as the foundational moment for humanist man, and

---

[2] To be precise here, in this latter case, the remark is made only shortly after the character discovers he has a gay side.

continued through modernity, for these avatars, it is only the liquidity and ecstasy (understood etymologically) of *jouissance* that is the foundational moment (albeit slightly retrospectively) for the post-queer avatar of the self. And implicitly, here is another version, for to speak in this universe is to speak of sex: "'Je bande depuis que j'entends ta voix' [I have had a hard-on since I heard your voice]" (Quérec 203). Third, and quite bizarrely at first thought, the definitional point of post-queer avatars may be considered to be the HIV virus itself, something non-human, between organic and inorganic, something that potentially makes each person a kind of hybrid or a cyborg, a figure among many in what a variety of writers today are calling the "post-human." As we have seen previously in the analysis of Dantec, post-human cyborgs and post-human avatars are merely two different names for the same figures, for there is no surprise in a world in which we are all, always, now potentially plugged in, potentially trackable, and never fully independent. It is not the information within the system, but the possible insidious corruption in the system that defines an individual's current subjectivity, as Dantec and Jones-Gorlin have shown, as well as the impossibility of unplugging.

I have already alluded to a shift in representational paradigms and that shift can, to a great extent, be attributed to the consequences of a single medical breakthrough: the possibility (in the West) of combination therapy: "On ne dira jamais assez combien la house est, avec les trithérapies, la raison essentielle du retour au sexe [You can never say enough about how house music, along with combination therapy, is the essential reason for the return to sex]" (Jonard 209). Suddenly, infection no longer means being ill and dying young; AIDS becomes declassified as a galloping syndrome that gives way to opportunistic infections and becomes redefined both medically and socially – morally, even – as a chronic condition whose negative sides can be forestalled by combination therapy. During that delay, an individual can still continue to have sex to his heart's content and no longer necessarily feels obliged to give moral or medical weight to the consequences of barebacking: "Après la peur de mourir, la peur de vivre. Il m'arrive de baiser sans capote. Et de faire le test régulièrement [After the fear of dying, the fear of living. Sometimes I fuck without a rubber. And take the test regularly]" (Duroi *Retour* 93). But all the test will do is determine whether the character needs to start combination therapy, not change his behavior. Here and there, one does find evidence of the earlier paradigm, a space at which there is a time bomb, if not exactly an atomic bomb; in any case, it is viewed as a site of massive death, the death of a community: "les séropos au centre de notre monde. [...] Hirosidashima. Nagasidasaki [Poz guys at the center of our world. Hiroshimaids. Nagasakaids]" (Saron 106). But generally speaking, the dying, death, and mourning associated with the first phases of AIDS have been replaced by a nonchalance or even a jubilant celebration; rebirth in the mid-nineties after the promise of certain death in the eighties. Sex returns with fewer consequences than in the first fifteen or so years of the AIDS crisis. And while a writer such as Rémès may argue in his fictions – he has taken a different point of view in his non-fictional narratives – that one *must* be seropositive to be *truly* gay and that it is the responsibility of the one accepting the vulnerable position to decide whether he wants to have bareback sex or not, it is in fact the case that seroconversion is, after the mid-nineties, an act with far fewer direct consequences. The practical consequence is that there is lots and lots of sex; it is often a marathon: "Jamais Yan n'avait été pris dans autant de positions en si peu de temps! [Yan had never been screwed in so many positions in so little time]" (Chuberre 47). Some random statements are testimony to this: "Je ne sais pas où je l'ai rencontré. J'ai couché avec tellement d'ombres! [I don't know where I met him. I have slept with so many shadows]" (Duroi *Retour* 52). Or again: "Je n'arrête pas de baiser. [...] On a l'impression d'un porno géant [I don't stop fucking. It's like a giant porn film]" (Sebhan 27). Or again, just for fun, "Je me suis branlé deux fois en dix minutes [I jerked off twice in ten minutes]" (Polver *Ogres* 27).

Again, these avatars of the post-queer man are an assemblage of the alphabet soup available to them within the paradigm: multiple encounters, anonymous sex, one-night stands, sexual variety, pornographic imagery, and multiple orgasms. The post-queer avatars enjoy – "jouir" in the old-fashioned sense of the word – the very fact of having their being defined as sexual being, a figure of the avatar that is primary. But that figure is enacted only when coupled with the cyborgian feature of man twinned and entwined with the virus. This is a new double helix, strands of protein intertwined. It is perhaps an accident of United States' puritanism that the most recent euphemism for semen is "DNA," but here, in this world, it is no euphemism: strands of protein intertwine, human DNA mixing with HIV to create the locus from which these new cyborgian men can speak, act, write, and have sex.

I shall return to the body of questions raised by the omnipresence of pornography below, but I should like to detour through the place and its cast of characters as well as the accompanying mechanisms that keep the machine running before turning back to that. The place, as I have indicated, is Paris, a gay Paris that is usually set as a world apart, a gay Paris made in the image of its denizens and which informs and shapes them in turn in a symbiotic evolution. Though there are some exceptions, it is rare for straight men to appear as characters in these novels and equally rare for any women to appear, except of course in the few novels in which the character is a practicing bisexual or in those few in which there is some version of homoparentality. In the latter case, the matter is, in a certain sense, beyond sexuality:

> Et voilà que nous nous retrouvions face au casse-tête chinois de cette grossesse, un écheveau d'émotions fortes et inconnues où le désir d'enfant s'inscrivait hors de la sexualité. (Vilrouge 119)

> [So we are face to face with the Chinese puzzle of this pregnancy, a tangle of strong, unknown emotions in which the desire to have a child is inscribed outside of sexuality.]

Arguably, women and straight men generally have no place here; this is a singular world in which the entire population has come to Paris to be gay in the ways I have described: sanctuary, utopia, or *hortus conclusus*, but one that includes the disease as essential to the running of the system. And those who just happen to be there, those who have not come to Paris for that purpose, are essentially invisible. The characters have entered a special, singular universe that does not obey the laws of the world with which it necessarily co-exists, but that functions in a semi-automatic way, semi-detached from the outside world.

So the sense of place necessarily moves the construction of Paris into a zone in which the sense of republican universalism, so fundamental to the foundation of modern French identity, is essentially absent. A communitarian sense of identity, anathema to the Republic, is at the heart of the definition of place and space. Yet while many of these novels are set in one specific neighborhood, or even in the generally recognized features of gay Paris beyond the Marais, the sense of communitarian space does not depend on this older notion of territoriality, on what amounted to a gay ghetto. Rather, like the world described by Hardt and Negri in *Empire*, or that described by writers as diverse as William Gibson, in *Neuromancer*, Dantec, or Alan Liu, in *The Laws of Cool*, this is essentially a world based on networks, cybernetics, exchange, and the possibility of establishing place and subjectivity at any given time, place, or moment. So even when the subject matter is not "gay" in these novels, we are reminded of this systemic interconnectivity and the effect it has on any individual's sense of identity and subjectivity: "En ville, il y avait des caméras à tous les carrefours [In town there were cameras at every intersection]" (Duroi *Retour* 19).[3] In these works, we are always figures of the specular, figures in the society of spectacle, and combined with the figure of the pornographic, this specular locus will quickly and easily become a virtual reality, a projection of and from constructions of cyberspace. In fact, one author (Gaubert) goes so far as to present his novel as a set of television seasons, with the chapters given episode numbers. We will see this specularity at length when we turn to the figuration of pornography in these novels.

In the simplest of senses, this means that contemporary technology is central to these works: the Internet, streamed videos, porn, and email; one writer writes that he is in a cybercafé (Sebhan 27) and another talks of the "telephone network" (Vilrouge 87). These are, of course, standard features of everyday life in the West, along with mobile phones, computers, BlackBerrys, GPSs, iPods, and DVD players. Of note here is the *naturalezza* with which these recent inventions are incorporated as essential parts of the discourse about the gay self: one could not imagine these characters being themselves without cybercafés, the Internet, easy access to porn, and so forth. The interpellated position of the subject is always *branché*, in both senses of the word: both plugged in and "in the know." Yet they are never themselves, they are always playing the role of the day, one that comes out of a range of pop cultures from porn to music: "Pas de quoi s'étonner qu'après tout ça il m'envoie un mail signé *ton soumis du cul* [No surprise that after all that he wrote an email signed *your sub bottom*]" (Saron 101). Or again: "Yan, à côté, est plus plastique,

---

[3]   On the panopticon, see not only Foucault's *Surveiller et punir*, but also Iain Sinclair's commentary on these cameras in *Lights Out for the Territory*.

plus *boysband* et tellement plus cruel [Next to him, Yan is more plastic, more boyband, and so much more cruel]" (Chuberre 33). Still again: "Le sauna comprenait différents univers à fantasmes [the baths had different universes of fantasy]" (Batlo 143). Gay identity, in the most essentialist sense, tied to same-sex desire, has given way to a technology of self – to use Foucault's expression – that depends on the plugging in not so much of Deleuzean *machines désirantes*, but of *machines désirées*, aided and abetted by a whole bag of technological tricks.

In at least one case (Saron 68), the author provides a Rabelaisian list of paraphernalia, just as he has previously provided a list of sexual activities: it would seem that queer sex cannot happen unless you take an inventory of the possibilities. But, one might add, inventory and *stockage* are fundamental to networks. Just as the networks and seropositivity have become defining factors instead of identity and desire, the materiality of existence in a "smart" world has in part replaced what we might consider to be face-to-face connection. The bars exist, but they tend to be more often the backrooms than loci for social conversation or interaction: "ma première backroom, mon premier bar à ours, ma première baise en public [my first backroom, my first bear bar, my first fuck in public]" (Polver *Ogres* 42). Or again: "les bars à cul avec leurs dédales et leurs backrooms empestant la sueur et le sperme [sex clubs with their mazes and backrooms stinking of sweat and sperm]" (Chuberre 31). So within the communitarian model mentioned above, there is a kind of Deleuzean rhizomatics for sex: bars are labyrinths in which one finds someone to bugger or, given the paradigm, by whom to be buggered.

There is thus a double constraint or even contradiction of the contemporary, the post-post-modern, the post-queer, or alternately, what one novelist terms "le post-sida [after-AIDS]" (Saron 73), significantly without capital letters. Let us consider that the seventies and the eighties were, at least in terms of gay culture, part and parcel of the post-modern: no grand narrative, rhizomatics at play, free play of the individual subjects who would plug in their *machines désirantes* in various ways. Fatally and ironically, the eighties see the rise of a master discourse, a discourse of death, and a turn toward mourning, both singular and generalized. By the mid- to late nineties, mourning is again displaced bit by bit; there is no return of desire as desire, no return to *machines désirantes*, but rather a turn toward a displaced desire of desire, or, as I have already indicated, a turn toward *machines désirées* and away from *machines désirantes*, objects desired by the system, objects desired because they are validated by the system. And those objects, to be sure, are reduced to one and one alone; being post-queer or post-AIDS in this world means being the passive "bottom." It is a turn toward a Lacanian incompleteness and specifically, to the impossibility of fulfilling desire completely, so that the orgasm becomes a telos, endlessly to be sought anew: "En revanche, question cul, il était bien 'parisienne.' Il ne désirait qu'une chose: m'enculer vite fait bien fait [On the other hand, as far as sex goes, he was really 'Parisian.' He wanted only one thing: to fuck me fast and really well]" (Duroi *Retour* 54). To my mind, the ontological and epistemological nature of being a "top" is not adequately addressed in these novels. I would argue that the collective, with its porn, its networks, its paraphernalia, and so forth, is the impossible yet omnipresent top: the protagonist is bottom to the system and each individual top is merely a synecdoche of the system as a whole.

Destabilizing the system, this displacement of desire, born out of the migratory pattern that is the fulfillment of the Baudelairean *flâneur*, since it can no longer be free-flowing, but is always monitored or *contrôlé*, ends up rendering permanent the impossibility of independent subjectivity. So ironically, the assumption of a queer identity means never being able fully to assume that queer identity as such. And the only one who can assume identity is the one who says his identity is elsewhere, or at least partially elsewhere:

> Mon tendre amant qui a combattu pour le droit à l'orientation sexuelle dans le monde n'a pas pu comprendre que je ne m'assume pas totalement dans mon identité. J'ai passé des heures à lui expliquer que mon père ne s'en remettrait jamais s'il apprenait que son fils unique était "*zamel*." (Trabelsi 16–17)

> [My tender lover, who has fought for the right to sexual orientation throughout the world, was not able to understand, that I am not on completely good terms with my identity. I have spent hours telling him that my father would never get over it if he learned that his only son was a "*zamel*."]

This last word is a pejorative Moroccan word for "faggot." So the post-queer discourse obtains only within a select (and self-selecting) group; in other words, not everyone is free to form his own avatar as he sees fit. One finds that there is an "in" group and that the others are outsiders: "J'avais l'impression qu'on me prenait pour un Arabe. Peut-être avais-je attrapé quelque chose là-bas? Un accent, à force de parler avec Nouri, une attitude? [I thought people thought I was Arab. Maybe I caught something when I was there? An accent, from talking with Nouri, an attitude?]" (Legrand 105). The other is very close; the other risks perverting the identity of the self that is always already other. But in this post-post-modern world, the double negation of identity does not lead to a return to the same, but rather to a further alterity.

As I indicated above, the population of these works is by and large uniformly gay male – and I would add that, with very few exceptions, it is a young population. Yet, given the last two quotations, it is obvious that the only sense of identity that can come out of this situation occurs precisely when the given locus for identity is put into question. In some cases, this happens because of general cultural otherness. The previous two cases put identity and stability into question by having the character face the otherness of North Africa. Other works variously involve a half-Finnish, half-French young man who moves early on to France, a traveler who goes to Istanbul, and a protagonist who goes to Italy and then time-travels with his Italian boyfriend back to ancient Rome and conveniently to Hadrian's Villa, which was known in ancient times for more perverse fun than anyone could possibly handle.

But this destabilization of identity can happen through several other mechanisms. The first, which I shall pass over rather quickly, involves the introduction of male heterosexuality as a destabilizing factor. This is a rare occurrence in these works, not only because the appearance of heterosexuals is itself rare, but also because the bulwark of stability of male heterosexuality – of phallogo-centrism and heteronormativity – is fundamental to the repositioning of gay men in these works: *la France profonde* – the provinces – is heteronormative; this Paris, or at least this topography and cartography of a particular part of Paris, is not. Yet occasionally there will be a straight guy who is gay-friendly or a family in the know, ready to accept the queer son. This remains a minor theme throughout the works; more importantly, it is not a contributing factor to the recoding of male identity for these characters, who do not get their sense of identity from heteronormativity and who ultimately, whether they announce it or not, buy in to some version of the Gidean pronouncement, "Familles, je vous hais [Families, I hate you]." In this post-modern world, hatred of families cedes its place to indifference more along the lines of Rhett Butler's exit line, "Frankly, my dear, I don't give a damn."[4]

Two other phenomena tell us far more about the situation. First, there is the dissociation of reproduction from any model of heteronormativity, in order to figure the position of *homoparentalité*. Clearly a figure relevant to the real world, the civil union (PACS [Pacte Civil de Solidarité]) and, specifically, its consequences in questions of *homoparentalité* have literary consequences as well because of the way they can dissociate, for example, the desire to be a father from what we would otherwise have thought of as bisexuality: the desire for paternity is not necessarily combined with the desire for the feminine other. So for example we read that, "Christine et moi repensons la famille comme d'autres se lancent dans l'invention de la solitude [Christine and I are rethinking the family as others hurtle towards the invention of loneliness]" (Vilrouge 16). In such works that stray across the border of homoparentality, there is sometimes a scene (or several) of comic relief in preparation for the characters having a baby the old-fashioned way: "Un onguent anti-âge au rétinol actif spécifié en caractères incrustés dans le verre réclame mes attentions, mes faveurs. Je trempe ma queue dans le pot. Bien que l'érection fût immédiat [...] [An anti-aging cream with active retinol specified in characters etched in the glass, gets my attention and favors. I soak my dick in the pot. Although the erection was immediate]" (Vilrouge 19).[5] But in any case, the divorce of desire and mechanism allows characters to queer their own homosexuality and move it away from any normalization, at least in this respect if not in those that relate to questions of communitarianism: "Je refuse d'être figé à une place d'òu il est impossible de se remettre en question ni de se situer ni même de s'éloigner [I refuse to be stuck in a place where it is impossible to put oneself into question or to situate oneself or even to distance oneself]" (Vilrouge 60). Strangely, put in these terms, *homoparentalité* becomes a weapon against the disidentificatory mechanisms of homonormativity. Returning to reproduction

---

[4] See the discussion of *Juste une question d'amour* below for the take of this film on Gide's line.

[5] Of note here, ironically, is the use of the imperfect subjunctive, a sign of a world thousands of miles away from this one.

means moving away from the categorizations typically associated with reproduction: it is, to be blunt, an additional, albeit different, means of queering heterosexuality and requeering homosexuality in the process.

The third mechanism here is one that destabilizes the act of sex by introducing something unexpected, something queer, that will, of course, return us to the system. We are all familiar with Michel Foucault's famous pronouncement on the function of what were then perceived to be rather fringe sexual practices such as S/M and especially fisting: they were inventions of the twentieth century; for Foucault, they functioned as renewals of sexuality, while destabilizing to some extent normative sexualities. Yet at the same time, if, between 1981 and 1995, ordinary unprotected anal intercourse comes to mean death and then begins no longer to mean death, it stands to reason that such extreme sexual practices are not really so extreme because the meanings of sex and sexuality have been radically altered by that double shift. So rather than using sexual practice itself as a radicalization of sex and sexuality, these writers often choose gender definitions to blur the lines and to queer the matter: "Et une lesbienne qui couche avec un pédé dans un backroom, c'est un act homo ou hétéro? [And a lesbian who has sex with a fag in a backroom, is that a homo or hetero act?]" (Jonard 35).

The point is well taken. The collapse of sexualities as fixed categories seems to have been ushered in along with the concepts of queerness. With a destabilized identity, any individual character is no longer subject to the heteronormatizing or homonormatizing notions of essentialist categories of sexuality. In a strange way, there is a return to the notion of the act, i.e., anal intercourse, for example, coupled with a lifestyle, a set of beliefs and categories into which that act fits. In other words, sexualities defined by social constructivism as a combination of medical, juridical, and psychiatric discourses held sway for a period of two centuries. But we could argue that while same-sex desire existed before that categorization and still exists after that, it is integrated into the enunciation of the self and into the episteme in different fashions before, during, and after the period of sexualities. One could easily imagine an individual in the Middle Ages fully conscious of his desire for a member of the same sex, but the locus of that desire or its articulation was not necessarily the same locus as that of the era of sexualities with its essentialist notion of desire. Similarly, as we move into a moment after sexualities (post-queer and post-straight), the articulation of that position moves away from the psychologically self-reflective into a deconstructed semiotics of sex(uality) and a somatized, verbalized, and "imagized" version of the self that is far less psychologically driven than it is driven by the recognition that culture has made a place for that desire. Indeed, all the writers studied in this volume relate to that change, regardless of the sexuality to which they belong(ed) or about which they are writing.

The final mechanism of destabilization attacks our notion of identity from within the sexual act. As I have indicated, sexuality is paradoxically destabilized along with identity by the changes undergone over the past quarter of a century through the evolution of the interrelation of sexuality and society and through the impact of various agents such as AIDS, already discussed, and pornography, to be discussed below. Before arriving at that point, I should like to examine this final figure of destabilization. Gilles Sebhan starts his novel in the following way, likening sex to a quest or scientific field trip:

> Pour certains, le sexe est le sexe. Point final. Mais pour Luc, c'est une espèce de chasse au trésor permanente. Ou une manie d'entomologiste. Dans son appartement, les garçons sont épinglés au mur comme des insectes. Encadrés une bonne fois pour toutes. Jeunes, en érection, pris au flash comme dans un bloc d'ambre. (Sebhan 9)

> [For some people, sex is sex. End of discussion. But for Luc it is a permanent treasure hunt. Or an entomologist's mania. Boys are pinned to the walls of his apartment like insects. Framed once and for all. Young guys, with erections, flash-frozen, as if in a block of amber.]

He is not alone here, for elsewhere we read a similar statement that likens the man to a scientist out in the field: "Je suis un naturaliste devant une espèce inconnue [I am a naturalist faced with a new species]" (Polver *Ogres* 44). In both these cases, sex is translated into a different discourse that invokes a subjectivity that is radically other from the two already mentioned: the independent subject and the destabilized partial subject in the network. The gay individual becomes a knowledgeable searcher, not exactly the independent hunter described by Michel Tournier in *Les Météores*, but rather an individual with intimate knowledge of the workings of his object of investigation. The post-modern gay man must change subjectivities.

There is both a changing relation to language and a changing relation to number that move away from the individual and toward a kind of Fourieresque madness. I shall come back to Fourier shortly.

In terms of language, the relation to and the relation of language is intrinsically and inherently queer, or, to use equally charged terms, but in a different register, language is always already deconstructed and then retrofitted into a new social construction. We have moved far beyond Barthes's comment that denotation is simply the last connotation. If language is seen traditionally as been supported by and as reflecting a social structure that it describes, then certainly the language of the French contemporary queer is both a retrofitting of the emerging new paradigms and a means of creating them by destabilizing any inherited *disjecta membra* of older paradigms: "Comment l'homosexuel ne se sentirait-il pas frère du linguiste, sa doublure roturière, trafiquant de mœurs comme l'autre est tricheur de mots? [How would the homosexual not think himself the linguist's brother, his vulgar double, trafficking morals as the other cheats with words?]" (Zagdanski 50). At a meta-level, we read of "[les] commentaires du narrateur (qui anticipe, qui brouille, qui déflore et fout la merde comme par plaisir dérisoire) [the comments of the narrator (who anticipates, mixes up, deflowers, and fucks things up, as if by some derisory pleasure]" (Quérec 15). Language here – queering and deflowering – is for the cognoscenti, and the cognoscenti are all marked by it and the acts it describes. The acts, both named and unnamed, and the language, twisted and perverted in skewing its object, intercombine to complete the destabilization. And yet they are there precisely to offer a kind of stability to an emerging social structure in which ritual has a place and in which those who are not "players" can be reduced to a functionality, whether it is "l'hétéro beauf [the hetero brother-in-law]" (Duroi *Retour* 18) or someone within the community necessarily reduced to a state of non-being and who is merely defined by a stereotypical and derogatory category: "L'arrivée au *Chant des voyelles* à Châtelet se passe dans l'euphorie et sans histoire. Une tapette nous demande combien nous sommes à dîner [Arriving at the *Chant des voyelles* at Châtelet happens in euphoria and without a hitch. A fag asks us how many of us there are for dinner]" (Gaubert 84).[6] But aside from

---

[6] *Le Chant des voyelles* is a well-known gay-friendly restaurant on the rue des Lombards just a few minutes' walk from a number of gay bars in the Marais.

that, everyone speaks the same language; indeed, it is a requirement: "'Exprime-toi donc comme tout le monde' [Express yourself like everyone else]," one character says to another (Quérec 7).

As any reader will have concluded, much of this new language does in fact concern the intimacies of sex, both the acts and the results. The sexual act, the exploration of the sexual, and certainly the result – "au sommet du jouissif [the super-orgasmic]" (Saron 9) – reconfigure language to make it both more and less intimate. This is a world without the polite form of the second-person pronoun to be sure, with very few exceptions. One of the novels, which is epistolary in form, starts as the correspondence between a teacher and one of his former students, and necessarily starts with the formal second-person pronoun, "vous." Another of the novels that features none other than Marcel Proust himself in the Charlus-like role of admirer of a younger man has the two of them using "vous." But basically we find the familiar second-person pronoun, "tu," everywhere, and were French, like Thai, a language in which even more degrees of intimacy were possible, we would undoubtedly find them: "Dans le cul, un plaisir tutoie l'autre, l'attire ou le repousse [In the ass, one pleasure says 'tu' to the other, attracting or repelling it]" (Saron 159).

And yet, the *travail à la chaîne* turns into *travail à la ronde*, as the series and sequences of events became a virtual Fourieriste *phalanstère* peopled with his queer creatures, every one of them engaged in various permutations and commutations: "Éric me dit qu'il pense que quand on baise à deux, on est plus de deux, qu'il y a aussi tous les autres avec qui on a niqué qui t'accompagnent [Éric tells me that when two people fuck, they are really more than two, that it is everyone else with whom one has had sex who is there as well]" (Saron 119). Obviously, at one level, this is merely a reflection of scientific reality insofar as sexually transmitted diseases (STDs) are concerned: the mechanisms by which STDs, including, but not limited to, AIDS, are transmitted are linear and sequential in nature, an echo of the famous patient zero theory proposed by Randy Shilts, author of *And the Band Played On*. Following the findings – later repudiated – of William Darrow at the Center for Disease Control in Atlanta, Shilts hypothesized that a Canadian flight attendant, Gaëtan Dugas, was the first to become infected with the HIV virus in the West and then spread it through repeated sexual activities. So in addition to pointing to a kind of pornotopia or sexual utopia, it also points to a mythic beginning, a fall into a sexuality that is necessarily marked by the twinning of intimacy and death; and even if combination therapy has thwarted the inevitable, the figure of death remains solidly a part of the imaginary of this world. This position, the texts seem to be saying, is Janus-like: if we did not have intimacy, we would not be queer, but the price of intimacy, the intimacy of this sexual utopia, may be death.

This is a pornotopia, a world in which the informing master mechanism is not literature but the visual world of pornography, its language, its material, its ubiquity, and its redetermination of the spaces and discourses of contemporary French queer sexuality. To say that Proust and Gide are no longer the master leaders, the icons, or the archetypes of gay discourse would be an understatement. The ground-breaking *Tricks* by Renaud Camus appears once, but to little effect (Duroi *Kotoba* 86), as do Hocquenghem (ibid.), and Dustan (Saron 35). And there are even brief stylistic turns reminiscent of Genet's prose and processes of naming characters: "Les obsèques de Momo les Grandes Oreilles avaient transporté Ami de moi dans les hautes sphères du deuil. [...] Je l'entendais [...] magnifier la vie de saint Momo [The funeral of Momo with the Big Ears took Ami from me and into the highest spheres of mourning. I heard him magnify the life of Saint Momo]" (Amstel 141). Yet this is not at all a literary world, despite the profusion of these books. The contradiction is that in this world of books, little reading is going to go on; as one narrator writes, "il me faut un mec qui aime le dialogue cérébral avec un poing dans le cul [I need a man who likes brainy chat with a fist in his ass]" (Saron 65). Fisting replaces literacy in this world in which the gape of the real, in the Lacanian sense of the locus into which language does not go, is usually marked by a language that is nothing more than grunts and moans, quotations from porn films, and here and there the irony of "brainy chat" from an impossible locus of enunciation.

As with any post-modern or post-post-modern phenomenon, there is no archetype nor are there any master discourses, and this same author, Antoine Saron, continues his ironic commentary by making sex a changing, temporal phenomenon: "je nique l'archétypal; non, le sexe n'est pas défini depuis toujours à tout jamais [I screw the archetypal; no, sex has not been defined since the beginning and forever]" (100). Definitions change and there are no absolutes. The discourses have become fragmented, led in part by the idea of gay literature, a communitarization of discourses that is, in its own special way, anathema to traditional concepts of French universalism and citizenship: "On parle de littérature gaie. Je lui dis que je comprends pas comment un écrivain gai pourrait avoir des lecteurs straight [People talk about gay literature. I tell him that I don't understand how a gay writer could have straight readers]" (Saron 62). In passing, readers will have noted the increasing Americanization of these discourses, something that is pervasive in straight and gay contemporary writing, but particularly so in French gay writing, because the discourse is incorporated along with a particularly Americanized version of homosexuality: "Tu me parles de quoi? Lui avait demandé son boy friend [What are you talking to me about?, his boyfriend asked him]" (Duroi *Kotoba* 13). Or again: "Un escort boy français assassine Yoko Ono [a French escort boy assassinates Yoko Ono]" (Amstel 8). This is due in part to the fast-tracking of US discourses about queerness and in part to the globalization and marketing of queerness, made in the USA, easily packaged and transmitted, much like the virus itself.

Simply put, the world is defined by porn: "Le sexe appelle le sexe. Je me branle devant *Scandaleux Volume 3* [Sex calls for more sex. I jerk off in front of *Scandalous*, volume 3]" (Jonard 67). Another writer, Pier-Angelo Polver, describes someone as "un adepte de la branlette devant l'écran [an expert in jerking off in front of the screen]" (*Ogres* 57). Sex cannot occur without the intervening mediation of porn; thus great attention is paid to reintroducing the necessities of phallocentrism, endlessly reaffirmed in the omnipresence of names of porn stars and of large dildos named for porn stars: "Sarah aimerait me goder avec le Jeff Stryker que j'aime tant [Sarah loves to dildo me with the Jeff Stryker I like so much]" (Jonard 52); or again, writing of a well-known contemporary porn star, Rocco Siffredi, who has actually made a transition to more mainstream films, one author writes: "Ce n'était pas encore aujourd'hui qu'elle sortirait le nouvel appareil perfectionné aux dimensions de Rocco Siffredi [It won't be today that she'll take out the new tool, modeled on Rocco Siffredi's dimensions]" (Chuberre 107). And another notes, admonshingly, "je suis pas un animal à cirque à la Rocco Siffredi [I'm not a circus animal like Rocco Siffredi]" (Saron 29). And yet they all are creatures of a kind of porno-circus of the mind. Porn is always nearby, both on screen and playing out in the mind's eye of these characters: "Il n'y avait rien de pire pour notre héros que de baiser avec un mec et de sentir que l'esprit du partenaire était ailleurs, en train de mater un film porno imaginaire, seul dans son coin [There was nothing worse for our hero than to have sex with a guy and to feel that the partner's mind was elsewhere, in the process of looking at an imaginary porn film, alone in his corner]" (Batlo 115).

What does this mean? How does this inform the universe? I have saved porn for the end of this part of the chapter because, in its way, it is as unifying an element as the matter of potential seropositivity and is ultimately the specular figure of this world. If seropositivity is the marker of belonging, the ubiquity of porn is nevertheless the sign of the virtual world we are in – a world of teledildonics, which are objectively defined as sex toys that are remote-controlled by computer, but which we could extend in meaning to encompass a virtual sexual reality safe from STDs and physical encounters. Here, ironically, the presence of pornography, that two-dimensional version of sex, counterbalances the immediacy and presence of potentially viral bareback sex. Porn is the figure of safety internalized within this world, as if modeling oneself on pornography, seeing oneself as the subject of pornography, and becoming part of the world of teledildonics were somehow that magical, oppositional antidote to the position of immediacy defined by bareback sex. That internalized and glorified other is also that specular, phallic other, the sign and seat of phallic presence presented as if it were there, when we know that it is not. To say that the characters introject themselves into a pornotopia is the bare minimum, so to speak: this is a world in which plot is accidental, in which the next lay is around the corner, in which all men are gay and well-endowed, in which pleasure goes beyond language to the primal, and in which the only real activity is sex. And yet this screen presence, going well beyond the literary, is the illusion that the world is like that, that sex is zipless, that sex is its own representation.

What then can we say about the world of these novels as a conclusion to this part of the chapter? The renewed liberation afforded by combination therapy creates a world in which the microscopic no longer matters and in which the macroscopic, the "big screen," is the ideological substitute for reality, or better, that which replaces reality. No longer is literature – popular, to be sure, and reasonably transparent – the product of earlier literature. Tied more directly to a social situation that is interpreted within pornography, these books reinterpret the present as the eminently readable and trope-free verbal version of those screen images. No tropes then in this internalized pornotopia, but only a viral marker that seems endlessly to delay the last reel of the film that is their lives.

II. Queer Images

Whether to watch films, to look at them, or to read them: that is the basic and century-old question relative to interpreting this genre. If in its infant stages at the end of the nineteenth century, spectators were called to by the spectacular and specular object of film, they were soon brought to a more active interrelationship with the object when cinematic narration began, a moment that we could conveniently associate with the genre change represented by the role of narrative in *The Birth of a Nation* (Griffith, 1915). As active participants, spectators had to change their passive act of looking at a spectacle into an active act of reading it. With *The Birth of a Nation* and other films from the same time period, film begins to demand that the spectators read a story, understand actions, and react to representations. So, even in its youth as a genre, film stages representations – real, realist(ic), fantastic, or impossible – of us or of others: representations to which the active spectators must react and with which they must establish an intersubjective relation. It is impossible not to look or watch; it is useless to try to remain illiterate when faced with film.

During the twentieth century, film, along with all audiovisual arts that have the same common heritage, becomes the most popular genre for representing identities, be they stable, unstable, emerging, or newly minted representations, in a far more effective and efficient way than any other genre. For example, the novel published in 1929 by Vicki Baum, *Menschen im Hotel*, staged the representation of a single woman who conforms neither to the traditional moral values of the nineteenth century nor to the representations of a prostitute or even a "loose woman." But it is only with the Hollywood (MGM) film, *Grand Hotel* (Goulding, 1932) that the world could see the incarnation of this modern, flapper-like, single woman, played to the hilt by Joan Crawford in one of the first versions of the role of the social-climbing "female" (as this character was described at the time) in which she would be so often typecast.

What I am concerned with here, though, is not the emergence of the social-climbing woman, but rather the emergence, some seventy years later, of the gay male in contemporary French cinema. And for that another literary example is even more relevant. Let us think about the number of readers of Marcel Proust's *A la recherche du temps perdu* or even of André Gide's *Les Faux-Monnayeurs* and compare those numbers to the number of spectators of film who, from the beginning of this art form, have seen the representation of a gay male, stereotyped or not, on screen. The number of people who have seen *La Cage aux folles* (Molinaro, 1978) certainly far outweighs the number of people who have actually read the *Recherche* or even just the first volume.

Among many critics who offer analyses of the representation of gay characters in film, often organizing their work along cultural lines, Vito Russo considers Hollywood from the silent era up to the 1980s. These representations were chaste and castrated, hidden, closeted, caricatural, but they were there, even during the long years of the production code (1934–1967), which prohibited the representation of sexual "perversion."[7] Still, even in the United States during this period of censorship, many more people saw the representation of gay characters on screen than read about them in novels, whether canonical or popular. And clearly the case was even more obvious in France, though as Alain Brassart has shown, there was a kind of closet. In Germany during the Weimar Republic, one might think of *Anders als die Anderen* (Oswald, 1919), written by no less an imposing figure than Magnus Hirschfeld and starring Conrad Veidt, who would become best known for playing Major Strasser in *Casablanca* (Curtiz, 1942). Even in films from the somewhat conservative United Kingdom both before and after the Wolfenden Report in 1957, one could see gay characters. For most people, the representation of the gay man in the twentieth century was visual, cinematic, and specular, and only minimally literary.

More recently, gay men have been represented more and more frequently in film, in a variety of roles and with fewer stereotypes than in the case of the pansies of yore. The scourge of AIDS, of course, was a pivotal moment, adding to the emerging images of the "normal" gay male the tragic or dramatic figure of a sick or dying

---

[7] The production code, created in 1930 and put into practice in 1934, established the rule for "good taste" and especially prohibited images or language deemed to be obscene, immoral, or otherwise harmful to the American way of life.

young man – for that, we should think of *An Early Frost* (Erman, 1985), *Les Nuits fauves* (Collard, 1993), and *Philadelphia* (Demme, 1993). Previously, with few exceptions in the history of film, the figure of the protagonist dying young from illness had usually been conjugated in the feminine; young men died in battle, with their boots on: think of Lew Ayres's character, Paul Bäumer, in *All Quiet on the Western Front* (Milestone, 1930), as one archetype, and Bette Davis's character, Judith Traherne, in *Dark Victory* (Goulding, 1939), as the other. At the same time, and perhaps only coincidentally, as queers, after the beginnings of gay liberation, began to be more visible, the age of AIDS is also that of queer film, depicting the gay man and homosexuality in all their aspects and multiple avatars, through normalizing images, as well as readings and representations that took some distance from the pathology that had reigned for so long.

Yet there is another change that has occurred more recently, in films from the late nineties and the beginning of the twenty-first century. As the representation of gay men and homosexuality has become so commonplace of late, at least in the big cities of the West, it is no longer remarkable. What middle-class citizen of Paris, London, New York, Montreal, or Sydney would think twice, wandering through the streets of the city, about a gay couple walking together, holding hands, or kissing? And this, even if some of the internalized images that observer would have come to her or him directly from what Guy Debord so aptly called the "society of spectacle"; they are images that have come out of film. We have entered a post-queer moment, one in which the gay neighborhoods of the eighties and nineties, whatever specific form they took in each city, may still exist, but are morphing into loci of a gay identity without homosexuality, as Florian Grandena has put it. It is one thing to have a gay ghetto; it is another to have the city of Chicago officially recognize a neighborhood as "Boystown" and Manchester officially name a neighborhood the Gay Village. Could the specular and spectacular side of this be in the process of disappearing? It is a hypothesis worth retaining, but we cannot yet be sure of it.

Yet the fact that there is such a change is recorded in film, and it is to that I now turn. First of all, in this part of the chapter, I shall try to analyze what is not remarkable, what no longer exists, what is not unique. For, nowadays – and I am not speaking of experimental films like those of Lionel Soukaz that include *Ixe* (1980),

La Télévision nous encule [Television Fucks Our Asses] (2002), *Fist Power* (2002), and *Notre trou de cul est révolutionnaire* [Our Assholes are Revolutionary] (2006) – though I am including *auteur* films, such as those of Olivier Ducastel and Jacques Martineau, or Sébastien Lifshitz – we are considering films that, in general, ask the audience to look things squarely in the eye. Here they are, take them or leave them. However, this non-confrontational attitude, which is also non-explanatory, leaves out the bonds of affect that had been present previously, either in the caricatural figures before the 1980s or in the sympathetic ones thereafter. The gay male figure in contemporary films is not necessarily bad (as before) or good (in the AIDS era).[8] And thus we are moved to question what form the look of the spectator (who is not necessarily coded as gay or straight) takes, when characters are shown to be gay, or to discover their own homosexuality. These are figures we would not look at twice for their homosexuality in the streets of any metropolis or college town, but we are asked to look at them, to focus on them, and to understand them, when we are sitting in the dark of a cinema.

So we should understand the situation as follows. On the one hand, again in the big cities of the West and among the middle classes, homosexuality is totally and completely dedramatized, its aberrant singularity having been removed. On the other hand, we have a representational situation in which phenomena are visible everywhere, wherever one looks in the urban, middle-class cultures of the West. What happens then to the spectator's look, given this thematic, psychological, phenomenal, and temporal reframing? What happens to the filmic gaze, that forced specularity, through which we look at something in the movies that does not concern us and that we do not bat an eye at in daily life, when gay men and

---

[8] François Ozon's stunning film *Le Temps qui reste* (2005) reworks the delicate balance of melodrama and disease as it engages questions of sexuality, heteronormativity, filiation, and a world in which AIDS is refigured. For the first time in a quarter of a century we have a film in which a character is gay and dying, but the entire discussion of AIDS consists of the following: "'J'ai le SIDA?' Non ['Do I have AIDS?' No]." Ozon offers a film in which the dynamics of the homo/hetero divide have changed rapidly, in which concepts of filiation, reproduction, and continuation have been challenged not merely by changing legislation – the PACS is not even mentioned – but by changing mores. *Le Temps qui reste* is a film in which interpersonal relations, concepts of mourning, and ideas about sexuality no longer fit neatly into categories that have had two centuries' worth of currency.

homosexuality are represented without any *Entfremdungseffekt* or defamiliarization (*ostranenie*)?

One does not often remember that there is an iterative aspect to the etymology of the French verb "regarder" [to look]. While one sees only once, the look is double, a redoubling of consciousness about an object that demands active and awake attention be paid to it. Etymologically, in French (different in this respect from Italian, Spanish, German, and English), the look is necessarily double; this is yet another version of the French exception, but it gives us all pause in the West, and it is a useful tool for the analysis that follows. To look in French – "regarder" – means to look a second time or, to make a macaronic pun, to look attentively or even to ogle, "reluquer." It is a way of reworking vision, of seeing something "in my mind's eye," as Shakespeare put it. It is, in short, to make it mine.

So here then is the problematic: an exploration of this redoubled look at homosexuality as it is represented in several contemporary films and made-for-television films. Later in the chapter, I shall focus on two films in depth, the dark film *Wild Side* (Lifshitz, 2004) and the lighter, gayer summer love comedy, *Crustacés et coquillages* [Crustaceans and Shellfish] (Ducastel and Martineau, 2005).[9] The other films that will serve here as a mini-corpus will be *Presque rien* (Lifshitz, 2000), a made-for-television film, *A cause d'un garçon* [Because of a Boy] (Cazeneuve, 2002), the stunningly aberrant *Ma vraie vie à Rouen* [My Real Life in Rouen] (Ducastel and Martineau, 2002), which takes a unique point of view in talking about the question, and another film for television, *Juste une question d'amour* [Just a Question of Love] (Faure, 2000).[10]

If we return to the beginning, we notice that the look, within a film, necessarily double, is redoubled by that of the spectator who looks, who cannot help looking at what she or he would not usually look at. Interestingly, and perhaps not at all coincidentally, a comment comes back over and over again, "ça ne me regarde pas";

---

[9] This was released in the UK as *Cockles and Muscles*, a play on the refrain from James Yorkson's song of the same title, but better known as "Molly Malone." In the US, it was released as *Côte d'Azur*, a misnomer, since the film is set in the Bouches du Rhône. Marseille, the *préfecture* of that department, is some 185 kilometers west of Nice.

[10] Films by André Techiné would also fit this corpus, as would works by a number of other film-makers. On Techiné, I refer the reader to Bill Marshall's excellent work.

a standard expression that literally means "that doesn't look at me," it can be translated more idiomatically as "it is not my concern" or, better yet, "it is none of my affair." But what is this affair? I would be rushing if I said that what is of no concern is "homosexuality," even if there is no other word to describe the phenomenon. But frankly, we cannot be sure that we are looking at homosexuality or looking at the representation of homosexuality, even if we all think we know what it is. Nevertheless, we can be sure that, most of the time, with exceptions made for the two films I shall treat singly, we are looking at the representation of a young man who has sexual desire for another young man or other young men. These films thus ask spectators to be the witnesses – if not to say voyeurs – of sexual behavior that is normally no concern to them, but which, when all is said and done, does concern them even if it does not concern characters in the film other than the protagonists.

This sexuality, if it is a sexuality – and I am using the word for lack of a better one – is necessarily specular then: as much as it does not concern other characters within the film it is of concern to the interested spectator of the film. And from that, I should like to make a claim: if the representation of this specific sexual desire is of concern to no one other than the desirer and the desired, by definition there cannot be homosexuality. For this sexuality, like any other, exists only through the collective, in the plural set of representations that frame the desire. In these films, the event is always singular, ready to be represented for the spectators, but not for those, intradiegetically, who might have affective relations to the character who reveals that desire or acts on it. Thus we can say that the non-look redoubles and is doubled by the looks of the spectator, who must look: that non-look is the blind gaze of the community of characters within the film, characters who know all without knowing, looking, and seeing. This is a far cry from the famous closet, if this closet ever existed, and this in spite of the fact that everything in these films is done under the sign of normalizing heteronormativity. It is not that every spectator is forced to look the way others do, but rather that the norms against which this discovery of homosexuality is set up are "naturally" those of society.

Clearly the expression "ça ne me regarde pas" could be considered to be spoken as a sign of the French concept of freedom: what one does freely with one's body should not be of interest to anyone or determined by anyone (if one sets aside certain societal or legal limits that engage matters like rape, pedophilia, incest, bestiality, and so forth), as long as the other is or the others are consenting adults. As the father, Marc (Gilbert Melki), says in *Crustacés et coquillages*, in relation to the sexual activity of someone else, "c'est pas mes oignons [those are not my onions]," which means the same thing as "ça ne me regarde pas," though with a higher level of slang and just a whiff of a double entendre. "Oignon," in French slang, means ass or anus, as in the expression "lui carrer dans l'oignon," which means "to put something in his ass." Thus, Marc is saying, in a way, that since it is not a question of his posterior, it does not concern him. What we learn, however, toward the end of the film, to be discussed below, is that it will precisely be a question of his ass, for he will rediscover his attraction to his former (male) lover and will end up back with him; but until then, it is none of his affair.

Still, there is another way to read this standard phrase and I shall take as the first example a scene from *Presque rien*. This film is about a family of Parisians on holiday in August at the beach. It is a somewhat dysfunctional family, with a mother who is still mourning the death of a child three years earlier and a father who remains in Paris, as he is unable to take a holiday with the family, something that is sacred in French culture. It is thus a family that is both too little and too excessively heteronormative. However, the film-maker is not suggesting that this familial dysfunctionality is the cause – if there is a cause – of the homosexuality of Mathieu (Jérémie Elkaïm). Mathieu discovers that he is gay precisely during this summer stay at the beach, during which he meets a local guy, Cédric (Stéphane Rideau). They fall in love with one another, an event that affects family relations. One day, when Mathieu returns to the house, his older sister Annick says: "Tu fais ce que tu veux avec ton cul. Ça ne me regarde pas [Do what you wish with your ass. It's none of my affair]."

One might speculate on the meaning of her comments. At a basic level, she is supporting republican values: everyone is the master of himself or herself and must have the right of enjoying freedom. As sodomy itself was long ago decriminalized thanks to the efforts of Cambacérès, everyone must be able to enjoy it if he or she wants. No one else has a right to say what one can and cannot do with one's body parts, even if the act of being sodomized is considered by many (including, undoubtedly, Annick) to be among the most abject. It little matters what role one actually plays; and the spectators, if not the sister, learn at one point that Mathieu is the top. But for the other, who chooses not to know and who puts family ahead of pleasure, the other who never leaves the realm of the heteronormative, the homosexual is always figured in this representational imaginary as the bottom in anal intercourse or as the fellator. So, in principle, Annick does not give a damn what Mathieu does sexually with his body, even as she champions family values and heteronormativity. But, in a film that is realistic, we need to think about this a bit more. What Mathieu does with his body is no affair of Annick's, but it is our affair. It is not that we desire to know exactly, and in strict anatomical detail, who does what to whom, but it is that we, the spectators, desire to know what happens, in order to be able to say with some assurance that this character or these characters are gay, that there is homosexuality in the room. With that guarantee, however, we are perversely thrust into a situation of aberrant knowledge and misplaced, prurient looks. Mathieu's affairs are our affairs too. We may be sympathetic or indifferent to his plight; we may reject, accept, or tolerate him; we may, as good liberals, be more or less neutral about questions of gender and sexuality, but if his affair were not ours as well, we would not continue to watch the film. We must be interested in it; we have to be interested in it; we are gayed by the film.

Let us continue by looking at three examples from the made-for-television film, *A cause d'un garçon*. Vincent (Julien Baumgartner), a handsome, seventeen-year-old athlete, is outed by other students after he has been seen meeting with the openly gay Benjamin (Jérémie Elkaïm). Even though nothing happens between them, aside from a kiss that is more or less refused by the latter, the rumour goes around that Vincent is gay as well. In this more or less conservative society set in the middle-class Paris suburbs (Val-de-Marne), what we think of as homophobia seems almost ubiquitous, even if Vincent's closest friends seem to accept him for who he is. But the homophobia is everywhere: at home, in the form of a rather brutish brother, among many of his co-students, and especially among the other teenagers on the swimming team. Parenthetically, one can think of other characters from the middle-class Paris suburbs who seem far more open-minded, such as the holiday-makers in *Crustacés et coquillages*, who come from Melun (Seine-et-Marne) – although their open-mindedness is in part a strategy for hiding other secrets. As for life out in the provinces, one family will be quite homophobic in *Juste une question d'amour*, while the other, consisting of a widowed mother, will be understanding. Further on, I shall return to questions of the geography of homophobia, heteronormativity, and homosexuality as they are all represented in these films.

In *A cause d'un garçon*, the look of the other, or the absence of this look, is shared by three characters: Noémie, Vincent's girlfriend; Vincent's literature professor, who is gay as well; and Vincent himself. After having seen the graffiti written by another student, "Molina est un pédé. Il suce [Molina is a fag. He sucks]," Noémie does not know what to think, as they have already slept together and he did not come out to her. Vincent eventually musters up the courage to tell her what he could not tell her earlier, to which she replies: "Ce qui me blesse, c'est pas que tu couches avec les mecs. Ça ne me regarde pas [What bothers me is not that you sleep with guys. It's none of my affair]." What bothers her, of course, is that he did not tell her, that he did not make it her affair, something that she must look at again. Later, in a meeting between two high-school administrators and the literature teacher, the former ask the latter to talk to Vincent, for they do not want him to lose the chance of getting a sports scholarship. One might guess that they ask him to do so because, as everyone knows, literature professors are sensitive and work more intimately with their students. But we may also think that the reason they ask him is that they suspect or know that he is gay, for it seems to be something spoken about in the hallways: disappointed in his grade in that class, Vincent's best friend calls the teacher a "pédé [fag]"; someone else writes graffiti saying "Molina couche-t-il avec le prof de français? [Is Molina sleeping with the French teacher?]" But the teacher balks, indicating that his students' sexuality is no more his affair than his is theirs. When he changes his mind, and finally decides to talk with Vincent, he comes out to the teenager, and as he does so, the latter starts to smile, almost impertinently. Vincent replies, "Excusez-moi. Je ne savais pas. Et je pense que ça ne me regarde pas. Vous êtes mon prof quand-même [Excuse me. I didn't know. And I think that it is none of my affair. You're my teacher, after all]." The homosexual is alone in the world, seemingly *sui generis*, and he does not participate in the shared, collective representations of homosexuality of our era.

It is easy to understand what these characters mean: even in feeling hurt by Vincent who slept with her without telling her that he had a boyfriend, Noémie in no way wants to limit his freedom or pursuit of happiness or even "tolerate" him as a homosexual; he lives his life as he sees fit. As for the French teacher, he does not want to be in the tricky situation of limiting his own freedom, for, in order to speak to Vincent, he would have to tell him that he too is gay. And having accepted himself as well as the actions and self-representations associated with his desire, Vincent does not seek to be complicitous with someone who plays a completely different role in his life, nor does he want to be forced into accepting a personal relationship with his teacher simply because they are both gay. However, at the same time, we must wonder why this has to be said at all, and said by these characters in particular as they announce their distance with the same five-word phrase. Each time the spectators, who are watching with interest, hear this lack of interest announced, they must effectively question the look and interest they bring to this affair. This occurs and goes beyond an enforced voyeurism, quite Sartrean in nature, whereby neither the homosexual nor homosexuality exists without the look of the other. The spectators are asked to interrogate their own behavior; the characters are not.

Let us take this from another angle, this one more geographic than linguistic in nature. Most of these films, as well as other films by Ducastel and Martineau (with one exception) that treat this subject, films by François Ozon, and others, are set almost entirely in the provinces. Paris does not dominate. Significantly, *Jeanne et le garçon formidable* [Jeanne and the Wonderful Boy] (Ducastel and Martineau, 1998) is set in a Paris that is easily recognizable to all: the first encounter between Jeanne (Virginie Ledoyen) and Olivier (Mathieu Demy) takes place in a metro carriage. But, while there are gay characters in this film, they are secondary, and the focus of the film is on a heterosexual relationship. Dying of AIDS, Olivier says that his HIV$^+$ status comes from his having been a drug addict. *Drôle de Félix* takes place in the provinces; *Presque rien*, at the beach in Brittany; *Crustacés et coquillages*, at the beach in the Bouches-du-Rhône; *Juste une question d'amour*, in the North of France; and *Ma vraie vie à Rouen*, obviously, in Rouen. *Wild Side* is the most Parisian of these films, through its characters, one of whom is a transsexual who works as a prostitute in Paris, but the film is divided between Paris and the provinces.[11] *Presque rien* speaks of

---

[11] Even the "post-AIDS" film *Le Temps qui reste*, which starts in the metropolis, becomes a road movie of sorts in the provinces.

Paris, but only to announce that the father is there and cannot come to the beach. And in *Ma vraie vie à Rouen*, significantly, Paris is the locus of a demonstration against Jean-Marie Le Pen. The characters leave Rouen, spend the day in Paris, and go back to Normandy.

The case is clearest with *A cause d'un garçon*, which is set, as I have indicated, in the Paris suburbs. There would be nothing easier than having the young protagonist get on the RER, get off at Châtelet-Les Halles, walk a few short blocks into the Marais, and discover gay Paris for himself. And his boyfriend Bruno (Nils Ohlund, who will also be in *Presque rien*) does just that. But for Vincent, this overly dramatic and garishly lit locus, where gay Parisian night-life takes place, where everything consists of unexpected caresses, sex, and forced sexualization, is odious, and he stays only a few minutes before going back to the suburbs. As he remarks, "Le Marais m'a foutu la trouille. C'est comme si j'étais devenu une marchandise [The Marais scared the shit out of me. It was as if I had become a piece of goods]." That is the answer to the double question: Paris is where the collective is, not only this garish night-life or the transvestites of the Bois de Boulogne, but also the demonstration in *Ma vraie vie à Rouen* against Le Pen and an Act-Up demonstration in *Jeanne et le garçon formidable*. Paris – specifically the Marais – is thus the locus of the homosexual collective, of its practices, discourses, and representations; it is the locus where the gay man is named as a gay subject. It is the locus of the "us," that is to say, of homosexuality. And that is exactly what is missing in the provinces, at the beach, or even in the suburbs where these films are set. It is not that there is no homosexuality in the provinces, but that a specific Parisian homosexuality does not exist there; or, perhaps, simply that the film-makers do not choose to show it, because they need that disjunction for their films to work.

Spectators are asked to look at the homosexual outside Paris, as if he were a subject before, aside from, or beyond homosexuality taken as a commonplace or an ideological position. Two interpretations are possible here: that the gay man stands outside of collective homosexuality by remaining a unique case, or that the gay man, staying at home, among his family members or in small-town life, remains "normal," and simply someone subjected to an innocent love. What is offered in the Marais would be a kind of homonormativity to the extent that certain behaviors and representations are mandatory and others are formally excluded.

Perhaps these film-makers are suggesting that the Marais brand of homosexuality has become in turn a kind of pressure, a stare at the gay man by the collective whose affair it is. Or perhaps there is something else at work.

There is thus a big difference between the geography of these films and that offered by the novels of arrival discussed above. The peripeteiae of the protagonists of these texts lead them to Paris and ultimately to a seroconversion that makes conversation, dialogue, and a recognition of self possible for the complete gay man. And this takes place, as we have seen, as if they were living in a pornotopia, a porn film in which each of the protagonists plays the lead role, and porn films code much of their behavior. Obviously, the form of the genre forces the representation to go in certain directions. The novels speak while the films have to show. There is nothing more normal for the writer than to describe, expatiate, or create dialogue. There is nothing more normal for the film-maker than to show the gay man in the process of discovering himself or looking at himself. For practical reasons, of course, both pragmatic and deontological in nature, these films that we are looking at must be clearly different from the porn films that are the medium upon which the novels are based.

Certainly there are naked bodies in the films, but they are dedramatized, erotic at times, but never pornographic. There is no better example of this than that offered by Ducastel and Martineau in *Ma vraie vie à Rouen*. The video camera that Étienne (Jimmy Tavares) totes everywhere both eroticizes and fragments the bodies of those he films. At the same time, the video camera does not fetishize the erotic body: Étienne films his friend Ludo (Lucas Bonnifait) as well as his geography teacher (Jonathan Zaccaï). In the dressing room, Étienne lowers his underpants, but the camera stops filming. Later on, Étienne wants to show some skating jumps to Laurent, and proposes taking his pants off to show him the last jump, but the latter, the same geography teacher who is now his mother's partner, does not accept; some lines cannot be crossed. Even later, having won a medal, Étienne films himself naked, as if, through that win, he could finally give value to his body and sexualize it for himself, but the shot does not last long. And when Laurent starts to lower his pants in a fake strip-tease while Étienne films him, Laurent realizes that the young man is actually interested and stops lowering his pants, asking, "T'as pas honte? [Aren't you ashamed?]"

Taboos can be approached, but one cannot transgress into pornotopia. The extremely eroticized body becomes the object of the gay gaze, and this is not permitted in this world. If, in the last scene, Étienne ends up finally having sex with another man, it is only at the end of the film and we will never again see the gay body.

If it is not permitted for the body to become too fetishized or eroticized in these films, there is nothing more normal than one character discovering other gay characters, as if the visibility of the other could occur in spite of the acts performed by the gay body, acts that are no one else's affair. Thus there are two scenes in *Crustacés et coquillages* that perform the visibility of the homosexual. In one, part of a running joke about the shower, Charly is going to take a shower but lets something fall on the floor; Martin hears the water running and goes out. Charly follows him, and the father, Marc, hearing the running water, figures out that both have left. Charly follows Martin to a cruising area and meets Didier, a plumber, who, we will learn, is Marc's ex-lover. Charly, confused, says that his name is "Charles Marc" and the plumber replies that he adores that name. Having returned to the house, Martin has an emotional moment and he and Marc spend the night chastely in bed together, after which Marc masturbates in the shower. Later, towards the end of the film, the truth of these confusing situations is revealed through the vision of the other, when a character finally recognizes that the situation is his affair. Martin flees towards the cruising area and finds Didier again; they begin to kiss. Having followed Martin, Marc separates them and replaces him in Didier's arms, as they kiss. Martin reveals the truth to Charly, which is the truth of the latter's father's homosexuality.

In all these films, the look or gaze ultimately reveals the truth of the homosexual, showing him to the other characters whether they like it or not, and putting into question any position previously espoused that demands a normalization or a framing of the acceptable of homosexual behavior, like the homophobia of Laurent's family in *Juste une question d'amour*, where the subject concerns the attitudes of a lower-middle-class family in which the father is a pharmacist in a small city in the North, while the gay son, Laurent, lives in Lille. Or, in another form, it is the tolerance found in more open-minded milieus. The look that accommodates the gay in the frame is also the look that discombobulates the others. No matter how blind they are at first, they cannot remain terminally indifferent to what they see; there is no way, however, to take it all in without erring in one way or another, and this is due to the omnipresent hetero-normativity accompanied by the ubiquity of the specular. To see the act, the object, or the behavior, means necessarily entering into a relation with this other, and particularly, with the identity of the other to itself and not to its specular image, and yet, it also means not knowing how to conceive of this other.

The desire to know through the look is something we could call voyeurism or scopophilia, but is accompanied only indirectly by a scotomization, that is to say, by a defense mechanism that would be a willful blindness to what is being seen. The others do not want to see or know: Laurent's family, blind to his homosexuality, truly wants to believe in the charade of his non-existent heterosexuality as it is played out by Laurent, who uses his friend Carole as a beard for a while. Carole even quotes André Gide's most famous statement, already mentioned, as if to evoke for the spectator the ubiquity of the repressiveness of heteronormativity: "Familles, je vous hais [Families, I hate you]." Laurent answers this classical reference with a verbal shrug: "Même pas [Not even]." The problem goes further than the classical definition of heteronormativity, which is seen to operate at the local level, to reach a generalized heteronormativity on the one hand, and the inability, because of the specular, for the gay man (in this case) to have an image of himself that is truly his and not internalized from some represented source, on the other.[12]

Families or society at large normalize and are normalized by conformity. In *Drôle de Félix*, the protagonist reconstitutes his missing family relations by giving these roles to people he meets during a trip to the South to meet – or discover – his father, whom ultimately he will never find (Grandena). By fetishizing filiation, the families, and even the gay sons, refuse queering, even when the gay couple is accepted within the familiar. In *Ma vraie vie à Rouen*, for example, while he is looking for what we might term his sexual identity, Étienne normalizes relations in a classic *fort/da* scenario, like the one used by Félix in *Drôle de Félix*: if the relations are normalized then all is well with the world; it little matters that Félix

---

12 Here, I am making a kind of Hegelian or Girardian argument with a twist. It is not simply that the desire is the desire of the other's desire, but rather, the desire (for an image of self, for an identity) is the Lacanian lack produced by the internalized and therefore ultimately foreign representation of the self.

is openly gay and partnered and that Étienne is only in the process of discovering his sexual identity. So, while his mother is his biological mother, his grandmother is rather the mother of his late stepfather, and thus not a blood relative. Later in the film, when the geography teacher has become his mother's partner, Étienne speaks of him as his "stepfather." But his friend retorts that Laurent is not Étienne's stepfather because he is not married to Étienne's mother. The word is wrong, but the discourse is clear: families and society normalize discourses. This addressing of the subject – whether by others or by the subject's own internalized voice or superego – is a way of making him or her more normal, less different, less queer.

In *Juste une question*, Cédric (Stéphane Guérin-Tillié) calls his mother by her first name, Emma, instead of calling her "Maman"; one could ascribe this discourse to his relative independence from the heteronormative system. However, all of Emma's discourse is based on family relations: she accept's Cédric's homosexuality because she does not want to lose him after her husband's death. She talks as a mother to Laurent's rather unfriendly parents; she talks anew to Laurent's mother and so forth. Comparable to this character named Cédric, there is only one other contender for escaping heteronormativity, and that is another character named Cédric, in *Presque rien*, who says of families "c'est pas trop mon truc [they're not really my thing]." He is one of very few who is able to take his distance. Still, after an accident, he accepts a visit from his father. In general, families normalize discourses and distribute relations and roles under directives from a heteronormative optic, the mirror image of the one that determines the relations of the spectators to the protagonists.

The film-makers often stage an accident as a plot device, whose role would seem to be a questioning of the presumed relations between or among characters in order to right the ship and put everything back into order in the family. Insofar as these accidents are concerned, the champions are Ducastel and Martineau. In *Ma vraie vie*, for example, characters refer to someone who fell – or who jumped – off a cliff, after a rockslide. Later, Laurent falls – or is pushed by Étienne – and breaks his leg, an accident that serves to tighten relations among the members of this family. And at the end of the film, Étienne seems to waver at the very same spot, as if he too were going to jump; it is only the arrival of the person who will have sex with him that shifts the dynamic, but this time, clearly it is away from the heteronormative and toward the queer. In *Jeanne et le garçon formidable,* Jeanne literally falls into Olivier's lap in a metro carriage; in *Drôle de Félix,* the title character witnesses a racist attack and murder; in *Crustacés et coquillages,* apart from a fake flat tire, a disabled water heater, random telephone calls, and other such events, there are the accidental meetings in the cruising spot, where Martin falls.

In *Presque rien,* Cédric falls in a cave on the beach; in *Wild Side,* by the same director, random meetings abound, involving eventful, communicational, and biological accidents, something to which I shall return below. In *Juste une question,* Laurent lets some plants fall by accident and in gathering up what has fallen, he and Cédric bump heads. In the same film, Laurent's father has to go to hospital after having fallen off a ladder. And even before the plot of this film starts, a gay cousin of Laurent has died, not from AIDS as the "thoughtful" family believes, due punishment for his homosexuality, but from hepatitis caught in Vietnam during he trip he has taken there with his partner, after his parents had thrown him out for being gay. Although Laurent and Charly get very drunk and Mathieu, in *Presque rien,* tries unsuccessfully to commit suicide, it is necessary to say that no gay character dies during the course of these films; in *Wild Side,* Stéphanie's mother dies, and in *Jeanne et le garçon formidable* Olivier does die from AIDS, but he, precisely, is not gay.

Each of these accidents leads to a bifurcation at which the character has the chance of realigning himself with the heteronormative order or of moving further away from it. In other words, these films are not declined in a tragic mode: the accident moves or changes things and the unexpected meeting reorganizes relations and dynamics. But if the locus is not tragic, how then do we understand the discourse and language used here? We need to reconsider the role of language in these films, not for the spectators, as above, or for those who dwell in heteronormativity, as is the case for most members of the protagonists' families, but for those – the protagonists – who are not quite sure of how the system addresses and identifies them. For it is only through understanding that address and identification that they can learn what role is played by their desire and what representations they can use to frame it.

In order to frame this better, I shall refer, albeit briefly, to a 2005 film that does not fit at all into the corpus at hand, for obvious reasons. In Ang Lee's very well-known film, *Brokeback Mountain,* there are chance meetings as well, but as soon as the events begin to unfold, there is no escape mechanism whatsoever, through language, act, or the gaze of the other. It is a gaze that is fatal and tragic: we know that Jack Twist (Jake Gyllenhaal) is bound to die and that Ennis Del Mar (Heath Ledger) will end up alone. In these French films, however, nothing is fatal or tragic – "fatalitaire," as Arletty's character, Raymonde, famously says in *Hôtel du nord*. The protagonist always finds the right language to confirm or reaffirm his sexual availability and personal presence, and this speech act moves him away from the suffocation imposed by heteronormativity. Sooner or later, the gay protagonist's speech act becomes a challenge to the moral order of society.

I am not suggesting for a moment that the characters always succeed in describing their situation or representing their desire to themselves. For example, Martin, the gay high-school student in *Crustacés*, has a mini-nervous breakdown one night when he cannot get over his unrequited love for his straight friend, Charly. And Étienne spends the entire time in *Ma vraie vie* unable to articulate what he feels or to put his desire into words. In *A cause d'un garçon*, Vincent sleeps with his girlfriend, Noémie, after which he tells her that he has something to tell her, but cannot find the words to tell her that he is gay, and the matter is dropped. In *Presque rien*, the spectator feels the difficulty that Mathieu has in expressing what he thinks and feels, in describing his relations with Cédric, in representing his stress, and even in saying why the two are no longer together. Thus, personal discourse can be used to realign the possibilities for the future and to give the characters the possibility of getting to know themselves better. So this discourse redoubles the position of the camera by deforming it: each personal comment is a challenge to the permanent nature of visibility and allows both the speaker and listener – often the same person – to redefine his point of view as a unique one by requeering it for his own purposes.

It is precisely this change of discourse that brings me to a discussion of some aspects of two recent films: the light, Hollywoodian film by Ducastel and Martineau, *Crustacés et coquillages*, on the one hand, and the very dark and brooding film, *Wild Side*, by Lifshitz. The title of the latter, it should be noted, is in English in the original, and is, among other things, a reference to the classic heterosexual story of illicit love, *Walk on the Wild Side* (Dmytryk, 1962), as well as to Lou Reed's song "Walk on the Wild Side" from his 1972 album *Transformer* (Rees-Roberts 145). I consider these two films in detail because each in its own way breaks away from the more recent films already discussed; each challenges the ubiquity of heteronormativity as it puts into question the idea of spectacular and specular homosexuality. In other words, though one film is rather rosy and the other is very bleak, they are both queer films, as opposed to merely films with gay themes or subjects. One is in part a coming-out film and the other most certainly is not; *Wild Side* could easily be described as being post-queer.

I shall begin by quickly revisiting the plots of each, in order to frame and situate them but also to see what elements are retained in a post-queer world, be it a comedy or a drama. *Crustacés et coquillages* is set at a summer home in the South just inherited by a family from the Île-de-France. Familial and heteronormative stability disappear during the course of the film, in part due to the unnerving presence of Martin, the straight son's gay friend, whose actions and open gayness serve as a prod that destabilizes the system. Béatrice, the mother, has a lover, and she plans to leave her husband. Marc, the husband, rediscovers his gay side in the arms of his former/first lover, Didier, to whom he had written many love letters years before. After they see each other again, Didier looks for the letters that Marc had written him and in rereading one of them, he hears Marc's voice. Just as Étienne's video camera tells the truth that he cannot yet articulate in the earlier *Ma vraie vie à Rouen*, here it is the voice-over of Marc, projected as that of a younger gay man, that tells the truth of who he is. In the epilogue to the film, which is set during the following summer, the couples have split up, changed partners, or otherwise re-paired themselves. They have constituted new couples according to their real sexual and emotional identities and feelings and everyone joins in a song and dance of celebration, the carnivalesque upheaval of the hypocritical nuclear family song and dance that Marc and Béatrice have earlier performed during a rainstorm. Everyone is gay, in both senses of the word, and then some; the film closes with a Hollywood-like happy ending, with each couple symbolically equal to the others. And even if they did not have many children, as the French expression goes, the viewer can safely assume that they lived happily ever after.

There is nothing so gay, in the sense of happy, in Sébastien Lifshitz's *Wild Side*. Each of the three main characters finds his or her own truth somewhere off the beaten path, in an uncomfortable locus at times; a queer space that is theirs alone, but one in which each determines language, look, relation, filiation, and genealogy relative to others; Todd Reeser rightly calls these phenomena "disruptions" in narrative, time, and sex(uality). In this film, which is more episodic than plot-driven, except for the event of one character's mother's death, it is a question of a variety of interpersonal relations in a *ménage à trois* that depends on mutual affection and on, as Nick Rees-Roberts puts it, "the characters' shared alienation from the stability of secure employment" (148). In that trio, one of the characters, Stéphanie, is a transsexual with both breasts and male genitalia. The second figure is Djamel, a presumably bisexual *beur* gigolo who has sex with clients of both genders, as well as with Stéphanie and Mikhaïl. This latter character is an ethnic Russian, from Odessa, who barely speaks French, and who sleeps with the two others, out of love, but in one case in a perverse theatricalization of the performance of sexuality to which I shall return below.[13]

Sexual differences multiply in *Wild Side*, a film that promotes the deconstruction (or the queering) of any and every category for sexual identities. Thus, from the very first scene, spectators see Stéphanie's fragmented body while, on the soundtrack, one hears a rather androgynous or epicene voice – it is the voice of Antony Hegarty, the lead singer of Antony and the Johnsons. The voice is singing in (British) English and is often in falsetto; the song, strange because of the language, for the average French listener, is about a "beautiful boy." But as all speakers of English know, this is not an exact translation of "beau garçon," since the word "beautiful," when referring to people, is gender-specific in English. The more expected modifier would have been "handsome," while "beautiful" as a modifier for "boy" would be used for an epicene ephebe. The queering of the events multiplies. Djamel successfully cruises a woman in a train station and asks her for fifty euros after having had sex with her; at a later point he gets fellated by another man, presumably for money as well.[14] Elsewhere, in the scene appropriately entitled "Night in Paris," Stéphanie is the active top penetrating a married man.

[13] I would presume that Mikhaïl is gay and that Djamel might be as well, but it cannot be guaranteed, in part because those stable categories are based on middle-class values and in part because they need the stability that comes from the collective of homosexuality.

[14] Scenes like this are post-modern versions of scenes in films such as *L'Homme blessé* [The Wounded Man] (Chéreau, 1983) and *Les Nuits fauves* [Wild Nights] (Collard, 1992).

The queering of positions reaches its apogee in the last scene (which, however, seemingly takes place much earlier chronologically), in Paris. It is set in a discotheque, where a man sees Stéphanie and cuts a deal with her: rather than sodomizing her himself, he leads her out and they pick up another man, who will then sodomize Stéphanie in front of the stranger. Yet this third person is Mikhaïl, who is already quite familiar to viewers. Arguably, then, this scene perhaps depicts the origin of the relationship between Mikhaïl and Stéphanie. At the same time, however, all remains ambiguous, since no frame is given. Thus, at a deeper level, this queered sex act is a multiple performance among the characters, including the voyeur, who screams "Fuck her" in English to Mikhaïl, and for the spectator, cast anew as voyeur in a strangely queered scenario. Through this scene in particular, through the character of the transsexual Stéphanie, and throughout the film in general, Lifshitz goes far in proposing a queering of identities which, in earlier films, have had to remain stable in order for the characters to develop. Here, on the contrary, it is in that very fragmentation and bending of gender, identity, and performance that a character assumes his or her multiple, and often contradictory, roles.

This fragmentation of identity and deconstruction of fixed categories are accompanied by a destabilization of identity in general, signaled and signified by the use of English both in this film and in *Crustacés*. In the latter film, some of the use of English is predictable as a sign of the transnational nature of the Euro-English gay discourse (Provencher) and of the imposition of an American model, at least from a consumerized and globalized point of view, on middle-class gayness in the West. So Martin speaks of "coming out," using the standard American term, something that has itself become a banality in the West, a term universally understood at least in the major cities, regardless of the language spoken. But it is only at the moment that Didier uses English – and that Marc speaks of Didier's return to see his father in California – that we can begin to understand.[15] For the film insists somewhat heavily on the fact that Béatrice's mother was from the Netherlands, because it is a simple way of encoding the progressive social attitudes found among the citizens of that country. There is a difference here between the two films: *Wild Side* recodes queerness, while *Crustacés et coquillages*

---

[15] Parenthetically, Jean-Marc Barr's English is excellent, as his father is American.

offers enlightened dual citizens instead of taking on the thornier problem of sexual identities. Still, the happy ending of *Crustacés et coquillages* is a literal reinscription of the discourse of coming out of the closet, for it depicts windows opening on the newly rearranged couples as each couple comes out of the closet of the closed room.

As for *Wild Side*, life imitates art – or vice versa. The director insists here not on people who are bicultural or who have dual nationality but rather on the permanent non-Frenchness that is inscribed in the lives of the characters. This could be taken as a metaphor for the destabilization of identity, as opposed to the more catholic, multicultural, trans-European identity espoused in the Ducastel and Martineau film. It is a significant difference from all the other films, where most of the characters are French of French heritage and where there is hardly a regional accent to be heard. If *Drôle de Félix* seems to figure someone who is of mixed origins (French and North African), he is more Norman than anything else, reared by a French mother deep in Normandy; he knows neither his father nor anything of his father's culture. With *Wild Side*, however, Lifshitz puts on screen three characters whose voices are as singular as they are, and whose idiolects are individual queerings of both the neutrality of the standard French accent and of the universalism associated with that accent and identity.

Stéphanie has a unique voice, a mixture of deep tones and sharp ones; it is a voice that would typically be associated with MTF transsexuals who have had hormone therapy but who still have their Adam's apples. At a moment late in the film, Mikhaïl asks her to speak with her "other voice," the one she had when she was a man. She tells him that she has only one voice and that it is the one she is using now. As for Djamel, he has the accent typically associated with the children of North African families living in the projects; it is an accent that to French people of French background may sound aggressive.[16] Finally, Mikhaïl speaks little French and understands not much more. Aside from the scenes in which he is communicating with other Russian speakers, he is spoken to with signs and hand signals or in broken English. At a particular moment in the

[16] The actor playing Djamel, Yasmine Belmadi, was from Aubervilliers (Seine-Saint-Denis), and seems to be have been typecast as a young *beur*, i.e., a Frenchman of North African descent, with at least three roles in films and televison in which his character is named "Djamel."

film, which gains importance only retrospectively in the mind of the viewer, Djamel tries to explain to Mikhaïl the origin of a scar on his arm. In rather faulty Franco-English, he translates the word "sang" incorrectly and says that he had "single" everywhere.

This sums it all up. Blood recalls the universal, that which everyone shares, that which is easily categorized or classified. Blood is also the symbol of a nationality and an identity that are squarely identified as being identical to themselves and to each other, the Frenchness found in the classic expression "nos ancêtres les Gaulois [our ancestors the Gauls]," the famous first line of a history textbook. Opposed to this universal blood that spills out of Djamel's wound is the "single," the singular and unique that each one of us is, not in an identitarian fashion, but in the sense of what there is of us that refuses categorization by the author or other or authority that seeks to determine.

Other events in this film reinforce the questioning of any project of collective identity. First, the film takes place partly in Paris, showing an ambiguity in the relations of each of the individuals to the collective homosexuality epitomized by the Marais, a homosexuality that has become very queer in this film. Whereas in *Jeanne et le garçon formidable* and *Ma vraie vie à Rouen* the Paris we see is by and large the Paris seen by tourists, here scenes alternate between the loci of popular Paris, including neighborhoods in the outer, more modest *arrondissements*, and the sexual cruising grounds of the Bois de Boulogne, and the unchanged life in Picardy, deep in the provinces, where everyone is of the same Franco-French heritage. Second, one sees a scene of bareback sex, the only one, to my knowledge, in this group of mainstream films: when Mikhaïl sodomizes Stéphanie in front of her client, it is clear that there is no pause for putting on a condom. In a continuous shot, Stéphanie fellates Mikhaïl and when the client orders the latter to have sex with the former, there is no cut in the montage: viewers know that he passes directly to bareback penetration.

What might one think of these two events? In one way, the film returns to the contemporary gay popular novel. It is beginning to create a multiply fragmented world, one in which everyone and anyone might be HIV⁺, one in which categories no longer function: sexuality, nationality, language, and culture are all cast aside. And that points us to a third issue which puts identity into question: Stéphanie, Djamel, and Mikhaïl cannot be clearly classified, for the sexuality of each one is variable and may or may not correspond to a real desire, whether momentary or more permanent. It certainly does not and cannot correspond to the figures allowed by hetero-normativity, based on middle-class values. The customer is always right, even when one is one's own customer.

It is not only in this rather somber world that the questions and answers are all mixed up, for they are also, albeit in a much lighter fashion, in *Crustacés et coquillages*, where, once queered, everything becomes post-queer. Marc rediscovers his gay nature about two decades after having left Didier. Béatrice allows that she is more bizarre than Marc because it was she who chose him; he did not pursue her to be a beard for him. Didier, the champion of cruising, turns out to be quite sentimental, as he has kept Marc's love letters and as he had sex with him exactly as they did the first time, out of sentimentality and nostalgia. (I should add that to create a bit of spiciness this sex act involves handcuffing Marc to the bed.) And finally, Charly's high-school friends think he is gay, as does his mother, even though he is not.

At the heart of all this, however, is one trick used by the film-makers: the frequency with which the male characters masturbate in the shower. This is the "McGuffin," as Alfred Hitchcock called it, the plot device that moves the story along and furthers the action. It is what provokes the encounter of Marc and Didier, as well as the final plot developments: the discovery of Mathieu as Béatrice's lover, the settling of accounts between Béatrice and Marc, and so forth. And it is here that *Crustacés et coquillages* joins up with *Wild Side*, no matter how different the two films are: autosexuality is the only sexuality that really exists, even when one is playing with another. It is the only definition of sexuality, the only one that is outside the collective, in this version of film in which gay men have become so visible. It is also at this juncture that these two films meet the contemporary novel, for this new avatar of gay cinema refuses categories in favor of the singularity of each individual. In that, these films actually go further than the novel: in their own way, these films are a *camera lucida* for the post-queer, for the self-deconstruction of stabilities and identities, in order to rediscover, at the end of the road, desire to be fulfilled by jouissance.

Both these popular novels and these mainstream (popular) films take received notions of gay male identity and push them in new directions. While the novels are concerned with the deconstruction of identity through the double mechanism of virology and pornography, they manage to destabilize the positions of identitarian politics, even as they adhere to communitarian standards, through an undoing of the self. The gay mainstream films we have considered are themselves not revolutionary, nor would any viewer expect them to be. But, considering the whole gamut of films here – and one could easily add work by other directors, including André Techiné –we recognize that, even without graphic sex or many references to HIV infection, the camera itself, in turning on the protagonist and his ambivalence and ambiguity, also remodels the episteme and moves it away from sexualities as abstract categories and toward lived experience – that of an integrated individual who comes to terms with his own self outside the institutions of homonormativity.

CHAPTER FOUR

Perversions of the Real

I. Nabe and the Rhetoric of Sodomy

Comment ai-je réussi à assassiner tous les êtres humains de notre ignoble planète? Rien de plus simple: en passant de la haine à l'extase [...] [How have I succeeded in assassinating all the human beings on this ignoble planet? Nothing easier: by passing from hatred to ecstasy.] (*V* 35)

At the beginning of his somewhat biographical, somewhat autobiographical, and somewhat jazzy essay on the singer Billie Holiday, the author, Marc-Édouard Nabe, offers a rhetorical conceit that places him, though as yet unborn, as a sentient being at a performance by the singer. Though he is "moins 3 mois [minus three months old]" (*BH* 11), he reacts to the concert viscerally, as he drinks in the sound of the blues singer at her famous New York concert at Carnegie Hall. This conceit points to Nabe's self-assessment that he is one of the true jazz *mavens*, one of the few people able of great discernment, so talented that he is able to appreciate excellent jazz even *in utero*. But the initial conceit goes beyond that. Here and elsewhere in his writing, he points to his unique position, as an only child, as a solitary being, as a singular man; in this case, he is underscoring that jazz – and the author's father, Marcel Zanini, is a pop and jazz musician – is a native language for him.[1] He is solipsistic, egotistical, and self-aggrandizing to the point that he can retro-project his talents to a point before he was born, while still in the womb.

This is, or would be, all well and good, were this conceit not

---

[1] Marcel Zanini is best known for his hit "Tu veux ou tu veux pas," which was based on a Brazilian original, "Nem vem que não tem." The song was also recorded by Brigitte Bardot.

itself moderated by a second one that is so aberrant that it throws the project immediately into question. For the Billie Holiday concert in question took place on November 10 1956. And Marc-Édouard Nabe, who, by his own accounts, was conceived in New York, was born in Marseille on December 27 1958. Wherever he was conceived, it was in late March 1958, at least one and one half years after the concert. I am less concerned as to the whereabouts of his parents in November 1956 or in March 1958, for that matter, than I am about this odd juxtaposition of conception, gestation, and impossibility. Nabe places his embryonic self at an impossible moment at which he can neither see nor hear, for he does not exist. He is not. And while a position of impossible narration is entirely plausible for a work of fiction, the technique is less believable and far more problematic in a non-fiction text. How, one wonders, does Nabe believe he can justify this impossible position of narration? But as we shall see, this impossibility is translated into other forms in later work as he projects an impossible universe in order to justify his reading of contemporary society and to posit his own masculinity. So why not write before one is conceived?

Let us pursue, albeit briefly, the literary model. This impossible position of narration is arguably a valid literary technique for works of imaginative fiction in which the narrative position can be an impossible one, be it that of the omniscient third-person narrator that was the backbone of realism, the first-person narrator who says "I am born," or even a dead narrator who pens his posthumous memories, as is the case in Machado de Assis's novel *Memórias Póstumas de Brás Cubas* [Epitaph for a Small Winner], among many others. Fictional narrators need not be consistent or coherent; think of Benjy in Faulkner's *The Sound and the Fury* or of Joyce's *Finnegans Wake*, not to mention Robbe-Grillet's *Les Gommes* [Erasers] or *La Jalousie* [Jealousy]. In Proust's work, the omniscient, Balzacian third-person narrator of "Un Amour de Swann" is ostensibly and impossibly the same figure as the limited, first-person narrator of "Combray" and of the rest of the *Recherche* to follow as well. And if there subjectivity and intermittence are associated with autobiographies and even autofictions, there is still an autobiographical pact, as Philippe Lejeune put it, an agreement with the reader to tell the truth insofar as it is possible. But a biographer, even an adulatory hagiographer, which is not exactly the case here, has an obligation to be writing from a believable position. And this is the case even when the biography is written in the first person. On such occasions, it is more likely than not that the author is writing a combination of biography and autobiography, that he or she knew the principal subject. Yet here, Nabe immediately breaks ranks with the reader by casting himself in an impossible and unbelievable narrative position. He does not serve the reader by doing this, but the reader recognizes the obvious: that even in this early work, appearing a year after the extremely polemical *Au régal des vermines* [At the Feast of Vermin], which, along with *Une Lueur d'espoir* [A Glimmer of Hope], will form the basis of this part of the chapter, this is all about Nabe. Billie Holiday is merely an excuse for Nabe to construct himself as a writer. On the rare occasions that Nabe chooses a subject other than himself, such as in the novel *Printemps de feu* [Spring Fire], set in Iraq with a Nabe-like figure as narrator, the work is wildly uneven and often without much interest.

Nabe constructs himself as the product of a second virgin birth, a presence of self before fertilization, coitus, or penetration. I list those in reverse order because this is a palinodic position, one that seems to say that Nabe conceives (of) himself textually as a kind of antichrist, a figure of the apocalypse, not as the redeemer of civilization but as its destroyer. From the early work of *Au régal des vermines*, a long diatribe that is arguably a fiction but that in retrospect, given his production to date, seems to have been written with a voice that is little different from his authentic voice, through the shorter, though no less vehement, polemic of *Une Lueur d'espoir*, written and published in the weeks after the events of September 11 2001, Nabe's writing is endlessly about himself, interminably political and polemical, and decidedly politically incorrect. It is about the construction of an impossible self in place of the one determined by the cards one is dealt at birth: the one determined by a real conception in a given time and place, the one determined by a real lineage, by a real society, and most importantly, by a changing society in which the assigned roles of nineteenth-century bourgeois propriety, place, class, and gender apply less and less.

From Nabe's very earliest writings, among which we can classify *Au régal des vermines*, we see a will to inflame any right-thinking non-extremist readership. It is perhaps a Céline-inspired polemic against all that is bourgeois, all the features of modern society that seems to have forgotten good behavior and aristocratic upbringing, what in French has been known as "la politesse des rois [the politeness of kings]" or "noblesse oblige." This nostalgia for the past, seen in writers such as Nabe and Renaud Camus, as well as in Dantec, already discussed, seems by and large to be nostalgia for a retrospective fiction, a past that never was: a past that was pure, and one that was never corrupted by middle-class morality, modernity, and contemporary mores. In *Au régal des vermines*, then, as well as in all of his subsequent work, Nabe seems to be constructing a work in which he – or his narrator (and I shall discuss this shortly) – can rail against a society of information and spectacle-peddlers and argue for a return to order, one in which biology, nature, essence, and propriety all have their synergistic roles to play.

In *Au régal des vermines* Nabe offers his readers – a group that does not collectively yet exist – a set of opinions on everything from A to Z. Much of his subsequent writing is like this early work: arguments loosely strung together that form a compendium or a primer of his wide-ranging, but seldom changing, opinions. *Morceaux choisis*, published in 2006, is precisely an A to Z: twenty-six topics, from "A comme Actualités [N is for News]" (*MC* 21) through "Z comme Zannini [Z like Zannini]" (*MC* 479).[2] In the case of *Au régal des vermines*, the reader is at first tempted to see the work as an elaborate fictional autofiction, i.e., as the creation of an imaginary character who writes these polemics and diatribes. But even a cursory reading of the twenty years' work that follow leads the reader to understanding that while this may not be absolutely "Nabe," and while the author has the right to create a fictional character different from himself, the differences are so minimal as to be imperceptible. And while, for the sake of literary criticism, one refers to the narrator as such and not as Nabe himself, I do not in fact see any differences, except some changes over time.

In this early work, Nabe's narrator, who is ostensibly telling the story of his life or his own *raison d'être*, shows the same concerns that the author, speaking in his own voice, will eventually show in his later work, focusing on the structuring of masculinity, the role of writing in general and literature in particular, and the interrelations of masculinity and literature. Clearly, the literary world, with its enthroned icons, has it wrong. Speaking of crowned canonical writers, Nabe's narrator states: "Rien n'est plus gueulable

---

[2] Nabe's real name is Zannini; his father's stage name, however, is spelled "Zanini."

que ces vieilles tantouzes viriles [Nothing is more screamable than those virile old queens]" (*V* 16). Separating sex and gender, Nabe's narrator seems also to be separating, at least here and now, the act of same-sex copulation from the affects or the perceived affects of homosexuality. One of these authors, whoever they may be, may be heterosexual in his sexual activity, but is nothing more than a butch homosexual in his affects in life and his effects on the world. And yet the categories are vague, because, in speaking of Barbey d'Aurevilly, whose work he admires, Nabe calls him a "tantouze hétérosexuelle [heterosexual queen]" (*V* 146). Seemingly ambiguous, Nabe's characterizations of others float in and out of abusive language, in and out of sodomy, and in and out of diatribes about sexualized activity.

But before turning to an analysis of the important features of this polemical rant, I should like to pause to consider its literary genre. It certainly reads like an autobiography, though it is short on facts. While no attempt is made to distinguish the narrator's voice from the author's own, it is not clear that it is intended to be understood as the voice of Nabe; one might consider it a rhetorical figure of the author, but one cannot state with assurance that the narrator as protagonist and the narrator's mother and father are in fact Nabe and his parents. At the same time, the positions taken by the narrator of this work are totally consonant with those taken by Nabe in his subsequent works. The polemical positions taken by this voice – for to say "narrator" implies that he actually tells a story – are those that the reader will find in subsequent fictions and nonfictions. The work reads like a compendium, or alphabet book, of things to come, and while there will be some evolution in thought as Nabe's work becomes increasingly apocalyptic, this starting point basically contains the germ of everything he will eventually write. It is perhaps *Une Lueur d'espoir*, while continuing so many of the patterns inscribed in Nabe's work, that will at times sound the most different, simply because the writing is itself precipitated by the events of September 11 2001.

The object of study in *Au régal des vermines* is double, but it can be summed up in the phrase "how I came to be an author." Embedded within that phrase are a whole host of psychological, biological, and intellectual factors that, as I have just implied, work in consonance for Nabe to make him the unique being he is. From the fantasized gestation period in the work on Billie Holiday through notions of literature and masculinity, Nabe or his narrator, here and elsewhere, constantly strives to show the interrelationship of these parts of him that synergistically combine to make a whole. In particular, Nabe is concerned with intertwined notions of masculinity and of the literary. As much as they might initially seem to be two somewhat separable notions of identity and performance, in Nabe's work one cannot be taken without the other. Arguably, at times he will substitute one for the other, and again, in later work, such as *Une Lueur d'espoir*, the political will replace the literary to a great extent.

Let us return to a previous citation, noted only in passing. Early in the volume, while speaking of crowned canonical writers, Nabe's narrator, vague about whom he is incriminating, says what has already been quoted: "Rien n'est plus gueulable que ces vieilles tantouzes viriles [Nothing is more screamable than those virile old queens]" (*V* 16). In one fell swoop, Nabe begins to dissect homosexual and heterosexual behavior and existence. No argument is made that such and such an author is gay (or straight). Rather, the oxymoronic category of "tantouzes viriles," implying virility and effeminacy at once, marks the objects of his scorn as "pédés [fags]" whether they are gay or not. Giving in to the exigencies of the modern, and in particular, its metonymic, symptomatic, and affective incarnation as literature, or what passes for literature, marks the author as coding as a "pédé." In fact, at least since the dawn of the modern, literature and its practitioners have had it wrong: they chose Rimbaud over Lautréamont, for example. That Rimbaud was gay and Lautréamont straight only adds heat to the argument. Nabe's article on Lautréamont is a straightforward rereading of Lautréamont's pure poetry: "Sa littérature est celle qui parle pour ne rien dire, et c'est ce rien à dire qui dit ce qu'elle veut dire, c'est-à-dire rien d'autre que ce qu'elle veut dire, c'est-à-dire rien. Et ce n'est pas rien [His literature is the kind that speaks to say nothing and it is that nothing to say that says what it means, that is to say nothing other than what it means, that is to say, nothing]" (83). That is pure writing and, as Paul Verlaine notes, "tout le reste est littérature [all the rest is literature]."

Significantly then, from the very beginning of *Au régal des vermines*, the narrator seems to be operating a separation of the homosexual affect or component from any practice of homosexual sex; straight men can be as gay as gay men, and some gay men can be as straight as upstanding heterosexuals. There are important writers and artists who were homosexual, and the honesty of their art is what lifts them up, for Nabe, above homosexuality, as if it were a state to be transcended; but it is also a state into which the gays of today have permanently exiled themselves by their behavior:

> Pas un des pédés étalés sur les quais de la Seine quand il fait soleil n'est capable de goûter l'ouverture de *Sodome et Gomorrhe*, la rhétorique suave d'hérissons broyés de Jean Genet, les saillies d'Oscar Wilde ou les gros plans de Pasolini sur la ronde-bosse des braguettes. (*Chacun* 10).

> [Not one of those fags spread out on the banks of the Seine when it is sunny is capable of understanding the opening of *Sodom and Gomorrah*, the smooth rhetoric of crushed hedgehogs of Jean Genet, the wit of Oscar Wilde, or Pasolini's close-ups of bulges in crotches.]

One might in fact go no further than to take issue with the choices here by saying that the beginning pages of *Sodome et Gomorrhe* could be read as homophobic or at least essentialist, and certainly the work of the other three could be read as essentialist, not queer at all, and that this, in and of itself, provides solace to Nabe – for it is definitely Nabe in this case – who wants to be comfortable in his hatred of homosexuals; a homosexuality that is as diverse as he would have heterosexuality be is a threat to his own essentialist order.

Nabe's narrator seems to have somatized his difference, from the very beginning, as the figure does not seem to have the stereotypical proportions of a he-man. And this difference is marked, somatized anew in his mind and on his body. The discourse of difference is doubly directed: against himself in a kind of self-loathing and as a lashing out about others. While the former position seems to dominate in the early part of this work, it will fundamentally be the second part that fills the pages and that marks the narrator's view of the world. Significantly, Nabe's narrator packs a number of things into each of these references, with layer upon layer of complex refigurings of the body: "Mais après tout, je ressemble surtout à un pédé préhistorique. Je suis comme une femmelette de Neandertal! [But after all, I really look like a prehistoric fag. I'm like a girly Neanderthal!]" (*V* 22). So, in one sentence, he manages to erect, suitably at an absent node that is easily understood as that of the *nom/non du père*, the image of a strapping individual, against whom are set a weak, primitive homosexual or little woman, and a somewhat apelike Neanderthal. Nabe's narrator distances himself from the ideal position, a distance that will continue to increase until he is confirmed in his abjection of self. Once that happens, he will build a chain of words back to that imagined position to construct a verbal object in the locus of the phallus.

If the narrator has it in his mind to reconstruct that path to masculinity through language, he is not yet in the totally abject position requisite for building that linguistic phallus, the Nabean tower of Babel. And I am not using the term "phallus" loosely, for, as will become clear in the rest of this chapter, the construction through language does not become the pure, authoritarian *nom du père* that the narrator has already sought nostalgically; it is a construction of our modernity and post-modernity that Nabe sees all around him. Like Dantec, he was probably not surprised by the events of September 11 2001. Here, however, we are over a decade and a half earlier than those events, and Nabe – or his narrator – is constructing his position of abjection. The first part of that construction is the opposite of the will to the phallus. In its stead is a frankly stated will to be a woman, to be marked as a woman: "Manquer de vagin me tape sur le système. Ça me gêne. C'est comme une épine: j'ai en permanence un clitoris planté dans la littérature [lacking a vagina gets at me. It bothers me. It's like a thorn. I always have a clitoris implanted in literature]" (*V* 31–32). With this statement, Nabe brings into question the very construction of the position of the subject. Wanting to have a vagina, it seems to me, at least from this vantage point, is a desire to have the possibility of playing the traditional role performed by a woman in an act of heterosexual, non-anal intercourse. But it is also the possibility of being fecund, of giving birth, of being both the genetrix and the genitor. For, if that bother is a thorn in his side, we can also scan it as "une (é)pine": the absence of a vagina is, at this level of the imaginary, also a penis, "pine" being a slang word for penis, albeit one that is not the size of the imagined phallus, but one that, like this non-existent clitoris, can penetrate. Literature itself becomes the woman he wants himself to be and with his linguistic version of the phallus, a modest tool at best, he will start to penetrate. Yet, since he cannot have the phallus or be the phallus, since his act of penetration cannot ever be as masculine as the one he imagines, he has to settle for a production of monstrosity: Nabe's narrator is in the position of having, blindly, to create the world that he so loathes. Or rather, he is condemned with his prose to repeat that world. The Nabean narrator is both sterile and impotent, incapable of creating anything new for himself, unable to create difference, and condemned to repeat the path to Armageddon he sees as being ubiquitous.

It should come as no surprise to any reader that the act and the language on which Nabe focuses here and elsewhere are those relating to homosexual anal intercourse, although he will vary the discourse in certain moments to include heterosexual anal intercourse. I begin with the clinical term, even though Nabe's language, which gravitates toward variants of "enculer" [to buttfuck or bugger], is anything but neutral and clinical. Nabe's language would be considered, in most contexts, vulgar and offensive, even if in certain situations it could be used in a tacitly or explicitly agreed way that would not be considered offensive by the speaker or the listener/reader. But in general, to call someone an "enculé" is to insult him with a vulgar term that is also a statement that challenges his virility or his masculinity. The language moves quickly between the denotative and the connotative, and, as Roland Barthes showed long ago, these two categories cannot always be separated. In this realm, I would argue, they can never be separated.

The long history of considering anal intercourse as a prohibited act goes at least as far back as Leviticus (18:22), with its injunction against lying with another man as with a woman, traditionally interpreted as the prohibition in question. Yet this prohibition is one of many – sources list 613 binding ones within the Jewish faith – and it is undoubtedly less important within Judaism than it is as a political tool for some contemporary evangelical homophobic groups in the United States. Still, the discourse takes on body and form in the Pauline interdictions found in Romans (1:26–27). Leviticus merely states a prohibition, albeit one whose transgression was punishable by death; the act is forbidden because it cannot lead to procreation. Paul, however, introduces the aporia of a sin "against nature [contra naturam]," which will continue to operate in the almost two thousand years that follow of the sodomitic tradition through recent times.

I say aporia, because the breach introduced – sodomy, being in this universe, comes from divine creation, yet it is against nature – allows for a rhetorical position, a language, figural in nature, that will accompany the sodomitic act, will describe it, will distance it from that which is apt, normal, natural. This breach is figured in language and on the body of the sodomite. It is this rhetorical version of sodomy that is figured in the late Middle Ages, in the work of Alain de Lille, the anonymous *Roman de Silence*, or even *Le Roman de la Rose*.[3] Dante will take the scholiasm and rhetoric associated with the sodomitic body and mind and use it in his discussion of Bruno Latini. And if, to go very quickly, the Renaissance uses the term "sodomy" for a myriad of situations (Goldberg), one perpetuated as late as the twenty-first century in the United States, until the US Supreme Court struck down all remaining anti-sodomy laws, it is Sade himself who seizes on the term, the action, and the consequences thereof, to turn the tables on nature. In his own way, Sade stands as the figure who turns the rhetoric of "anti-nature" on its head, preferring to see the natural as unnatural and pushing for the "anti-natural" as the *sine qua non* of modern existence. Procreation is futile; living fully for today in the fulfillment of the *carpe diem* means, among other things, not thinking about consequence or tomorrow. Thus, in the Sadean universe, anal intercourse, both heterosexual and homosexual, is, or should be, far more important and far more central to the construction of his modernity than the act of heterosexual intercourse that might lead to procreation. Sade is reversing a two-thousand-year-old argument in favor of procreation, in favor of the continuation of the species, in favor of the future.

When Nabe's narrator says "Sade encule Freud [Sade buttfucks Freud]" (*V* 42), he is turning civilization over or saying that civilization has always already been turned over in a position of submission, with forced entry or not. Today's will to power is the superior force that dominates through an act of humiliation the attempts at adequation, at being together, at overcoming the neuroses and discontents in civilization. From the beginning to the end of the Freudian process, including especially *Civilization and Its Discontents*, originally published in 1930 as *Das Unbehagen in der Kultur*, thus literally, "Uneasiness in Culture," among the later works, there is a sense that Freud recognizes that the perfection, the return into grace from the Fall, is certainly not possible and that any movement in that direction is benighted at best. At the same time there is, in Freud, a *Mitsein*, a living with oneself and with others, that is a compromise that works. This *Mitsein*, which was, of course, named by Heidegger a few years before in *Sein und Zeit* [Being and Time] (1927), and which is the

---

[3] Michael A. Johnson has eloquently demonstrated this in his study of *Le Roman de la Rose*.

foundational ethical position (Olafson), is obviously contrary to the anti-anti-nature group that can be traced back to Sade.

In having Sade bugger Freud, then, Nabe's narrator essentially buys into the position already hinted at in the title of his book, which is simply that since we cannot ever aspire to being the humans that we want to be, we are no better than beasts, and vermin in particular, and given that, we had might as well have fun, for all attempts at being human are nothing more than a sham or hypocrisy. Late in the book he will summarize his sense of *Mitsein* with the following: "J'ai horreur des amis [I am horrified by friends]" (*V* 225); in so saying, he is joining with writers such as Renaud Camus and Fabrice Neaud, already discussed. Nothing summarizes better the anti-humanism and the radical misanthropy that mark the polemic, a combination that Nabe sums up in his figure of buggery. This position, he hastens to add, is not a political one in the current sense of the term, but rather a philosophical one, in the eighteenth-century sense of the expression; it is a way of life, a way of being in the world, a difference from the *Mitsein* of the bourgeoisie – Renaud Camus would say the *petite bourgeoisie* – that is all-controlling. So when Nabe's narrator here says that he is not political in the standard sense – though he clearly has and will have political positions – we can believe him and his article of faith, "Je suis d'extrême Sade [I'm Sade in the extreme]" (*V* 139–40). This is the staking out of a philosophical position that goes beyond the accidents of daily life.

Sade then acts as the prototypical figure of the "enculeur," and this despite the fact that the historical figure of the Marquis de Sade was probably more polyvalent than Nabe would make him out to be. But that is also part of the deal and Nabe does not see the possibility of polyvalency or versatility. The only acceptable position is that of the person who buggers other people, for to be buggered is despicable and irreversible. It makes men and women into "women," versions of the "pédé" or the "femmelette" already described. But whereas Sade's anti-humanist vision implied an opposition to reproduction, Nabe's does not. Aside from any symbolic value of acting in a willful effort to be *contra naturam* and to reduce the two sexes to one symbolically, as everyone can be buggered, Sade proposes an act that cannot lead to pregnancy, gestation, and birth. Opposed to that, while clearly understanding the physiology of reproduction and while following Sade to some extent in the unisexuality, Nabe reforms the paradigm.

There is no contradiction between buggery and reproduction. In fact, one suspects the contrary and that for Nabe, those who are the "enculé(e)s" of the world are precisely the same people who have the bad taste to reproduce. This is not, I hasten to add, some fantasmatic biology, but rather a recategorization of being according neither to sex nor to gender, but rather according to whether Nabe's narrator believes someone to be an "enculeur" or an "enculé." That he aligns the first with traditional masculinities is clear, and the second, his reproach to the world, is aligned with everything that is not masculine, i.e., the feminine and the effeminate rolled into one. But, at the same time, this does not interfere with reproduction and could be considered the very cause of it. So, for example, both the mother and the father are in the same category. The description of the mother is a telling conflation of all that the narrator despises: "A force de traiter *pour rire*, devant tout le monde, mon père d'Arabe ignoble ou de Vieux débile et ma mère de Conasse Enculée [Having treated, for the sake of fun, my father as an ignoble Arab or a mindless Old Man and my mother as a Buttfucked Bitch]" (*V* 42). Aside from the racialization or blatant racism in the description of the father (to whom we shall shortly return), the blatant misogyny and homophobia in the description of the mother lead the reader to think that, for the narrator, there is not only conflation of the two sexes and of genders in general, but of all possibilities of penetration, or more likely, of being penetrated, in particular.[4]

This conflation is not the invagination of which Derrida writes in "La double séance," nor is it the fact of being penetrated, but rather, the position of "having been penetrated," of always already having been penetrated. The word "enculé," as adjective and noun, is a past participle for Nabe's narrator and it is this characteristic that is the functional one for Nabe. The buggered of the world are those who have already been penetrated and this will always have been the case. Consider then the description of the father:

> Mon père s'est toujours fait baiser. Mon père est un enculé. L'Anus en Chou-fleur, le type qui, lorsqu'il reçoit un coup de pied au cul, se retourne pour en recevoir un dans les couilles. (*V* 180)

---

[4] It should be noted, for purposes of accuracy, that Nabe's real father, Marcel Zanini, was born in Turkey, seemingly of mixed Greek, Italian, and Turkish ancestry.

[My father always got screwed. My father is an asshole. His anus spread wide, the kind of guy who, having gotten a kick in the ass, turns around to get another one in his balls.]

The violence and anality shift between the figurative and the literal, encompassing both, returning the literality of the expression to something that had essentially become a catachresis. Nabe's narrator makes no distinction here between the two positions and ironically tropes the catachresis into a return to the literal, thereby buggering language itself.

Even if the position he espouses is more philosophical than political, as I have indicated, this does not prevent Nabe's narrator from having teleological positions that have at least political ends in mind. His hatred of contemporary Western culture knows no limits and, as often as not, he uses the same figure to describe his vision of an apocalypse that should come sooner rather than later, if he is to have his way. But in a reversal of Dante's vision in the seventh circle (Canto 15) of the Inferno, where some sodomites are condemned to eternal hell-fires and the flames enter their open wounds, the people of this world are condemned to death by buggery: "Je suis très raciste. J'espère que les Noirs vont finir par enculer tous les blancs et les assombrir pour toujours [I am extremely racist. I hope that the Blacks will wind up buttfucking all the whites and spoil them forever]" (*V* 83).[5] Here, then, Nabe is adding to the simple act of anal penetration a racist dimension that we might already have expected from the earlier pejorative remark about the narrator's father. And while his relation to questions of race, religion, and ethnicity is a matter best dealt with when he firmly engages the political, it is important to note that the use of the word "assombrir" parallels his use of words relating to "enculer," for it too blurs the line between the literal and the figurative: it literally means to darken, but figuratively means to create a darker emotional position or to spoil.

Thus the narrator's concepts of race and sodomy parallel one another. At one level, one might think that, for the author, this is a way of letting the subaltern speak, that those disenfranchised by heteronormativity, by sexism, by racism, and by the metaphysics of

---

[5] The allusion to Dante is important. It is not by accident that Nabe entitles a chapter of this work "Béatrice enculée [Buttfucked Beatrice]" (223). Not even the metonymy of paradise is exempt from buggery; not even her presence in paradise can save him or anyone else.

the West in general, are able to acquire their own voice through this symbolic action. But, at a deeper level, that is not at all the case. The act of anal penetration, paralleled by an act of miscegenation, is seen as the destruction of white bourgeois culture, to be sure, but not to the benefit of any subaltern voice that might arise from a revolution in culture. The well-endowed blacks he imagines are an instrument for the destruction of society, but they are reduced to a primitive cannibalistic state in the process of serving the needs of the one person who may survive this apocalypse, the narrator himself, as he wishes for "trois ou quatre nègres bien membrés viennent nous bouffer [three or four well-hung Negroes to eat millions]" of Westerners (*V* 86–87). No redemption is in sight and no righting of the system will occur to rectify matters.

And if the blacks serve the needs of the narrator in his recounting of the end of the world, they do so in their roles of being less than human, for in his eyes, they are simian in nature. They are not Nietzschean supermen who will replace weak-minded Western humanity with something better; they are rather the figures of some *Untermenschen* who will be the tool of annihilation that, at least at this point, will be total and complete: "C'est en gardant leur simiesque génie cosmique que les nègres peuvent se défendre et nous ENCULER, car moi, je ne rêve qu'à ça: l'Enculage, l'Extermination totale des Blancs un jour ou l'autre! [It is in keeping their ape-like cosmic genius that Negroes can protect themselves and buttfuck us, as I dream only of that: Buttfucking, the total Extermination of Whites one day or another!]" (*V* 90). Interestingly enough, there is a rhetorical shift here, from calling everyone else a buggered individual to including himself in the collective "us." This deepening of tone, what he has just called darkening, no longer exempts the narrator from the invective and rant he has been performing but subjects him to the same law. And if in individual cases, such as those of his father or mother, the association was between buggery, bourgeois values, and reproduction, here the tables are turned. The act of buggery is an execution. Simultaneously the author seems to be suggesting that this transcendental buggery, associated with blacks, a racist position to be sure, is the sign of the complete death of humanity, a return to an ape-like existence that is pre-human and not post-human.

As we have already noticed, Nabe uses slippage between denotation and connotation to great effect in constructing the rhetoric of animosity and apocalypse around the word group of "enculé" and its kin. So too does he slip between a denotative definition of race, a concept that is certainly considered artificial as I write, but was not necessarily pervasively considered so when Nabe was writing *Au régal des vermines*, and an insulting, connotative one at the heart of classical racist paradigms. This connotative one associates people of color with inferior human status and underlies notions of white superiority. Various anti-Semitic remarks made by Nabe in his diaries would be products of the same kind of monstrous rhetorical move: between a denotative, descriptive, rather objective, even positivist definition to a subjective, connotative, hate-filled position. The "other" man, i.e., whoever is not a white, heterosexual male – women are by and large objects for the pleasure of the white, heterosexual male – is considered to be an amalgamation of his positivistically defined category and stereotypes and slurs about his otherness.

Still, there are moments in which the narrator pours his invective out on the specifically defined categories, without letting it spill over into a generalization or into an amalgamation of the other with his stereotype. There is a virulence, as one might expect, that could be characterized, quite simply, as extreme homophobia, pointed toward gay men, simply for being who they are. So "Il y a un snobisme du pédé, un symbolique de la nouvelle tante [There is a snobbishness of fags, a symbolic order of the new queen]" (*V* 136). But these apparitions of anti-gay rhetoric never last very long. They pop up in the midst of a longer argument that seems to be about the interference with personal freedom to which each white, heterosexual male is entitled by birthright, a freedom that seems to have been taken away by others with no mess of pottage offered in exchange: "Les pédés, je les hais, mais ils ne sont qu'une minorité parmi d'autres. Toutes les minorités empêchent les individus de prendre le pouvoir [I hate fags, but they are only one minority among others. All minorities prevent individuals from seizing power]" (*V* 137). Clearly when he writes "individuals," Nabe's narrator is referring to people like himself, the inheritors of Sade's vision and philosophy, those who believe that as white, heterosexual males they have absolute rights to everything, should have absolute power, and must be returned to that position if the world is to continue to exist, even though, as we have already seen, by becoming one of the "enculés," the narrator has essentially foreseen the impossibility of reversion.

What Nabe's narrator opposes here is similar to what Dantec assaults in his tirades against Fordism and Taylorism: the substitution of the inauthentic for what each believes to be the authentic. The difference between Nabe and Dantec is that the latter buys into an information network, a Deleuzean rhizomatics constructed of neuronal and informational matrices. And Nabe, in true Luddite fashion, does not. One might speculate that at some level, this is one of the things that bothers him about the gay male collective: that its pattern can be perceived as being more a rhizomatics than an arborescent, phallic tower of power. In any case, Nabe's narrator feels that this degenerate model has become ubiquitous in society and that, if the "enculés" are the most visible (for him) sign of this degeneration, they are not the only figures of it. For he likens people in advertising to "enculeurs de pimprenelles [buttfuckers of pimpernels]" (*V* 129). On the one hand, this is a way to approach an expression, "enculeur de mouches [buttfucker of flies]," without actually using the cliché. On the other hand, it is a way to distance himself from the details of that expression. An "enculeur de mouches" is a person who pays excessive attention to details and minutiae instead of seeing the bigger picture. Nabe could have chosen other expressions for a detail-oriented person or a hair-splitter, including "un pinailleur," someone "qui coupe les cheveux en quatre," someone "qui chipote," someone "qui cherche la petite bête," and so forth, but he chooses the most vulgar, and the anal one to boot. The problem here, for Nabe's narrator, is that the details to which attention is paid in this information-driven world are inauthentic and inconsequential; an "enculeur de mouches" pays attention to real details. So the pimpernel, an insignificant plant nowadays, though formerly used in cooking, becomes the sign of the inauthentic detail, the mass-market, information-driven, trend-setting moment that is meant only to increase profits.[6] Nabe's "enculeur de pimprenelles" thus becomes the symbolic messenger of the world of the buggered, the vehicle for transporting the (in)consequences fostered by a civilization of "enculés."

The narrator of *Au régal des vermines* (128–29), in a Célinian rant against all the information workers, as Alan Liu calls them, and others, the figures of modern life, suggests that they all be sent to the "Vél d'hiv." This is an unsubtle and outrageously obscene invocation

---

[6] According to *Le Trésor de la Langue Française*, "pimprenelle" (pimpernel) has often been confused with "pimpenelle"/"pimpenella" (saxifrage), which was thought in the Middle Ages to produce madness. I cannot be sure whether Nabe knows this or not.

of the events of July 16–17 1942, during which French authorities rounded up over eight thousand French Jews and sent them to the Vélodrome d'Hiver (an event referred to as "la rafle du vél d'hiv"). While a few escaped, most ended up in the death camp at Auschwitz and were murdered in the implementation of the Final Solution. So once again, Nabe's narrator makes equivalences among information workers, deported Jews, and "enculés." The world composed of his abjected people is one in which, ironically, the changing possibilities of categorization create a maelstrom to feed his hatred and to mark his lack of power. If only, he seems to be saying, we could set the world aright: "D'abord, l'homme ne sait plus où donner de la tête à l'envers. C'est le roi diabolique Dagobert: il a mis son cul-faust à l'envers. Où s'enverser? [First of all, (the) man doesn't know where to invert his head. It's good old, diabolical, king Dagobert: He put on his under-faust backwards. Where should I invert?]" (*V* 121).[7] This is a complicated substitution. One could separate "culotte" into "cul" and "lotte" and the latter would be the figure of Charlotte in Goethe's *The Sorrows of Young Werther*, the archetypical literary work of Romantic longing. Nabe then substitutes another figure in Goethe's writing, Faust, who makes, as all readers know, a pact with the devil. A pact with the devil is irreversible, and thus, setting the world aright no longer seems possible. Not even Léon Bloy, the fervently Catholic nineteenth-century writer, whom the narrator admires enormously, could do it, for he ends up performing a "frankensteinisation" (*V* 113) of the world through exegesis. No transformation is possible that does not lead to monstrosity or total perdition.

But perhaps there is one glimmer of hope, to employ the phrase that Nabe will use as a title for his essay on the events of September 11 2001: a return to the beginning, to the heterosexual couple that is there to define the man's pleasure and the use of the woman as an object for giving the man pleasure. No consideration need be given her here, for her redemptive quality is that she can give him pleasure where the others – the "enculés" of the world – could not. Perhaps, then, that fulfillment of heterosexual desire that is ultimately the autosexual, as I have called it in reference to *Crustacés et coquillages*, will be the solution for him. At least that is what he seems to believe:

---

[7]   As the song goes, "Le bon roi Dagobert / A mis sa culotte à l'envers [Good King Dagobert put his underwear on backwards]." St. Eligius straightens him out.

Je suis tellement fasciné par les femmes, si soumis à elles, béat de leur
béance, amoureux, inconditionnel d'avance que les glands me voient
d'un très mauvais méat! Ils me trouvent suspect: féminin que je suis,
je devrais être pédé, et c'est moi qui suis le plus obsédé, le plus atteint.
(*V* 231).

[I am so fascinated by women, so "sub" for them, so blissful faced
with their gap, loving, unconditional beforehand that other cockheads
see me with rather a bad meatus. They see me as suspicious: since I
am feminine, I must be a fag, and it is I who is the most obsessed, the
most afflicted.]

But even that fascination and gaping when faced with their gape
or gap, their invagination, is too much for him. He cannot stop his
obsession; cannot move away from his fascination with pederasty/
buggery/homosexuality/queerness, can never stop straying toward
that position that he claims is not his but that marks every page of
this work.

So the purported or would-be possessor of the phallus is subjected
to the feminine. There is no battle that he does not fail to lose,
no position that he is not himself ousted from created by himself
through his rhetoric of displacement. The masculine will not have
been possessed, will not have been possible, for it is always already
subjected to the power of the feminine as he finds himself irresistibly
drawn into that bewitching power. The lack that is the woman for
him is a lack that has power over him, over his thoughts, his body,
and his being: "Vous croyez peut-être que ça m'amuse d'être un
homme féminin totalement asservi à l'existence des femmes? [You
might believe that it's fun for me to be a feminine man completely
subjected to the existence of women?]" (*V* 232). So even this too will
be reversed and the reversal takes place exactly where one might
have predicted it: into "enculage," but this time it is heterosexual
buggery, so that, it would appear, does not count.

In a brio-filled passage marked by exclamation points and yet
another anti-gay jibe, Nabe's narrator confesses that he is the king
of heterosexual anal intercourse:

Et par-dessus tout, l'anus! L'olive! L'oignon mauve! Le Sot-l'y laisse!
Je ne comprendrai jamais les pédés. Ils n'amortissent pas l'extase.
C'est des candides. S'il s'agit d'exacerber un trou de balle, la femme
aussi a ce tour dans son sac. Les anus des femmes sont plus beaux.
Leurs nouilles sont splendides. (*V* 233)

[And above all, the anus! The asshole! The lavender onion! The nugget! I'll never understand fags. They never pay off their lust. They are ingenuous. If it is a question of exacerbating a hole, women have it as well. Women's holes are more beautiful. Their fissures are splendid.]

Nabe sets up a chain of signifiers that relate to food. Two do relate to the anus: "oignon," as has already been mentioned in chapter 3, is a slang word for the anus, and "nouilles," which here means the fissures of the anus or perhaps external hemorrhoids visible after a particularly violent act of intercourse, and meaning the same thing as the already mentioned "chou-fleur," has a figural anal meaning as well, for it is found in the expression "avoir le trou de cul bordé de nouilles," which means to have good luck, to be sitting in clover. Thus can we assume that this ecstasy is seen by this "feminine" man (V 241) who considers himself the luckiest of men because he gets laid the way he likes. And yet his metaphors are mixed, for "olive" has no anal references whatsoever, but is rather, when used in the plural, a slang word for testicles. Even more curious is the use of the expression "le sot l'y laisse," which literally means "the fool leaves it," but is the popular culinary term for what is known as a "chicken oyster" in English, the olive-shaped, tender morsel of meat that is nestled in the hollow of the hipbone (*ilio-femoralis externus*) where the thigh is attached. So just as he develops an anal vocabulary in celebration of heterosexual anal intercourse, he fantasmatically reintroduces testicles in the form of olives and chicken oysters, and this famous refusal of the homosexual in favor of this most celebrated of masculinities is once again turned over: "Je suis le contraire même de la pédérastie. Je m'étonne même qu'un être aussi féminin que moi n'ait jamais éprouvé ne serait-ce qu'une seule fois un désir pédérastique [I am the complete opposite of pederasty. I am even astonished that someone as feminine as I am has never felt, even once, a pederastic desire]" (V 241). But even if he has never felt such a desire, he seems to have compared the anuses of men and women often enough to reach aesthetic conclusions about them.

From one end of the book to the other, Nabe's narrator cannot avoid the endless reversals of fortune. Like King Dagobert, he is the last of his line to wield any power, but unlike Dagobert, he has no Saint Éloi (St. Eligius) to tell him that he has put his underwear on backwards. And even in his Faustian pact with the devil, this Dagobert will remain badly dressed, the opening of his underwear ever behind, placed squarely over his anus, expecting and perhaps hoping, from one moment to the other, to become the once and future bottom for a supreme top. With this in mind, I turn to what is, to date, Nabe's most radically invective-filled rant, his "analysis," so to speak, of the events of September 11 2001, ironically entitled *Une Lueur d'espoir.*

Insofar as the events of September 11 2001 are concerned, many, including Jacques Derrida and Jürgen Habermas, quickly came to understand why we should not have been surprised by the events. According to Derrida (in Borradori), for example, the events were part of the auto-immune sickness in the West: we produced the conditions by which "terrorists" saw the possibility of the validity of the attacks, but we also enabled the situation, given the ways of a society that allows anyone to register to learn to be a pilot, even when he (or she) turns out not to be very interested in learning how to land an airplane. Most, including Derrida, of course, do not suggest a turn from democracy toward some sort of police state or totalitarian regime, nor do these thinkers condone acts of terrorism, but they caution that events such as those of September 11 2001 are not external to the ideology of liberal democracies, but rather, at least in part, a by-product of those ways of thinking. Terrorism is not, as George W. Bush would have it, some external menace, but rather something that is inherently tied to liberal Western thought as well as to a continued Occidentocentric post-colonial political agenda. At the same time, while reacting differently to the events of September 11 2001 than even staunch conservatives who still speak, however perversely, in the name of Western bourgeois democracy, apocalyptic writers on the right, such as Dantec (as we have seen) and Nabe, seem not to have been terribly astonished by the events, which would have happened sooner or later according to their fatalistic reading of the decline of the West – a fulfillment of Spengler's vision of Western bourgeois democracies as Faustian civilizations doomed, because of their pact with the devil, to decline (Vico; Huntington). For such writers, this event is nothing short of the foreshadowing of the eventual apocalypse, coming, for them, sooner rather than later, and never a moment too soon. If, for Dantec, the events are tied up with the dehumanization of the West that corresponds to the aftermath of the Industrial Revolution, for Nabe, as one might imagine, while the cause itself is an amalgamation of Western behavior and "malaise," the affect and performance of the events are necessarily related to his view of the sodomization of the West in particular and its inevitable decline in general: "Quel intérêt de vivoter dans une époque qui n'en finit pas de crever? [What interest is there in struggling through an era that never finishes collapsing?]" (*L* 12).

Quite coincidentally, September 11 is the birthday of Nabe's mother. As is his wont, he calls her on the afternoon of her birthday, which corresponds to morning in New York and Washington, and she immediately responds by telling him to turn on the television. He does so and sees the events with which anyone reading this volume is all too familiar. Coincidence or not, this confluence of events immediately makes the political into the personal and the personal is transformed immediately into a question of sexuality, not so much the maternal, but the specularity of the events: "un avion de ligne américain vient de foncer tête la première sur l'une des Twin Towers. Un autre surgit dans le ciel très bleu et s'encastre à son tour dans la deuxième [An American airplane has just hurtled head first into one of the Twin Towers. Another emerges in the very blue sky and plunges into the second]" (*L* 11). Now while a certain minority position relates the etymology of "encastrer" to "castrare," i.e., "châtrer," and while it is more likely to be related to "castrum," i.e., castle, it is nevertheless clear that Nabe is using words such as "foncer" and "encastrer" to insist on the act of penetration. The phallic twin towers, archetypes of the West's erection of monuments to itself and monuments to its own erections, are themselves sodomized by a greater force, one, as will soon be seen, tied up with a Faustian decline and a messianic mysticism. At the same time, while disagreeing on principle in terms of their cause, Nabe would not disagree with Derrida's notion of the events as the consequences of an auto-immune disorder. While the matter does not come up directly here, Nabe would certainly not disagree with the likening of these events to the other well-known auto-immune disorder, AIDS. And while it would perhaps, even for Nabe, be over the top to enunciate this analogy, he would not disagree with the notion espoused by some on the evangelical right after the events, which was that New York was hit because of its homosexualization. He certainly comes close to this: "Cette ville (Babylone, Rome, New York) est pour saint Jean la *mère des abominations de la terre* [This city (Babylon, Rome, New York) is for St. John the mother of abominations of the earth]" (*L* 15). For if, according to John, writing of the apocalypse (Revelation 17:5), Babylon is the "mother of harlots and the abominations of the earth," as the King James version puts it, can the ubiquitous sodomy and subsequent sodomization of New York be far behind?[8]

These spectacular opening images of New York being penetrated as a sign of its effeminacy, its status as the city of buggery and the buggered city, are emphasized by the signs of the mystical that Nabe uses to underline the inevitability of the events. Not only is the maternal the sign of fatality, the recurrence of a date being inscribed into the eternal, the numbers themselves conspire to mark the apocalypse: "Et le onze septembre, il restait cent onze jours avant la fin de l'année! 11: deux 1 érigés comme des tours jumelles! [And September the eleventh, there were still one hundred and eleven days until the end of the year. 11: two 1s erected like the twin towers!]" (L 13). It is not yet the 666 of the Apocalypse, but it is one sixth of the way there; in Nabe's world, we are *en route* to the Final Judgement. The numbers are fated and fateful, but they have immediately become his numbers: "J'en ai plein les mains, de mes chers chiffres sacrés [...] 11.09.2001 [My hands are full of my dear sacred numbers: 9/11/2001]" (L 12). Just as his mother's birthday is fated to happen, these events are fated to become Nabe's own, as if he were John writing the Book of Revelation or as if he were giving a playbook for the apocalypse. And these numbers are sacred, their inevitability being a sign from somewhere, the beyond in any case, coming out of the blue, as it were, to mark this conjunction of Nabe, New York, apocalypse, and sodomy.

Nabe's text is solidly focused on the act of penetration, and, specifically, on the homosexual act of penetration that for him is the attacks on New York – the Pentagon is pretty much sidelined here – in part for themselves and in part, eventually, for their political power. But what marks his work is the figuration of the images of the event as a strange homosexual penetration of the phallic towers by an even more potent, albeit primitive, phallus. Each tower morphs into an anus as the airplane penetrates it; each tower becomes a gape as the plane rapes it, makes it a rectum, and invaginates it through an act of aerial sodomy: "Quelle pénétration! Aucun des deux sexes foudroyants n'est ressorti de ces matrices phalliques. Prises ainsi

---

[8] Obviously the play on words between Sodom and Saddam, in French or in English, comes to mind here. Nabe eventually entitles a chapter of *Printemps* "Sodomie chez Saddam [Sodomy at Saddam's]" (235); the chapter culminates (247) with an act of (heterosexual) anal intercourse. The matter is never far from Nabe's mind.

presque à leurs sommets, les deux tours de quatre cents mètres de haut n'ont plus qu'à s'envoyer en l'air [What penetration! Neither explosive penis came out of these phallic matrices. Taken almost at the top, the two towers, each four hundred meters high, have only to get it on]" (*L* 16). For Nabe, then, the key difference some decade and a half after *Au régal des vermines* is the transformability of the phallus into the matrix or the womb: the phallic tower that was once immutable as the position of masculine power becomes, at a moment's notice, the matrix that is instantaneously destroyed by another phallus. So the matricial nature of the WTC, unlike Dantec's neuromatrices which have some permanence, is immediately turned into an unproductive site of copulation that is no different from a rectum. And the towers then become two legs raised in the air, the space between them a symbolic vagina, as each becomes a rectum. As Leo Bersani asked so powerfully in the first years of the AIDS epidemic, "Is the rectum a grave?" For Nabe, it is clear that the answer is affirmative, as he speeds up the act of penetration, infection, illness, collapse, and death, all of which happen, as the expression goes, "in a New York minute."

Nabe's fantasmagoric and conflated geography and anatomy are an alchemical blend that situates the author as co-pilot of the planes, penetrating the towers and thereby assuming his manhood as he, with his words, transforms the phallus of the other into the penetrated. And it little matters at this point of the book whether this is an act of heterosexual or homosexual anal intercourse. For now, at least, Nabe has moved away from that opposition into a generalized act of sodomy that puts the act before the sexuality. He justifies this retrograde move by intimating that this has always already happened, that the act of penetration has already been there: "Évidemment, c'est sexuel! La Mort ne demande pas son avis à la Vie lorsqu'elle l'encule. Sodomie surprise! Pas le temps d'écarter les fesses: quelque chose est déjà dedans [Obviously, it is sexual. Death doesn't demand Life's opinion when fucking Life's ass. Surprise Sodomy. No time to spread one's thighs: something is already inside]" (*L* 17). So not only is this act sexual in and of itself, any action taken by the West is always already a call to an act of sodomy. The West will always have been a gaping rectum waiting to be sodomized by a real man, a man who has not given up power, a man who has not ceded ground to the effeminate mores of the West and its incarnation in the figures of the bourgeoisie, the market, pervasive liberalism, and tolerance. To have produced this auto-immune effect means that the West was always already screwed, in both the literal and figural senses of the word.

In this "castrated" city (*L* 17), now marked by the gap(e) of its phantom "imperial towers" (17), the sky has become the spectral locus of a cosmic Armageddon that is inscribed in three strands of discourse. First, there is the discourse of sodomy, which transforms everything into a rectum that is also a grave. No position in this clash of civilizations is that of the protected imperial phallus and no position in the West can henceforth be essentialized as transcendental truth; phallogocentrism is, in the end, a pierceable metaphysics. Second, it is also clear that the West's retreat from essence of its own free will and its move toward the spectacular (Debord, Baudrillard) is part of the cause of the problem. If Nabe, ever the misanthrope, is no friend to humans, here or elsewhere, it is in part because humans have decided to opt for a minoritarian position that substitutes existence for essence and spectacle for reality. When reality appears, a kind of reality that is spectacular, humans have to be told that it is reality: "Il faut dire aux Français qui nous regardent que nous ne sommes malheureusement pas dans le cadre d'un film ou d'une image virtuelle [The French people looking at us have to be told that we are unfortunately not in a film or a virtual image]" (*L* 15). And this piercing of illusion by reality is better than any special effects that Hollywood can offer (22); it is a spectacular erection of colossal proportions that only this author's words are capable of matching.[9]

The third strand, which is some fantasmatic teratological birth that comes from the coupling of the previous two strands, is a solipsistic, autosexual act in which Nabe can transcend the vanities of this world and be, in a freaky way, with Mohammed Atta and the others who perpetrated the events of that day. So the discourse becomes euphoric in its celebration of a combination of death and penetration, of sodomy and autosexuality, of self-pleasure and transcendence. Nabe is thrilled that his discourse of hell and damnation, of fire and

---

[9] The Hollywoodian spectacularity is a leitmotif here: "Les terroristes semblent avoir remonté le film à l'envers [...] Quel est le but? Détruire spectaculairement le Centre du Monde du Fric [The terrorists seem to have been screening the film backwards. What is their goal? To destroy in a spectacular manner the Center of the World of Cash]" (*L* 30). At times one thinks that Nabe's position is marked by nothing deeper than the possibilities of camera tricks, special effects, or PhotoShop.

brimstone, and of massive destruction is ubiquitous: "Bientôt, les mots que je préfère le plus au monde embellissent les lèvres pincées des journalistes: kamikazes, suicide, décombres, catastrophe, pirates, fanatiques [Soon, the words I like the most adorn the tight lips of journalists: kamikaze, suicide, ruins, catastrophe, pirates, fanatical]" (*L* 18). This massive change of discourse, this apocalyptic sign of total destruction, is ultimately what Nabe likes best, i.e., the equivalence between the act of anal penetration and the self-serving masturbation in which there is no other. For, in the last analysis, one of the things that works for Nabe in his world-view is precisely that there is no other; only the active bugger is a subject; everyone else is merely a tool for his pleasure. If some bugger others or if some masturbate, the non-productivity and the non-reproductivity are all the same. The world is a great masturbatory spectacle that transforms the false spectacles of the bourgeoisie into reality: "C'est la Grande Masturbation médiatique! [It's the great media masturbation]" (*L* 18). And the sky of New York becomes one enormous wet dream: "C'est le sperme des Boeing, pardon le kérosène, qui a déclenché l'incendie dans les étages et fait fondre les tours [It's the sperm of the Boeings, sorry, the fuel, that set off the fire on the upper floors and made the towers collapse]" (*L* 20).

It is not at all surprising that Nabe focuses on the event and its spectacular nature before turning to the simple fact that several thousand people died in the collapse of the towers. On the one hand, as we have already seen, Nabe relates surface to interior in his own particular way as they are marked by the phenomenon of anal invagination and by the peremptory association of figurality and literality in the idiosyncratic ways he chooses to associate them. Thus, the lack of aberration of same-sex desire is for him replaced by an aberrant model that focuses on his association of the manifestation of that desire with all that relates to being someone in society who does not assert his normality according to majoritarian positions. On the other hand, however, the "enculés" of the world, as we have seen in the penetration of the Towers as if they too were gaping rectums, is the sign that those who were in a parasitic position (Serres) of preying on others have now received their just deserts. In this case, he returns to the invective already discussed about information workers, transformed here into those who work on world trade, who fill their own pockets with cash, through a process, again named by an old word, that is nothing short of usury: "des *golden boys* qui [...] dans les tours de Babel du Veau d'Or, traficotaient sur leurs ordinateurs, au service de la grande Enculerie yankee [the golden boys who, in the towers of Babel of the Golden Calf, deal on their computers, on the job for the big Yankee Buttfuck]" (*L* 29).

It is obvious in this concatenation of anti-Semitic and anti-gay swipes that Nabe's invective is focused on those who worship false idols – the Golden Calf instead of the about to be declared Ten Commandments (Exodus 32). But it is, more importantly, yet another in the series of substitutions of an old-fashioned rhetoric for a contemporary one, in which we see, or feel we see, words such as "sodomy" and "usury" replacing "same-sex desire" and "trade": "Ce n'est pas à toute une société d'usuriers internationaux de lui faire le moindre reproche! Ezra Pound serait fier de lui [It is not up to a whole society of international usurers to reproach him in the slightest. Ezra Pound would be proud of him]" (*L* 60). These "golden boys," in Nabe's world-view, are parasitic upon the world of real people, and buggered them with profiteering and by using information instead of substance. In a sense, then, Nabe seems to be pining for a return to a pre-capitalist model of circulation, the famous C-M-C that defines a pre-capitalist existence, i.e., money being used as a universal medium to establish the rules of barter, instead of the capitalist model, M-C-M, in which money is used to make more money. The symbolism of the golden boys, the Golden Calf, the capitalist model of parasitism, the sodomy, and the usury are all summed up in his expression "enculerie yankee."[10] The US

---

[10] The anti-Americanism that is a profound dislike of the "American way of life" is a theme running through the diatribe: "La caractéristique des Américains est que tous les clichés qu'on colporte sur leur compte sont justes. Les Yankees civilisés préfèrent l'*American way of life* à ce qu'ils appellent la *Diarrhea way of life* [...] Le reste de la Terre est une Bougnoulie où l'on attrape la turista ! Les Américains vivent dans le plus petit pays qui soit: mon ghetto, ma maison, ma voiture, ma télé, mon chien, et mon frigo (le chien dans le frigo?). Tout est réduit à sa plus simple expression. Un grand vide habite ce vaste espace. Et ce vide, il faut le cacher [The characteristic of Americans is that all the clichés spoken about them are right. Civilized Yankees prefer the American way of life to that which they call the Diarrhoea way of life. The rest of the World is a land of savages where one gets 'turista.' Americans live in the smallest country around: my ghetto, my house, my car, my TV, my dog, and my fridge (the dog in the fridge?). Everything is reduced to its simplest expression. A big void inhabits this big space. And this void must be hidden]" (*L* 70).

is screwing the world and those who died in the bombings of New York are themselves finally and justly "enculés" by a real phallus, the battering ram of the jet plane that destroys the icon of the Golden Calf and the golden boys.

The opposition is endlessly played out in Nabe's mind between those who are real men and those who are buggered individuals and false prophets, earning or stealing false profits. So the image of the Golden Calf continues as Nabe sets an implicit opposition up between a real man, in this case Jean Genet, and a false prophet, George W. Bush. Bush is cast as the false Moses, worse than Aaron erecting the Golden Calf, someone who comes back down from the mountain with nothing to show for his forty days' absence other than an emotional incomprehension of transcendence:

> À Ground Zero, Jr emprunte un mégaphone et tient le brave pompier casqué no. 164 par le cou […]. En attendant le "Mémorial," le Texan est juché sur un monticule de verre et de béton. Sur ce Sinaï de gravats, Bush improvise un discours sanglotant. (*L* 38)

> [At Ground Zero, Junior borrows a megaphone and holds the brave fireman, helmet number 164, by the neck. Waiting for the "Memorial," the Texan is perched on a hill of glass and concrete. On this Mount Sinai of rubble, Bush improvises a bloody discourse.]

The politics and stances of George W. Bush are transparent; he is a little man for Nabe, prey to the same interests that keep capitalism and transnational liberalism afloat in the most hypocritical fashion. But Genet, despite his avowed and unrepentant homosexuality, is one of the greats: someone who was not afraid to take a true political position – presumably those he took relative to the Black Panthers and to the Palestinians. And in taking positions against the ubiquitous thought of the West, Genet transcends his status as "enculé" and becomes the bearer of the phallus.[11] In this case it is not so much an act of sodomy but an act of fellatio; yet it all ends up being the same:

[11] Similarly, Nabe reverses roles for the players when it comes to needing a good image. Here the Towers of Jericho are worthy of destruction, even though that attack will be accomplished by Joshua, who was Jewish: "On n'ose imaginer le diktat moral si les tours du World Trade Center de Jéricho avaient été détruites: 'Nous sommes tous cisjordaniens!' [One dare not imagine the moral diktat if the towers of the World Trade Center of Jericho had been destroyed: 'We are all West Bank Palestinians']" (*L* 44).

Les «lettrés» se gardent bien de faire référence à Genet, alors qu'il me semble entendre son rire et ses applaudissements devant les ruines du World Trade Center. Les moustaches de l'intelligentsia en ont plein la bouche de sa grosse bite littéraire, mais quand il s'agit de rappeler qu'il avait aussi des couilles politiques, il n'y a plus personne pour continuer à le sucer. (*L* 43)

[The "learned" make sure not to refer to Genet, while I seem to hear his laugh and his applause in front of the ruins of the World Trade Center. The moustaches of the intelligentsia have their mouths full with his big literary cock, but when it is a question of recalling that he also had political balls, no one keeps sucking him off.]

Opposed to them are those who are the true "enculés" of the world, the pundits who see the attacks as an auto-immune effect, "les enculés qualifiés [qualified bottoms]" (*L* 60) who attempt an analysis that sees the West as having forged the tool of its own destruction and those who, like Bush, perpetuated a situation in which the downtrodden had no option but to react in the way they did. For not having lifted the embargo, Clinton and W.'s names will not be engraved on American marble but on "la pierre ponce de la Yankeerie [the pumice stone of Yankeehood]" (69). Nabe goes on (69–70) to compare them to Foch and Clemenceau, who reduced Germany to a state of slavery, "jusqu'à ce qu'elle finisse par se donner, jambes écartées, au premier Führer venu [until it wound up offering itself, legs spread, to the first Führer on the spot]" (70).[12] Yet it is never clear how those who see the auto-immune response are "enculés," while Nabe's own explanation does not see the West as anything but guilty in the production of the matter.[13] And it also remains unclear where and how Nabe's own model of a parallel universe in which usurers and sodomites would be rapidly extinguished could have prevented the events.

---

[12] This could be taken as an example of Godwin's Law, developed originally by Mike Godwin in reference to Usenet discussions.

[13] The West's behavior is nothing short of moral oppression: "les milliards de Terriens qui ont compris que les symboles de l'oppression morale exercée par tout un système occidental viennent de sauter [The billions of Earthlings who have understood that the symbols of moral oppression exercised by the whole Western system have just exploded]" (*L* 32).

II. Houellebecq's Emasculations

Among the various dystopian worlds created by contemporary authors and film-makers to illustrate, rebel against, or otherwise illustrate the crisis in masculinity, the world of Michel Houellebecq stands alone as one that has been multiply invented in various avatars that move from a pseudo-scientifically based double autofiction such as *Les Particules élémentaires*, through a narrative about sexual tourism, to a science-fiction project such as *La Possibilité d'une île*, with its multiple avatars of the same DNA over the course of centuries. In all cases, however, even when Houellebecq strays from the paths of verisimilitude to illustrate his displeasure with the current world and stretches the limits of science to point the reader towards the possibility of a "brave new world" – there is, in fact, a chapter of *Les Particules élémentaires* titled "Julian et Aldous" – the world we see is our own, seen through a fairly precise lens, but one that has no warm, fuzzy side and no humanity to it.[14] Houllebecq's lens is as cold as a surgeon's or even a pathologist's; he seems to make no distinction between a living body which a doctor might cure and a corpse undergoing a forensic autopsy.

Houellebecq puts all of humanity on the operating table and takes his scalpel to it to remove the excess, the dangerous supplement foisted on mankind by capitalism, by communitarism, by the wiles of the "gauche bien pensante [the thoughtful left]," by the rejection of the natural, that is to say, the phallocentric and heteronormative order. Through his writing, he seeks to analyse the ills of Western society in what he will call "suicide occidental [Western suicide]" (295). He sets up a scenario, especially in *Les Particules élémentaires* [Elementary Particles], but also in the more recent work *La Possibilité d'une île* [The Possibility of an Island], in which the ills of modern Western men are caused, produced, and/or provoked by an intrusion of the feminine, of women's freedom and their claims to parity and equality (Crowley), but also by the intrusion of homosexuality and homosexuals, who make the same claims and who seek the same *jouissance* to which previously only heterosexual men had been entitled. This double challenge – which Houellebecq would in all

---

[14] On the relation of Houellebecq's work to *Brave New World*, see Varsava (158–60).

likelihood characterize as an attack – puts Western culture in danger and it brings to light both the crisis in masculinity and the effects and affects of that crisis.[15] Like Dantec and Nabe, Houellebecq lives the crisis in a very personal fashion: it is within him or within his narratives, and it is the synecdoche of a heterosexuality that has been placed into doubt by a new political agenda in the West and new positions of the subject that offer basic challenges to long-reigning phallogocentrism and heteronormativity.

Fairly late in the novel *Les Particules élémentaires*, which is the story of two half-brothers and their travails (very few other characters are more than sketched out – Houellebecq seems to be able only to offer incarnations of himself as three-dimensional characters), a minor character is involved in an anecdotal situation. A latter-day Holden Caulfield labeling others as the equivalents of the former's "phonies," David de Meola is a character to whom I shall return below in the context of his involvement with snuff films, a reference to and comment on Dantec. Here, David is key in discussing the epitome of contemporary culture:

> Ce n'était pas la version officielle, certes, mais David *savait* que Mick Jagger avait poussé Brian Jones dans la piscine; il pouvait se l'imaginer en train de le faire; et c'est ainsi, par ce meurtre initial, qu'il était devenu le leader du plus grand groupe rock du monde. (257)

> [It was not the official version, of course, but David knew that Mick Jagger had pushed Brian Jones into the pool; he could imagine himself doing it. And it is thus, through this initial murder, that he became the leader of the greatest rock group in the world.]

The entire history of pop culture from the second half of the twentieth century is found in this synecdoche that is also a symbol of the neo-Spenglerian decline of the West. The world is upside down, a carnivalesque universe in which the falseness embodied by a media star parading like some self-aggrandizing rooster on the stages of the world is applauded, Houellebecq would say, by a group of mindless, screaming fans cheering on Jagger's vulgar androgyny. Such is the Houellebecquian vision of the world, a world in which men – i.e. "real" men – have already lost to women, to the effeminate, to the jerks, and to the simians that we have all become. And the real man

---

15 For an excellent reading of the interrelations between Houellebecq's concepts of masculinity and an inscription of the abject, see Reader (105–33).

killed by the false idol who is applauded by the assenting vulgus is lying at the bottom of a swimming pool.

This swimming pool death combined with the erection of a false prophet, perhaps coincidentally, recalls two iconic moments in Western culture. In *Der Mann Moses* (1938), translated as *Moses and Monotheism*, Freud claims that, despite the fact that Moses had led his people out of Egypt and given them the law in the form of the Ten Commandments, they nevertheless sacrificed him as a scapegoat. René Girard, for one, writing in opposition to traditional psycho-analytical readings that tend to sideline this work, based his theory of the scapegoat partly on his belief that Freud was on target here: the crowd sacrifices an innocent individual to rally the community and restore order. As far as the swimming pool is concerned, it is not without an echo of the initial scene of Billy Wilder's 1950 masterpiece *Sunset Boulevard*, in which the narrator, Joe Gillis, played by William Holden, is floating dead in Norma Desmond's swimming pool. Norma (Gloria Swanson) has shot him because she cannot deal with the truth, and he tells the story (as is the case in Machado de Assis's novel) as a flashback told by a dead man. What is common in both cases, one epic, the other fairly tawdry, is that the prophet, the truth-teller, is killed for telling the truth. Here, in *Les Particules élémentaires*, Houellebecq has taken that basic motive and redoubled it: once it is given as an anecdotal aside about rock and roll, but more generally, it is given as Houellebecq's story: he will tell the truth, no matter how unpleasant it may be, no matter how many golden calves – here it will be the television show *Loft Story* – are erected where the truth of the Decalogue should have been.

Houellebecq shares some attributes with both Nabe and Dantec. Like Nabe in *Une Lueur d'espoir*, Houellebecq is obsessed with homosexuals and homosexuality. Part of *Les Particules élémentaires* is set in Paris, and the narrator does not waste a moment before moving from a scene between Michel and his director to a panoramic or telescopic shot of the area known as Tata Beach, that is to say the banks of the Seine below the Tuileries, a well-known gathering spot for gay men. The narrator takes great pleasure – though I suspect it is a kind of internalized *Schadenfreude*, either self-directed or at least directed at his two miserable protagonists – in describing the native fauna, their incessant need to touch their own crotches or those of other men, and so forth (24–25). Far from recognizing that gays may form a visible community – whatever the nature or definition thereof may be – in every Western city in the late twentieth and early twenty-first centuries, and that there is absolutely nothing remarkable or noteworthy about that fact as such, Houellebecq chooses to defamiliarize the situation in the Formalist sense: the author makes something strange in order to allow the reader see new aspects of the formerly familiar. Under Houellebecq's pen (or through Houellebecq's keyboard), homosexuals become not only other, but also, and more importantly, less than human. Certainly compared to the rants of Nabe, Houellebecq is charmingly moderate and restrained. But still, the obsession makes the text deviate and the Houellebecquian defamiliarization of homosexuality is, I think, the affective by-product of what can only be termed an underlying homophobia. The author seems to be saying to his readers: look at them, they are no better than dogs in heat.

Like Dantec, Houellebecq projects a fiction that takes on certain aspects of science fiction, that predicts a visible and understandable, though not yet accomplishable, future, without, at least in *Les Particules élémentaires*, violating the laws of science as we know them. While marked by elements of futurism and science fiction, most of which involve genetics or quantum physics, *Les Particules élémentaires* remains steadfastly in the realm of currently imaginable science. By this, I mean the same thing indicated about Dantec's science fiction. For example, forty years ago computers filled big rooms and could not do one-thousandth of what a laptop can do today. One can imagine a prescient writer in 1968 predicting the miniaturization of the computer, just as we ourselves can foresee the day in which a chip thousands of times more powerful than today's laptops might be implanted subcutaneously. Certainly Houellebecq twists and untwists science here in directions suitable to him, and the entire discussion of molarity and molecularity would not necessarily pass the Sokal litmus test, but the laws of science are not violated. However, in *La Possibilité d'une île*, the author seems to go beyond even Dantec and to transcend the laws of science as we currently know them – though the motif he uses, that of reincarnation with the same DNA, is not unrelated to some well-known leitmotifs used in films and novels as diverse as *Sleeper* and *Alphaville*.

In *Les Particules élémentaires* Houellebecq divides the role of the protagonist between the two half-brothers, Michel and Bruno. On the most basic level, the double story allows the author to write a longer novel in the most arithmetic way, for the narrator can shift between two stories, two biographies, and two sets of anecdotes. The technique is an old one and the stuff of which soap operas are made. Houellebecq is rather transparent in his unabashed use of this trick, and we would do well to see him not as trying to be duplicitous (even if he is) but as trying, in a *roman à thèse*, to set out Cartesian dualism between the body and the mind as one of the primary struggles that any individual (that is to say, for him, any heterosexual Western man) has to face. And in setting up this *agon* as primary, Houellebecq is also reminding his readers that the fragmentation is always already given, and that his "man" will always have been incomplete, inadequate, sterile, and fragmented, without, at least in current conditions, the possibility of the two parts fusing to form a whole.

Bruno, the incarnation of the physical and corporal, is pusillanimous and inadequate from a brutally macho point of view (Houellebecq is constantly struggling with the image of the heterosexual man as would-be super-hero). He is physically weak and sexually immature compared to other teenagers who have already gone through puberty. In the heteronormative world in which "boys will be boys" and in which cruelty is translated into vulgarity, Bruno is the object of taunting and is ultimately urinated and defecated on (56–57). He is the incarnation of the abject, the object of scorn who is not only not an alpha male (59) in a group of animals, already likened by the author to a troop of animals, monkeys in particular (59), but rather the omega man[16] in a horde of mutants. The physical world, for Houellebecq, itself becomes parodic, in which even the most banal creatures are sub-human versions of prancing B-movie versions of Mick Jagger. Nevertheless, Houellebecq makes his point clear: dehumanization and emasculation for him are absolute equivalents of one another. To resolve this will not be a question of returning to some mythic masculine human state, but of going beyond the impasse – not towards a rehumanization but towards a remasculation.

While fetishizing a kind of too-human masculinity in what would be for him a utopian heteronormative world of the near future, Houellebecq, despite himself, is finally drawn into a speculative,

---

[16] Houellebecq's use of the terms "alpha" and "omega" here seems coincidental. Still, there is a strange referentiality to the plot of the film *The Omega Man*, in which the immunized ex-scientist, played by Charlton Heston, fights the retro group of "The Family." The difference is that the Heston character is more like Michel than Bruno, as befits Hollywood's general rejection of duality for superheroes.

specular, and voyeuristic homosocial order in which his supposedly straight character is fascinated by male genitalia. In the case of the narrator's early remark about Bruno, that "[s]on sexe est petit, encore enfantin, dépourvu de poils [his penis is small, still that of a child, deprived of hairs]" (56), we seem to have simply the case of a child who has not yet crossed the threshold into puberty. But Houellebecq betrays himself through his use of language, for there is an ambiguity here. Instead of "dépourvu," the author could have written, for example, "glabre" [smooth]. But he chooses a negative or privative word, "dépourvu"; even if the word is often used without a privative meaning, that subtending deprivation is there, reinforced by the fact that there is, throughout the novel, an obvious tension between progress or what Houellebecq calls "mutation métaphysique [metaphysical mutation]" (10) and retrogression or degradation. Here, then, it is a question of retrogression instead of maturation towards some heteronormative masculine state. But this is because the stakes have changed, Houellebecq would argue. Bruno will not make progress, and "il avait une trop petite queue [his dick was too small]" (126), which the author, in his insistent voyeurism, will specify as measuring twelve centimeters (238). Freudian penis-envy, usually associated with women, is established within the realm of the masculine, as the latter has been perverted, so to speak, by the infiltration and infection of homosexuality that has stormed the heterosexual masculine sanctuary. As Bruno notes,

> Le problème, le problème nouveau, c'était mon sexe. Ça peut paraître fou maintenant, mais dans les années 70 on ne s'occupait réellement pas de la taille du sexe masculin; pendant mon adolescence j'ai eu tous les complexes physiques possibles, sauf celui-là. Je ne sais pas qui a commencé à en parler, probablement les pédés; enfin, on trouve également le thème abordé dans les romans policiers américains; par contre, il est totalement absent chez Sartre. (237–38)

> [The problem, the new problem, was my penis. It might seem crazy now, but in the seventies, people weren't really concerned about the size of male genitalia. When I was a teenager, I had all the physical complexes possible, except that one. I don't know who began to talk about it, probably the fags. But you also find the theme taken on in American detective novels. But it is completely absent in Sartre.]

The obsession with the size of male genitalia is the fault of homosexuals, to be sure, but they are not the only object of loathing, as black men, stereotyped as well-endowed, become the object of fierce hatred, fear, and envy, simply because of that. Once again, it is not a question of being more than a man, especially not a Nietzschean superman, but rather a sub-human, who happens to be more "male" on the level of animality. Bruno's self-loathing becomes other-directed, but it leads him and the novel into a dilemma that will be endlessly repeated: there is no turning back through nostalgia to some previous avatar of the masculine, for the human race has degenerated into sheer animality. But for now, there is no predictable future in sight toward which to turn.

Given their reduction in Bruno's eyes to a state of mere physicality, homosexuals – for the minor rant about men of African origin is a temporary interlude – do not have, in his mind, a conscious mental or intellectual status; they are an unpleasant mixture of physicality and animal drives, impulses, and instincts, and are incapable of changing themselves; their physical being is their essence. So even if the metaphysical mutation does take place – it will be described much later in the book and re-enacted in a somewhat different form in *La Possibilité d'une île* – it will be uniquely for heterosexual white men, for it is only they who are capable, in Houellebecq's mind, of a metaphysical dimension: women, blacks, homosexuals, and *tutti quanti* will be excluded. In a perverse way, homosexuals as such do not exist, for to give them that name – albeit, in the twenty-first century, a slightly quirky and macaronic relic of a nineteenth-century medical, psychiatric, and juridical discourse – would be at least to allow them full status as human beings; for Houellebecq, a direct homophobic rant is out of the question, where it is not for Nabe. So Houellebecq does not turn, as does Nabe, to a biblical or apocalyptic discourse, if for no other reason than that he is too much of a hedonist to do so, despite his perception of the perversity of homosexual behavior. It is not so much the act of homosexual sex that bothers him, but rather the perceived noxious effect on society itself. So rather than turn to hellfire and brimstone, Houellebecq inflects one nineteenth-century discourse with another, an even more pathological one, if taken literally. As Bruno says, "C'est tout à fait faussement, pensait par exemple Bruno, qu'on parle d'homosexuels. Lui-même n'avait jamais, ou pratiquement jamais, rencontré d'homosexuels; par contre, il connaissait de nombreux *pédérastes* [Bruno was thinking that it was completely false to speak of homosexuals. He had never, or practically never, met homosexuals; on the other hand, he knew lots of *pederasts*]" (131). And he continues: "La plupart des pédérastes, cependant, préfèrent les jeunes gens entre quinze et vingt-cinq ans; au-delà il n'y a plus, pour eux, que de vieux culs flapis [Most pederasts however prefer young men between fifteen and twenty-five years old; beyond that, for them, there are only old worn-out asses]" (132). Yet he is begging the question, for in redefining, in choosing the exact, appropriate word, he errs, as "pederast" literally means a lover of boys, not of adolescents, which would be the situation of the *erastos* described by Foucault in the first volume of *Histoire de la sexualité*, nor of adults. The correct word would be "ephebophile." Houllebecq's recourse to the word "pederast" means that readers will immediately think of the pejorative and vulgar insult "sale pédé," a phrase that carries a connotative value of scorn of the other.

In a moral judgment these homosexuals or pederasts are not just guilty of an "attentat aux mœurs [an attempt to corrupt morals]," for that would occur only at the level of the local in a one-on-one situation, as it were. Rather, they are collectively guilty of absolute corruption and leading the West, in a wayward fashion, down the "primrose path of dalliance." In Houellebecquian ideology, they are thus no longer the innocent scapegoats for a system gone awry, but rather the cause of sadness, evil, corruption, and the steep Lucretian *clinamen* toward perdition and animality; they are the source, *fons et origo*, of the mortal and earthly fall from grace:

> Comme en bien d'autres cas, les prétendus homosexuels avaient joué un rôle de modèle pour le reste de la société, pensait encore Bruno. Lui-même, par exemple, avait quarante-deux ans; désirait-il pour autant les femmes de son âge? En aucune façon. (132).

> [As in many other cases, the supposed homosexuals had served as role models for the rest of society, Bruno thought. For example, he was forty-two. For all that, did he desire women of his own age? No way.]

In Houellebecq's universe, as articulated by Bruno, we have all been homosexualized, not queered in the affirmative sense often used in the twenty-first century, but weakened and rendered impotent and effeminate. And it is all their fault.

Leaving matters where they are for the moment in terms of this obsession with the havoc wreaked by homosexual men on the West, I should add that the question takes on the full force of the abjection of the physical when conjugated with an anecdotal incident intercalated late in the novel and set in counterpoint to scenes between Bruno and his erstwhile girlfriend Christiane. Houellebecq kills the latter off slowly and cruelly, in a manifestation of a misogyny that will reach full force only in *Plateforme*, the novel of sexual tourism, by saddling her with a necrosis of the coccygeal vertebrae, followed by suicide, including as he does so references to the suicides of Guy Debord and Guy Deleuze. He does this, on the one hand, to set Christiane's illness and death in opposition to the desideratum of going beyond physical limitations for men (straight white men) to become Sadean supermen, and, on the other, to illustrate the expendability of women in this universe.[17]

To accomplish this multiple task, Houllebecq uses the minor character of David de Meola, who has been touted, as the reader remembers, as the man who knows the truth about Mick Jagger.[18] In this seemingly minor passage, de Meola is involved in snuff films. Human life, given the way it has evolved into its current form in the present, is worth nothing in and of itself; any individual life is worth something only in the process of becoming a corpse, and that value can be translated into cash: "[un] bon *snuff movie* pouvait se négocier extrêmement cher, autour de vingt mille dollars la copie [(a) good snuff film could sell for a lot, about twenty thousand dollars for a print]" (259). Snuff films, whether the stuff of urban legends or not, are said to include sex scenes as such as well as torture (or "supplice," i.e. torture up to death); they end with the death of the victim (usually a woman) that occurs simultaneously with the orgasm of the torturer (usually one or several men).[19] Thus "la petite mort," the French term for post-coital depression, literally "little death," is conflated with death, yet, as we know from novels like *Justine* and especially *Juliette*, there is no mourning, no regret: the

---

[17] On sexual tourism in *Plateforme*, see Ní Loingsigh.

[18] The Jagger reference is just two pages previous to this anecdote.

[19] French makes a useful distinction here between "torture," which is used to extract information, and "supplice," which is the abuse after condemnation or judgment and before death. Since we know that the culmination of the scene in a snuff film will be the death of the victim, this distinction moves us from the informational to the truly Sadean. In passing, this intercalated passage on snuff films, while providing a reflection on sexuality in a more general sense in this work, may also be seen as a commentary on Dantec's *La Sirène rouge*, published five years before.

corpse is merely the earthly remains of an instrument for the sheer pleasure of the one(s) remaining alive. The corpse, abject reminder of what it was, is a singular and monstrous combination of the human and the non-human.

With this set of juxtaposed abject sexualities, we are in the presence of a kind of multiple chiasmus, a crossroads of the anti-human and anti-humanist Houellebecquian philosophy or ideology in which human life itself is worth nothing; it is only in the moment of transfiguration into death, the turning point of the chiasmus, that this life has a value. Strangely, here as elsewhere, the author falls into a reinscription of the Debordian society of the spectacle in which the institutions that represent capitalism and further its interests are seen as inevitable. Thus does Houllebecq strangely reinscribe the old Hollywood commonplace, as articulated by the Lionel Barrymore character Mr. Potter in *It's a Wonderful Life*: "You're worth more dead than alive." This cliché of mainstream comedies, melodramas, and *films noirs* is taken over by the industry of snuff films, as Dantec shows in *La Sirène rouge*; the difference is that in mainstream films, the cliché is made as an announcement of things to come (or not); here, in snuff films, it is a question of fulfilling the promise and accomplishing it without the *morituri* knowing at first that this possibility will become a definite event. The zero point, the ground zero of the chiasmus, is that moment between life and death, between non-orgasm and orgasm, an undecidable, indeterminate, and unannounceable moment that is the explosion of the Lacanian Real.

In figuring the Lacanian Real, here and elsewhere in his work, Houellebecq takes the commonplace of Hollywood and seemingly stands it on its head. One could argue that traditional Hollywood mainstream studio films have no place for that Real, and that one has to go back either to the classic Anglo-American modernist novel or to independent films (or some post-studio films) to find the insertion of that category in film.[20] Still, in reaching out and bringing in the real to create a scene beyond norms and taboos,

---

[20] For reasons not particularly germane here, I would argue that while French modernist writers such as Gide, Proust, and Colette seldom, if ever, let the Lacanian Real occupy any high point, Anglo-American modernism is rife with such moments. Not the least of these is Molly Bloom's "yes oh yes oh yes," but there is also *To the Lighthouse*: "She had had her vision"; *The Great Gatsby*: "So we beat on, boats against the current, borne back ceaselessly into the past"; and *Heart of Darkness*: "The horror! The horror!," among others.

Houellebecq ends up banalizing the obscene, which becomes nothing more than another episode shrugged off by all in a dreary world: "Dans cette cassette, tournée un mois auparavant, il sectionnait un sexe masculine à la tronçonneuse [On that cassette, filmed a month before, he was cutting off a penis with a chainsaw]" (260). In this world, it little matters who the victim is or whether it is a man or a woman. Narrative repeats anecdote: it is all just grist for the mill:

> Après avoir épuisé les jouissances sexuelles, il était normal que les individus libérés des contraintes morales ordinaires se tournent vers les jouissances plus larges de la cruauté; deux siècles auparavant, Sade avait suivi un parcours analogue. En ce sens, les *serial killers* des années 90 étaient les enfants naturels des *hippies* des années 60; on pouvait trouver leurs ancêtres communs chez les actionnistes viennois des années 50. (261)

> [After having exhausted sexual pleasures, it was normal that individuals freed from ordinary moral constraints turn towards the wider pleasures of cruelty; two centuries earlier, Sade had followed an analogous path. In that way, the serial killers of the nineties were the illegitimate children of the hippies from the sixties; their common ancestors could be found in the Viennese activists of the fifties.]

In this world then, it is perfectly normal to go beyond the limits imposed by society if one is in search of the real (or the Real) and orgasms of any sort, be they onanistic or with another person. It is simply a continuous and unfiltered process of a feeding frenzy based on the cannibalistic devouring of the other, the freedom of the other, and the rights of the other: it is not so much the Hobbesian "homo hominis lupus," but rather "homo hominis cibus" – and this for the real on demand, the real as fast food.

As I have indicated at the beginning of this section, the division of the role of the protagonist between Bruno and Michel, between the bodily and the intellectual, the corporal and the cerebral, and the physical and the metaphysical, is an old trick, arguably one used to great effect in stories of twins and in medieval allegory. Here it is a short-cut to lengthening the novel without necessarily imposing the forms, plots, and structure of a long nineteenth-century novel or even the aesthetics of a modernist text. Houellebecq makes the relation to the "twins" plot ever more acute by having the two half-brothers in the same year in school. Having examined the abjection of the bodily as a sign of the crisis in masculinity, a physicality from which there is seemingly no relief, we now turn to the cerebral and metaphysical as a possible solution, through an analysis of the character of Michel and his import for the development of the larger ideology of the novel.

This is the moment of metaphysical mutation, of a paradigm shift through thought and scientific knowledge. In comparison with the passages in which Bruno is the protagonist, those about Michel are far more complex and wide-reaching, and are the sign of the crisis having taken on metaphysical proportions. Next to the inadequacies and the excesses of Bruno and in spite of the temporary solution offered by the Sadean snuff film episode, each moment at which Michel is on stage is the narrative and novelistic translation, in multiple forms, of the crisis. This is clear from the beginning of the novel: "Ce livre est avant tout l'histoire d'un homme, qui vécut la plus grande partie de sa vie en Europe occidentale, durant la seconde moitié du XXe siècle [More than anything else, this book is the story of a man who lived most of his life in Western Europe during the second half of the twentieth century]" (9). Thus, the narrator makes it clear from the beginning that the use of a double protagonist is a feint, with Bruno serving, as it were, as a body double; Michel is the subject, the illustration, and the ideological force of this novel that is the enactment of the beliefs and positions of the author, not coincidentally named Michel as well. The position is staked out from the beginning: "Les mutations métaphysiques – c'est-à-dire les transformations radicales et globales de la vision du monde adoptée par le plus grand nombre – sont rares dans l'histoire de l'humanité [Metaphysical mutations, that is to say, global and radical transformations of the vision of the world adopted by the majority, are rare in the history of humanity]" (10). And while it would be too simplistic a move to make a direct identification between the author and his character and while the narrative vacillations and vagaries are too constant to render "identification" possible, even were that desirable, Michel is the standard-bearer for the author, while Bruno, alas, is the catch-all somatization of Houellebecq's traumas, neuroses, preoccupations, and affects.

The starting point for the two characters is the same, and necessarily so, in order both to dramatize their difference and to mark Michel's *Aufhebung* that seemingly gets him beyond the impasse of the physical. We would have expected a similar beginning, and Houllebecq wastes no time in offering nothing short of a mid-life crisis, "souvent associée à des phénomènes sexuels [often associated with sexual phenomena]" (28). Emasculated by society in general and by youth culture (again, as we have seen, this is the fault of homosexuals), Michel's "bite lui servait à pisser, et c'est tout [cock was used for pissing and that is all]" (28). As far as Michel is concerned, the author has him start in a mixture of monstrosity and abjection, as he dreams of "poubelles gigantesques, remplies de filtres à café, de raviolis en sauces et d'organes sexuels tranchés [giant garbage cans, filled with coffee filters, ravioli in sauce, and severed sex organs]" (20). Here the mid-life crisis is duly noted, rather transparently, with droopy images like the ravioli, images of castration, and an image of the abject: the coffee filters, undoubtedly used ones, remind us of Zola's "marc de la veille [the previous day's coffee grounds]" in *Germinal*, used to underline the abject poverty that reduces Catherine to using yesterday's coffee grounds to make some wan coffee. The scene of castration speaks for itself, and literally so, for there is no displacement of condensation; it is more a direct hallucination than the Freudian image that would invade the unconscious and be translated somehow by the conscious mind. Once again, it is a kind of fast-food version of the Lacanian Real: an entry into the unnameable and unspeakable that the author has to articulate directly. There is no refuge in a neurotic scenario of castration anxiety fed by an Oedipus complex, but a direct plunge into the world without language that Houellebecq feels to be his daily reality.

If the author leaves Michel's alter ego, Bruno, to wallow in the "slough of despond," as he is imprisoned by the banal reality of the physical and obsessed with the reality of castration, he allows the cerebral Michel to go beyond the physical, literally and etymologically, into the metaphysical, in which he interrelates thought, physical, biological, and chemical actions of particles and quanta, and the meaning of life. Houellebecq enters into somewhat dangerous territory here, for in addition to going directly to scientific sources for information on particle physics and quantum physics, he seems to have mined the pseudo-scientific concepts of molarity and molecularity from Deleuze and Guattari, who use the concepts to vastly different ends in their quest for rhizomatics and endlessly renewed deterritorialization. Houellebecq's use of science would not, in and of itself, withstand the scrutiny of Alan Sokal. Yet, at the same time, given that this is a fiction, and that it does not purport, as Deleuze's writings might, to be a theoretical analysis of some reality or truth, it is easy to go beyond the pseudo-science to see what worlds Houellebecq is dreaming of. Simply put, Houllebecq's goal for Michel is to surmount, go beyond, and even annihilate the physical in a leap into the metaphysical, to rewrite the limits of the physical as something temporary, false limits imposed by the structures of humanism and capitalism, limits blocking masculinity from realizing its full capacities.

As has already been indicated, Houellebecq does not found his metaphysics on the Nietzschean concept of the superman, in part because Nietzsche's concepts are born within capitalism and bear the marks of a relativism that the author finds untenable, for what he needs is an absolute position from which to wage his apocalyptic war on the institutions of the West. Strategically, then, he opts for an idealist Kantian scenario that is both universal and totalizing, the necessary base, or platform, to use a Houellebecquian word, on which he can erect his new physics and metaphysics:

> La pure morale est unique et universelle. Elle ne subit aucune altération au cours du temps, non plus qu'aucune adjonction. Elle ne dépend d'aucun facteur historique, économique, sociologique ou culturel; elle ne dépend absolumment de rien du tout. Non déterminée, elle détermine. Non conditionnée, elle conditionne. En d'autres termes, c'est un absolu. (46)

> [Pure morality is singular and universal. It does not undergo any alteration over time, nor any addition. It depends on no historical, economic, sociological, or cultural factor. It depends absolutely on nothing at all. Undetermined, it determines. Unconditioned, it conditions. In other words, it is an absolute.]

In choosing to found his system on a universal, absolute, transcendental, and achronic base, Houellebecq necessarily rejects the relativism that marks much of the Enlightenment and its aftermath (and that, parenthetically, marks even Kant, in his political writings, for example). In so doing, Houellebecq can eschew the existential turn and erect his morality as an essentialist and trans-historical *sine qua non*. He thereby establishes a redoubled time frame: an eternal, unchanging, and transcendental time on the one hand, and, on the other, human time in decline, on a Lucretian *clinamen*, a time of loss and absence, a time of emasculation and feminization. At the same time, this move re-establishes the base toward which, in a synthesis of the *termini ad quem* and *ab quo*, his scientific and metaphysical leap must take him, precisely that of an unchanging morality founded on essentialist masculinity. With that gesture, Houellebecq manages to push to the side all current incarnations of the relative, which we could put in theoretical terms: there is no need to think, with Foucault, about the social construction of categories of sexuality (among other things); no need to think, with Derrida, about the deconstruction of any and all transcendental "absolutes" as figures of an ideology of phallogocentrism; no need to think, with Lyotard, about the consequences of the libidinal economy; and no need to think, with Deleuze and Guattari, about the results of a rhizomatic pattern. And as we have seen, Houellebecq's intersection with Lacanian "beyonds" is retranslated into an all-you-can-eat buffet. The author's essentialist base, from which he operates and which he also uses as a *telos*, pushes his readers toward a reconsideration of an essentialist pattern for being and for sexes, genders, and sexualities, one that will seemingly be rediscovered through the transformative process of this "metaphysical mutation" (11).

As Houellebecq, even in outlining his desiderata, is not going to legislate morality in a privative manner, mores become an absolute for the author, but at a cost, which is a fairly liberal approach to the science and mathematics that he chooses to deploy in his explanation of the mutation toward the post-human figure of the male who is more masculine even than pre-Enlightenment men: mores are science-driven. His first hypothesis is certainly a tenable one that has often been considered as a thought-experiment [*Gedankenexperiment*], especially as an axiomatic position for thinking about the possibilities of extra-terrestrial life: "Michel prit conscience que les bases chimiques de la vie auraient pu être entièrement différentes [Michel learned that the chemical bases of life could have been completely different]" (49). But it quickly becomes obvious that the science he is using as the vehicle for this metaphysical and moral transformation is a floating set of signifiers that mixes molar and molecular models, and that ultimately transforms the molecular, that bane of his existence, into a version of the molar. And while Deleuze and Guattari, in *L'Anti-Œdipe*, in particular, oppose the two and favor the deterritorializing molecular over the stabilizing molar, Houellebecq will reject that position in favor of a rewriting of science.

It is precisely this point that is at the crux of the Houellebecquian counter-current in which he is going against the tide of the times. And to understand this, it is necessary to take a quick detour through the Deleuzean model. Taking their cues from quantum mechanics among other fields, the authors of *L'Anti-Œdipe* oppose the molar and the molecular. For them, the molar designates the whole object, perceived and understood as a *Gestalt*, an unchanging essence that is also unchangeable and identical to itself. Opposed to the stability of the molar is the endlessly changing molecular, of which the classic Deleuzean examples would be the "desiring machines," the plug-ins, the partial objects, and the concept of rhizomatic movement; these often contradictory forces, moving in and beyond the object – the text, the social aggregate, the system of desire, the film or cultural object – drift in random Brownian motion in all directions. So, opposed to the universalizing, globalizing Oedipus complex, erected as a universal through the ubiquity of capitalism, Deleuze and Guattari tout the drives of partial objects, the movement along rhizomatic lines, the needs, gaps and desires, all of which form, for them, a process of becoming, one that Foucault for one describes as being radically anti-fascist, a statement that we might translate into anti-totalitarian and anti-totalizing.

The goal of the Houellebecquian project is obviously the complete and absolute opposite of the Deleuzean radicality that flirts with anarchy, though it could easily be argued that Houellebecq's own position, in its singular foundation on the individual without the social contract, also flirts with anarchy, or perhaps just with a radical libertarian position. Even if we move away from the logical and intuitive extension of Foucault's comment in the negative, we can still see Houellebecq's system as opposed to the rhizomatic disorder of Deleuze and Guattari; and even if we do not see Houellebecq's desiderata as manifestos of totalitarianism, it is clearly totalizing desires that are also the vehicle toward a return to stability and toward an essentialism in which the reproduction of the same or a collective and generalized ipseity is devoutly to be wished. Molecules are ordered and there would be no difference between Houellebecq's version of the molecular and the molar. This identity, repeated at several points, is a return toward a past that has never existed; it is a nostalgia, played out in the future, for perfection that is not touched by the degradation, effeminacy, and emasculation of modernity.

Houllebecq takes the plunge with science, using it to multiply and divide positions in the narrative, so that he can ultimately reformulate the whole in his own fashion, and after his own conceptions of totality:

> Les histoires consistantes de Griffiths ont été introduites en 1984 pour relier les mesures quantiques dans des narrations vraisemblables. Une histoire de Griffiths est construite à partir d'une suite de mesures plus ou moins quelconques ayant lieu à des instants différents. Chaque mesure exprime le fait qu'une certaine quantité physique, éventuellement différente d'une mesure à l'autre, est comprise, à un instant donné, dans un certain domaine de valeurs. (84)

> [The consistent histories of Griffiths were introduced in 1984 to relate quantum measures in veritable narratives. One of Griffiths's histories is constructed based on a set of more or less random measurements taken at different moments. Each measurement expresses the fact that a certain physical quantity, different from one measurement to another, is made up, at a given moment, in a certain set of values.]

Not only has the author organized the deployment of his argument around the concept of regulatable quanta, and in so doing has avoided the messy problem of the molecular, he has also given himself the possibility of announcing this in literary or narrative terms. In this manner, he creates a complex literary space in which there is a homology between the narration in general, the mini-narratives about quanta, and the physics that will immediately mutate into what we might call an advanced version of biophysics – one that will also eventually have a component of bioinformatics, which will be the solution to creating the new man (Dahan-Gaida 109–11; Chassay). The stories he gives to his characters, which may once have seemed random or aleatory, if not to say (especially with the earthbound Bruno, who is the archetypal schlemiel) stereo-typical, now, while retaining the dynamic of the molecular, quickly become ordered, almost in goose-step fashion, so that he can use his tales teleologically in quest of the *summum bonum*, which, for Houellebecq, is the possibility of perfect reproduction.[21]

---

[21] The concept of "consistent histories" is one developed by Robert B. Griffiths (119–27) in his furthering of quantum mechanics. While "inconsistent families of histories" are "meaningless" (123), it is interesting to note that in some cases, consistent histories have "decoherence conditions" (122). For Houellebecq, then, this twinned consistency and decoherence is grist for his mill in his quest to reorient the problematic molecular disorder. I should like to thank my colleagues

It is normal and necessary that Houllebecq take a positivist point of view as a starting point, one from which his essentialist method can guarantee a logical, determined, and totally predictable trajectory and conclusion that develops out of a renewed and updated form of positivism:

Les conditions initiales étant données, pensait-il, le réseau des interactions initiales étant paramétré, les événements développent dans un espace désenchanté et vide; leur déterminisme est inéluctable. Ce qui s'était produit devait se produire, il ne pouvait en être autrement; personne ne pouvait en être tenu pour responsable. La nuit Michel rêvait d'espaces abstraits, recouverts de neige [...]. (113)

[The initial conditions having been given, he thought, the network of initial interactions having been measured, the events take place in a disenchanted and empty space: their determinism is unavoidable. What was produced had to be produced; there was no alternative; no one could be held responsible. At night, Michel dreamed of abstract spaces covered with snow.]

Nothing can change the determined path or progress of the narrative or its contents. No molecular action can upset the order of things, the essence of being or the *raison d'être* of the world. The author seems to revel in the idea, undoubtedly a comforting one for him in these troubled times, that an unchangeable future will be completely determined by a past or present moment. Given the fact that the current state of the West is not suited to him, he envisions a moment of transformation through the metaphysical mutation that will organize the future in an essentialist and positivist fashion; the order of the future will be fixed and roles will no longer vacillate. It is not so much that "boys will be boys," though that is true; it is that "men will be men." This future will resemble the imaginary order (albeit not in a Lacanian sense) posited by transhistorical phallogocentrism and heteronormativity, a utopian dream of someone who seems to represent, on an intellectual and emotional level, if not necessarily a physical one, the perpetual incarnation of a mid-life crisis or the status of what the French pithily call "mal baisé."

It is always about sex in Houellebecq's work. This was clear in the sections of the novel devoted to Bruno, a character who seems

at the University of Illinois, Ido Golding and Michael Bednarz, for pointing me in the right direction here.

to be reincarnated in various guises in *Plateforme*. In that work, it is a question of sexual tourism for Westerners who are sexually frustrated, people who seek to fulfill their desire exotically when they can no longer do so in the West, a West in which women pursue their own goals (and pleasures) instead of serving the needs and desires of horny, Western, heterosexual men. So it is not as if Houellebecq were turning to some puritanical or monastic model in order to reclaim masculinity. Rather, this rhyparographer – this painter of moral decay – or this supreme voyeur sees something positive in the sexual liberation of the end of the twentieth century, or rather something that could have been positive had the liberation of others – women and homosexual men in particular – not had a noxious effect on the singular stronghold of traditional macho masculinity as he envisions it. He admires sexual liberation without reservation: "Sur le plan de l'évolution des mœurs, l'année 1970 fut marquée par une extension rapide de la consommation érotique, malgré les interventions d'une censure encore vigilante [On the level of evolving morals, 1970 was marked by a rapid extension of erotic consumption, despite the interventions of still vigilant censure]" (63). With the appropriate metaphysical mutation, this event may still turn into a positive, liberating one.

The problem is not in sexual liberation as such, but rather in the ideology that accompanies the multiple liberations of the second half of the twentieth century. If "la génération précédente avait établi un lien d'une force exceptionnelle entre mariage, sexualité et amour [the preceding generation had established an exceptionally powerful link among marriage, sexuality, and love]" (69) and if the following generation unhooks these three categories (or ideological constructs, especially in their linkage) to concentrate on the independence of sexuality and sex, the problem for Houellebecq is that, through this uncoupling, all sexualities have become open to expression and not just the one he would favor. And that multiple liberation rubs Houellebecq the wrong way, so to speak, for his own conception of freedom and liberation is a reinterpretation of positivism in a post-Christian world: it is only heteronormative, heterosexual men who truly have a right to that freedom:

> Bien des années plus tard, Michel devait proposer une brève théorie de la liberté humaine sur la base d'un analogie avec le compor-tement de l'hélium superfluide. Phénomènes atomiques discrets, les échanges d'électrons entre les neurones et les synapses à l'intérieur

du cerveau sont en principe soumis à l'imprévisibilité quantique; le grand nombre de neurones fait cependant, par annulation statistique des différences élémentaires, que le comportement humain est – dans ses grandes lignes comme dans ses détails – aussi rigoureusement déterminé que celui de tout autre système naturel. Pourtant dans certaines circonstances, extrêmement rares – les chrétiens parlaient d'*opération de la grâce* – une onde de cohérence nouvelle surgit et se propage à l'intérieur du cerveau; un comportement nouveau apparaît, de manière temporaire ou définitive, régi par un système entièrement différent d'oscillateurs harmoniques; on observe alors ce qu'il est convenu d'aller un *acte libre*. (117)

[Many years later, Michel had to propose a short theory of human freedom, based on an analogy with the behavior of superfluid helium. Discrete atomic phenomena, exchanges of electrons between neurons and synapses within the brain are, in principle, submitted to quantum unpredictability. Most neurons, however, through the statistical annulation of elementary differents, make human behavior, both along broad lines and its details, as determined as that of any other system. Yet, in certain circumstances that are extremely are – Christians speak of the action of grace – a wave of new coherence arises and multiplies within the brain; a new behavior appears, in a temporary or definitive manner, ruled by an entirely different system of harmonic oscillators; one thus observes what people call an act of free will.]

There is certainly an evolutionary model here, an evolution toward a post-Christian, liberatory position, but I would argue that Houellebecq's use of the seemingly innocent expression "natural system" is anything but innocent. Rather, what Houellebecq conceives of as "natural" is based on a concept of nature as the eighteenth century conceived of it, an essentialist, masculine nature, even when it is a question of "Mother Nature," or of "marâtre nature [nature as step-mother]," as Ronsard put it in the sixteenth century; opposed to it is everything conceived of as being *contra naturam* (Doré). It is thus that he invokes, almost in spite of himself, given the religious echoes of the phrase, the "action of grace," the act of freedom that is the sign of the jump to a new system. Only the operation of grace can free us from the insistence of the molecular, whose anarchy is rampant. This operation of grace translated into a new or renewed *jouissance* can make the jump, but without it, we are condemned to an infernal future: "Michel médita plusieurs heures sur le message contenu dans les deux phrases qui définissaient la thématique de la collection: 'Optimisme, générosité, complicité, harmonie font avancer le monde. DEMAIN SERA FËMININ' [Michel meditated for several hours on the message contained in the two sentences that defined the thematics of the collection: 'Optimism, generosity, complicity, and harmony make the world advance. Tomorrow will be feminine']" (153).

Mark of Houellebecquian terror, the capital letters are a sign of the fearsome, castrating *vagina dentata*, the sign of the inevitable continuous decline if the metaphysical leap does not happen. Without the non-Christian miracle he is waiting for, the pleasures of the future will be merely illusory, *ersatz* orgasms faked for us by nature. While all sexual acts and sexualities are in principle accepted within the realm of the "normal," in fact anything that is not heterosexual, masculine *jouissance* is inferior to that model, held as the gold standard. At times, it would seem that everything else is not only inferior, but also false, temporary, and mendacious; as the narrator disdainfully remarks:

> Partout des êtres humains vivaient, respiraient, essayaient d'éprouver du plaisir ou d'améliorer leurs potentialités personnelles. À tous les étages des êtres humains progressaient ou essayaient de progresser dans leur intégration sociale, sexuelle, professionnelle ou cosmique. Ils «travaillaient sur eux-mêmes», pour reprendre l'expression la plus communément employée. (163)

> [Everywhere human beings lived, breathed, tried to have pleasure or improve their personal potentials. At every level, human beings made progress or tried to make progress in their social, sexual, professional, or cosmic integration. They were "working on themselves," to repeat the most commonly used expression.]

This illusion of progress, this move toward a feminine future, can only be a disappointment to an author who can conceive of nothing more than a masculine future with a perpetual orgasm. Opposed to the feminine, molecular future, Houellebecq posits a future in which the molecular collapses into the molar, into a series of erect phalluses, stiff and ready to ejaculate, as the order of things in the "natural system" decrees.

For scientific or pseudo-scientific reasons that depend on the valorization of presence, speech, and the visible and the relative devalorization of absence, writing, and the invisible (all of this discussed of course by Jacques Derrida in his epoch-making *De la grammatologie*), Houellebecq ironically cannot accept the consequences of his own theorization of the future without manipulating them toward a completely empty ontology. In so doing, he allows essence to become, bizarrely, the transcendental effect of the imposed mutation and new order of things, with no suggestion that there may be other possible futures:

> Soit les propriétés cachées déterminant le comportement des particules pouvaient avoir l'une sur l'autre une influence instantanée à une distance arbitraire. Soit il fallait renoncer au concept de particule élémentaire possédant, en l'absence de toute observation, des propriétés intrinsèques: on se retrouvait alors devant un vide ontologique profond – à moins d'adopter un positivisme radical, et de se contenter de développer le formalisme mathématique prédictif des observables en renonçant définitivement à l'idée de réalité sous-jacente. (155)

> [Either the hidden properties determining the behavior of particles had an instantaneous influence on one another at an arbitrary distance. Or one would have to give up the concept of the elementary particle having, in the absence of all observation, intrinsic properties. One would thus be faced with a deep ontological void, unless one adopted a radical positivism, and was happy with developing the mathematical formalism that is a predictor of observables, and one definitively renounced the idea of an underlying reality.]

Or again:

> [L]es équations de la mécanique quantique permettaient de prévoir le comportement des systèmes microphysiques avec une précision excellente, et même avec un précision totale si l'on renonçait à tout espoir de retour vers une ontologie matérielle. (282)

> [The equations of quantum mechanics allowed one to foresee the behavior of microphysical systems with excellent precision, and even with total precision, if one gave up any hope of a return toward material ontology.]

While the science is sound, the use of science as a vehicle for a deontology would certainly give pause to many informed readers. Moreover, the deontological position is dubious because it still depends on the re-establishment of a retro phallocentric model that is reinserted instead of "underlying reality." If reality and contemporary lived experience do not suit this teleological model (teleological because of the insistence on predictability), then they can be placed in Husserlian brackets, or just simply eliminated in favor of precision and mathematical prediction. In all cases, this evisceration of ontology by metaphysics allows the author and his text to wander beside or float above formal questions of categorization, as he decrees, from his own personal Mount Sinai or mount in Galilee, his version of the Ten Commandments or the Beatitudes.

There are certainly deontological consequences to Houellebecq's singular position. First, personal preferences, judged as being arbitrary (and perhaps fed by the structures of a consumer society or a society of consumption in which desires are instilled or imposed) should be rejected, if they produce a detour in the determination of the molar. In the chapter entitled "Julian et Aldous," already mentioned, we find the following:

> Comme la plupart des gens il [Michel] estimait détestable cette tendance à l'atomisation sociale bien décrite par les sociologues et les commentateurs. Comme la plupart des gens il estimait souhaitable de maintenir quelques relations familiales, fût-ce au prix d'un léger ennui. (177–78)

> [Like most people, Michel thought that this tendency toward social atomization so well described by sociologists and commentators was detestable. Like most people, he thought it desirable to maintain some family relations, even if it was at the price of slight boredom.]

There is a maximum of misanthropy here, but not because of the excess of honesty and the absence of diplomacy that characterize both the behavior and the philosophical position of Molière's Alceste. Rather, Houellebecquian misanthropy is based entirely on this wholesale rejection of the disorder of the molecular, except insofar as the molecular can be re-ordered by a transcendental game of identity. There are two moments in the last third of the novel in which the author, explaining more fully the mutation in question, finally engages the whole question.

Houellebecq finally gets around to naming the mutation referred to since the beginning of the novel in a few tightly written and dense pages in which he gets to the heart of the matter. Obviously, for reasons of plot and retaining readers' interest, it makes sense for him to defer as long as possible the magic formula for the metaphysical mutation that functions, oddly enough, as a sort of *deus ex machina*. The moment finally arrives, however, in which vague allusions have to be replaced by a hard mantra that is now the inevitability of the work, as the narrator indicates that his protagonist, since he was a child, "ne pouvait pas supporter la dégradation naturelle des objets, leur bris, leur usure [could not stand the natural degradation, breaking, or wear and tear of objects]" (203). On the surface, there is nothing remarkable about this. The desire that nothing change or get old from use is not just a willfully inserted antidote to the mid-life crisis of the present, nor is it just the fact that the present follows logically from the past; this all makes sense on a psychological level, even if, for most of the text, one could argue that psychological realism is sacrificed to the plot and, more importantly, to the expression of ideology in this *roman à thèse*. In this, both Michel and the narrator can be seen merely as spokespersons for the author himself; the commentary becomes a kind of inserted analepsis, a justification of hating one's mid-life crisis, as well as an explanation of the other crises sprinkled throughout the novel.

Yet on a larger scale, in spite of an argument by Houellebecq against youth culture and the generalized zeal of the West to search for the fountain of youth, this hatred of the abrasion of objects is also a sign of the desire for continuous, uninterrupted identity. That is thus the famous metaphysical mutation: a future without a cloud in the sky, a continuation of essentialism, and this, despite the fact that he has voided it ontologically, the permanent order of things. At the molecular level, the abandon, anarchy, and disorder foretold in the Deleuzean model can be replaced in a biophysical model in which every little part behaves: "Pour permettre la reproduction, les deux brindilles composant la molécule d'ADN se séparent avant d'attirer, chacune de son côté, des nucléotides complémentaires [To permit reproduction, the two strands of the DNA molecule separate before each attracts complementary nucleotides]" (203). Thus, even if "Michel eut l'intuition qu'une reproduction parfaite serait impossible tant que la molécule d'ADN aurait la forme d'une hélice [Michel had the intuition that perfect reproduction would be impossible as long as the DNA molecule had the form of a helix]" (203), one would still have to go beyond the current limitations of biology as we know it and sing the praises of some sort of metabiology or metabiophysics, which would be the science behind the metaphysical mutation that must take place. This is what Michel does, as he is able to "dépasser sa première intuition selon laquelle la reproduction sexuée était en elle-même une source de mutations délétères [go beyond his first intuition according to which sexual reproduction was itself the source of deleterious mutations]" (203–204). Biology yields to this metabiophysics: "[Il] rédigea sa publication la plus importante, *Prolegomènes à la réplication parfaite* [He wrote his most important publication, *Prolegomenae to Perfect Replication*]" (206).[22] The future seems to be ensured by the replication of identity, even without an ontological foundation or any real, logical reason for being. The future is clear, or seems to be.

In search of the eternal masculine, Houellebecq falls into a trap of science: perfect reproduction does in fact exist and is named parthenogenesis. Parthenogenesis is limited to the females of certain species. In search of the masculine, Houellebecq hits a pitfall in Mother Nature, a pitfall of the pure feminine. The Goethean *Ewig-Weibliche* leads him on, so to speak, as it castrates him anew. Yet in a long, complex, pseudo-scientific passage, the author seems to fall anew into pessimism, into the gape of the Lacanian real, no longer available as a quickie or a take-away meal, an abyss in which no order seems to be imposed on the molecular.[23] Following a long disquisition on Margenau, Fock, and Hilbert, whose works on quantum spaces seemed to resolve problems of disorder, the author admits that the questions that seemed to have been answered could no longer be asked – not now and certainly not in the future

---

22   Once again there is an intertextual reference to Kant here, and specifically to his 1783 work *Prolegomena to Any Future Metaphysics*.

23   "Selon l'hypothèse de Margenau, on pouvait assimiler la conscience individuelle à un champ de probabilités dans un espace de Fock, défini comme somme directe d'espaces de Hilbert. Cet espace pouvait en principe être construit à partir des événements électroniques élémentaires survenant au niveau des microsites synaptiques. Le comportement normal était dès lors assimilable à une déformation élastique de champ, l'acte libre à une déchirure: mais dans quelle topologie? Il n'était nullement évident que la topologie naturelle des espaces hilbertiens permette de rendre compte de l'apparition de l'acte libre; il n'était même pas certain qu'il soit aujourd'hui possible de poser le problème, sinon en termes extrêmement métaphoriques [According to Margenau's hypothesis, an individual consciousness could be assimilated to a field of probabilities in a Fock space, defined as the direct sum of Hilbert spaces. In principle, this space could be constructed by starting with elementary electronic events occuring at the level of synaptic microsites. Normal behavior could then be assimilated to an elastic deformation of the field, the act of free will to a tear: but in what topology? It was not at all obvious that the natural topology of Hilbert spaces allowed for the accounting of the appearance of the act of free will. It was not at all certain that it is possible today to set up the problem, except in extremely metaphysical terms]" (278).

– without recourse to metaphors. Thus the proposed models turn into a nihilist vacuity and if the "équations de la théorie du chaos ne faisaient aucune référence au milieu physique dans lequel se déployaient leurs manifestations [equations of chaos theory made no reference to the physical surroundings in which their manifestations played out]" (282), one could well argue the contrary: the rub in this novel is that the author tries to eliminate disorder, chaos, and entropy, when it is impossible to do so. Again, if, toward the end of the novel (337), the author recalls Pascal's commentary on Descartes, to wit, "tout se fait par figure et mouvement [everything happens by figure and movement]," the same could be said for *Les Particules élémentaires*, in which dualism comes back with a vengeance.

Clearly the Lacanian real and the anarchy of Deleuzean molecules can strike fear in the hearts of those interested in maintaining an order that is *status quo ante*, an order judged by many to be retro and a thing of the past, especially in terms of sexual categories and sexualities some forty years after the beginning of modern women's and GLBTQ liberation. To keep the flame of traditional phallocentrism burning would seem to many a folly. Yet this retro folly is also symptomatic of the crisis in masculinity that we can see in numerous novels, films, and essays on the contemporary French scene. It is one symptom among many in Houellebecq's work and it is no surprise if, in a work like *Plateforme*, he seems to resign himself to the inevitability of the fall and the fact that he will not change the world, the metaphysical mutation toward a future that is nostalgic for an imaginary past. So why not fuck until the end of time, in this hour before midnight, for there is no real future, no *jouissance*. The future is now and it is empty.

Bibliography

Amstel, Paul. *Le Tueur du Marais*. Brussels: Théglacé, 2003.

Anon. "Scientists trace AIDS virus origin to 100 years ago." CNN.com (1 October 2008). http://www.cnn.com/2008/TECH/science/10/01/aids. virus.origin.ap/index.html. Last accessed 2 October 2008.

Appadurai, Arjun. "Disjuncture and Difference in the Global Cultural Economy." http://www.intcul.tohoku.ac.jp/~holden/MediatedSociety/ Readings/2003_04/Appadurai.html. Last accessed 11 September 2009.

Batlo, Bruno. *Des baffes et du sexe*. Le Mesnil-sur-l'Estrée: CyLibris, 2001/2005.

Baudrillard, Jean. *Simulacres et simulation*. Paris: Galilée, 1985.

Baum, Vicki. *Menschen im Hotel. Ein Kolportageroman mit Hintergründen*. Berlin: Ullstein, 1929.

Bellin, Michel et al. *Le Premier Festin. Pour une littérature de la différence*. Béziers: H & O Éditions, 2003.

Bersani, Leo. "Is the Rectum a Grave?" In *AIDS: Cultural Analysis/ Cultural Activism*, ed. Douglas Crimp. Cambridge: MIT Press, 1988. 197–222.

Bloy, Léon. *Le Désespéré*. Préface de Maurice Dantec. Wilmington, DE: Éditions Underbahn Ltd, 2005.

Bontour, Brigit. "Nicolas Jones Gorlin: Pédophilie, jeunisme, la figure de Janus." *Écrits ... vains?*. http://ecrits-vains.com/romanciers/nicolas_ jones_gorlin.html. Last accessed 11 September 2009.

Borel, Vincent. *Un Ruban noir*. Paris: J'ai lu, 2000.

Borradori, Giovanna, ed. *Philosophy in a Time of Terror: Interviews with Jürgen Habermas and Jacques Derrida*. Chicago: University of Chicago Press, 2003.

Boyle, T. Corghessan. *The Road to Wellville*. New York: Viking, 1993.

Brunello, Thierry. *C'était au paradis*. Paris: Editions Gaies et Lesbiennes, 2005.

Chambers, Ross. *Facing It: AIDS Diaries and the Death of the Author*. Ann Arbor: University of Michigan Press, 1998.

Charauau, Benoît. *Ton aile*. Brussels: Editions Biliki, 2005.

Chassay, Jean-François. "Les Corpuscules de Krause: A propos des *Particules élémentaires* de Michel Houellebecq." *Australian Journal of French Studies* 42.1 (2005): 36–49.

Chuberre, Erwan. *Le Rôle de ma vie*. Le Mesnil-sur-l'Estrée: CyLibris, 2004.

Clarke, Arthur C. *2001: A Space Odyssey*. New York: New American Library, 1968.

Collard, Cyril. *Les Nuits fauves*. Paris: J'ai lu, 1991.

Corbin, Alain. *L'Harmonie des plaisirs. Les Manières de jouir du siècle des lumières à l'avènement de la sexologie*. Paris: Perrin, 2008.

Crowley, Martin. "Houellebecq: The Wreckage of Liberation." *Romance Studies* 20.1 (2002): 17–28.

Dahan-Gaida, Laurence. "La Fin de l'histoire (naturelle): Les Particules élémentaires de Michel Houellebecq." *Tangence* 73 (2003): 93–114.

Dantec, Maurice. *Babylon Babies*. Paris: Gallimard, 1999.

——. *Périphériques*. Paris: Flammarion, 2003.

——. *Les Racines du mal*. Paris: Gallimard, 1995.

——. *La Sirène rouge*. Paris: Gallimard, 1993.

——. *Villa Vortex*. Paris: Gallimard, 2003.

Dean, Tim. *Unlimited Intimacy: Reflections on the Subculture of Barebacking*. Chicago: University of Chicago Press, 2009.

Deguy, Michel. "R.B. by M.D." Trans. Robert Harvey. *The Yale Journal of Criticism* 14.2 (2001): 485–92.

Debord, Guy. *La Société du spectacle*. Paris: Champ Libre, 1971 [1967].

Deleuze, Gilles and Félix Guattari. *Capitalisme et schizophrénie. L'Anti-Œdipe*. Paris: Minuit, 1972.

Derrida, Jacques. *De la grammatologie*. Paris: Minuit, 1967.

Despentes, Virginie. *Baise-moi*. Paris: J'ai lu, 2000.

Doré, Kim. "Doléances d'un surhomme ou La question de l'évolution dans Les particules élémentaires de Michel Houellebecq." *Tangence* 70 (2002): 67–83.

Dubyaspeak. http://www.dubyaspeak.com. Last accessed 20 January 2009.

Duroi, Lionel. *Le Kotoba*. Villettes: Editions Bonobo, 2005.

——. *Retour à Calella*. Paris: Editions Geneviève Pastre, 2003.

Dustan, Guillaume. *Dans ma chambre*. Paris: P.O.L., 1996.

——. *Dernier roman*. Paris: Flammarion, 2004.

——. "Un Désir bien naturel." In *Ecrire gai*, ed. Pierre Salducci. Montreal: Les Editions Stanké, 1999. 83–120.

——. *Je sors ce soir*. Paris: P.O.L., 1997.

——. *LXiR*. Paris: Balland, 2002.

——. *Nicolas Pages*. Paris: Balland, 1999.

——. *Plus fort que moi*. Paris: P.O.L., 1998

——. "Tribu(t)." *Écritures* 10 (1998): 40–41.

de Duve, Pascal. *Cargo vie*. Paris: Livre de poche, 1994.

Ferry, Luc and Alain Renaut. *La Pensée 68. Essai sur l'anti-humanisme contemporain*. Paris: Gallimard, 1985.

Foucault, Michel. *Dits et écrits. 1954–1988*. Paris: Gallimard, 1994. vol. 1.

——. *Surveiller et punir. Naissance de la prison*. Paris: Gallimard, 1975.

Gantz, Katherine. "Strolling with Houellebecq: The Textual Terrain of Postmodern Flânerie." *Journal of Modern Literature* 28.3 (Spring 2005): 149–61.

Gaubert, Jean-François. *Gay Tapant*. Montigny le Bretonneux: Yvelinédition, 2005.

Gibson, William. *Neuromancer*. New York: Berkley Pub. Group, 1984.

Gilbreth, Frank Bunker. *Primer of Scientific Management*. With an introduction by Louis D. Brandeis. New York: D. Van Nostrand Company, 1912.

Girard, René. *Mensonge romantique, vérité romanesque*. Paris: Grasset, 1961.

Glissant, Édouard. *Le Discours antillais*. Paris: Seuil, 1981.

Goldberg, Jonathan. *Sodometries: Renaissance Texts, Modern Sexualities*. Stanford: Stanford University Press, 1992.

Grandena, Florian. "L'Homosexuel en dehors de l'homosexualité: Expressions de l'identité gay dans les films d'Olivier Ducastel et Jacques Martineau." *Contemporary French Civilization* 30:2 (2006): 63–86.

Griffiths, Robert B. *Consistent Quantum Theory*. Cambridge: Cambridge UP, 2003. Consulted online at http://quantum.phys.cmu.edu/CQT/chaps/cqt10.pdf, 26 October 2007.

Guénif-Souilamas, Nacira. "The Inflated Ego and New Games of Belonging." In *Turns to the Right?*, ed. Michael A. Johnson and Lawrence R. Schehr. *Yale French Studies* 116 (2009): 113–24.

Guibert, Hervé. *À l'ami qui ne m'a pas sauvé la vie*. Paris: Gallimard, 1990.

Guillory, John D. *Cultural Capital: The Problem of Literary Canon Formation*. Chicago: University of Chicago Press, 1993.

Halperin, David. *One Hundred Years of Homosexuality*. New York: Routledge, 1990.

Haraway, Donna Jeanne. *A Haraway Reader*. New York: Routledge, 2004.

Hardt, Michael and Antonio Negri. *Empire*. Cambridge: Harvard University Press, 2000.

Hocquenghem, Guy. *Le Désir homosexuel*. Paris: Éditions universitaires, 1972.

Homes, A. M. *The End of Alice*. New York: Scribner, 1997.

Houellebecq, Michel. *Extension du domaine de la lutte*. Paris: J'ai lu, 1994.

——. *Les Particules élémentaires*. Paris: J'ai lu, 2000.

——. *Plateforme*. Paris: Flammarion, 2001.

——. *La Possibilité d'une île*. Paris: Fayard, 2005.

Huffer, Lynne. *Mad for Foucault: Rethinking the Foundations of Queer Theory*. New York: Columbia University Press, 2009.

Huntington, Samuel P. *The Clash of Civilizations and the Remaking of World Order*. New York: Simon and Schuster, 1996.

Huxley, Aldous. *Eyeless in Gaza*. Harmondsworth: Penguin, 1955 [repr. 1972].

Johnson, Michael A. "Sodomy, Allegory, and the Subject of Pleasure." In *Queer Sexualities in French and Francophone Literature and Film*, ed. James Day. *French Literature Series* 34 (2007): 1–12.

Jonard, Pierre-Arnaud. *Parties*. Paris: Hachette, 2005.

Jones-Gorlin, Nicolas. *Rose Bonbon*. Paris: Gallimard, 2002.

King, Stephen. *It*. New York: Viking, 1986.

Legrand, Alexandre. *Le Garçon de Tunis*. Le Mesnil-sur-l'Estree: CyLibris, 2002/2004.

Lipovetsky, Gilles. *L'Ère du vide. Essais sur l'individualisme contemporain*. Paris: Gallimard [Folio], 1989.

Liu, Alan. *The Laws of Cool: Knowledge Work and the Culture of Information*. Chicago: University of Chicago Press, 2004.

Lowie, Patrick. *Au rythme des déluges*. Brussels: Théglacé, 2000.

Lyotard, Jean-François. *La Condition post-moderne. Rapport sur le savoir*. Paris: Minuit, 1979.

——. *Discours, figure*. Paris: Klincksieck, 1971.

Marchal, Hugues. "Chroniques de la vie sexuelle." *Magazine littéraire* 426 (December 2003): 56–58.

Marin, Louis. *Le Portrait du roi*. Paris: Minuit, 1981.

Marshall, Bill. *André Techiné*. Manchester: Manchester University Press, 2007.

Miles, Christopher and Thomas Kopp. "J'aime faire rigoler. Un entretien avec Guillaume Dustan." *La Revue h* 5–6 (1998): 28–34.

Moraux, Christophe. *Un Garçon d'un autre temps*. Paris: Éditions Lanore, 2005.

Nabe, Marc-Édouard. *L'Affaire Zannini*. Monaco: Éditions du Rocher, 2003

——. *L'Âme de Billie Holiday*. Paris: Denoël, 1986.

——. *Au régal des vermines*. Paris: Barrault, 1985.

——. "Cent phrases pour Paul Claudel." *L'Infini* 21 (1988): 76–82.

——. *Chacun mes goûts*. Paris: Le Dilettante, 1986.

——. "La Littérature de Lautréamont." *L'Infini* 23 (1988): 80–87.

——. *Une Lueur d'espoir*. Monaco: Éditions du Rocher, 2001.

——. *Morceaux choisis*. Paris: Léo Scheer, 2006.

——. *Printemps de feu*. Monaco: Éditions du Rocher, 2003.

——. *Zigzags*. Paris: Barrault, 1986.

Neaud, Fabrice. "Fabrice Neaud. Confidences sur le papier. Propos choisis." http://perso.orange.fr/soleille/fabriceneaud/auteur/propos.htm#sympa. Last accessed 19 January 2009.

——. *Journal (I). Février 1992–septembre 1993.* Angoulême: Ego Comme X, 2000.

——. *Journal (II). Septembre 1993–décembre 1993.* Angoulême: Ego Comme X, 1999.

——. *Journal (III). Décembre 1993–août 1995.* Angoulême: Ego Comme X, 1999.

—— *Journal (4). Les Riches Heures.* Angoulême: Ego Comme X, 2002.

Ní Loingsigh, Aedín. "Tourist Traps: Confounding Expectations in Michel Houellebecq's *Plateforme.*" *French Cultural Studies* 16.1 (Feb. 2005): 73–90.

Noudelmann, François. *Pour en finir avec la généalogie.* Paris: Éditions Léo Scheer, 2004.

Nye, Robert A. *Masculinity and Male Codes of Honor in Modern France.* New York and Oxford: Oxford University Press, 1993.

Polver, Pier-Angelo. *Ogres.* Paris: Balland, 1999.

Provencher, Denis M. *Queer French: Globalization, Language and Sexual Citizenship in France.* Aldershot: Ashgate, 2007.

Quérec, Arnaud. *Petite chronique du désir.* Bruxelles: Théglacé, 2002.

Ranskalainen, Mikko. *Comment te le dire?.* Paris: Editions T.G., 2005.

Reader, Keith. *The Abject Object: Avatars of the Phallus in Contemporary French Theory, Literature and Film.* Amsterdam/New York: Rodopi, 2006.

Readings, Bill. *The University in Ruins.* Cambridge: Harvard University Press, 1996.

Reeser, Todd. W. "Transsexuality and the Disruption of Time in Sébastien Lifshitz's *Wild Side.*" *Studies in French Cinema* 7:2: 157–68.

Rees-Roberts, Nick. "Down and Out: Immigrant Poverty and Queer Sexuality in Sébastien Lifshitz's *Wild Side* (2004)." *Studies in French Cinema* 7:2 (2007): 143–55.

Rémès, Érik. *Guide du sexe gay.* Paris: Editions Blanche, 2003.

——. *Je bande donc je suis.* Paris: Balland, 1999.

——. *Le Maître des amours.* Paris: Balland, 2000.

——. *Serial Fucker. Journal d'un barebacker.* Paris: Editions Blanche, 2003.

Roubaudi, Ludovic. *Le 18.* Paris: Le Dilettante, 2004.

Russo, Vito. *The Celluloid Closet: Homosexuality in the Movies.* Revised Edition. New York: Perennial Library, 1987.

Salsa, Patrice. *Un Garçon naturel.* Rodez: Editions du Rouerge, 2005.

Saron, Antoine. *Désir de nuit.* Paris: Editions Gaies et Lesbiennes, 2005.

Sartre, Jean-Paul. *La Nausée.* Paris: Gallimard, 1938.

——. *L'Être et le néant.* Paris: Gallimard, 1943.

Schehr, Lawrence R. *Figures of Alterity: French Narrative and its Others.* Stanford: Stanford University Press, 2003.

——. "Mr. Malaprop, or, No President Left Behind." In *AmBushed: The Costs of Machtpolitik*, ed. Dana D. Nelson. *South Atlantic Quarterly* 105:1 (2006):137–52.

——. *Parts of an Andrology: On Representations of Men's Bodies.* Stanford: Stanford University Press, 1997.

Schuerewegen, Franc. "He Ejaculated (Houellebecq)." *L'Esprit Créateur* 44:3 (Fall 2004): 40–47.

Sebhan, Gilles. *Presque gentil.* Paris: Denoël, 2005.

Serres, Michel. *Le Parasite.* Paris: Grasset, 1980.

Shilts, Randy. *And the Band Played On: Politics, People, and the AIDS Epidemic.* New York: St Martin's Press, 1987.

Simpson, Mark. "Here Come the Mirror Men." *The Independent.* 15 November 1994.

——. "Metrosexual? That Rings a Bell ..." http://www.marksimpson.com/pages/journalism/metrosexual_ios.html. Accessed 1 October 2008.

Sinclair, Iain. *Lights Out for the Territory: 9 Excursions in the Secret History of London.* London: Granta, 1997.

Sweet, David Lehardy. "Absentminded Prolepsis: Global Slackers before the Age of Terror in Alex Garland's *The Beach* and Michel Houellebecq's *Plateforme*." *Comparative Literature* 59:2 (Spring 2007): 158–76.

Taylor, Frederick Winslow. *Principles of Scientific Management.* New York and London: Harper and Brothers, 1911.

Tomso, Gregory. "Barebacking, Bug Chasing, and the Risks of Care." *Literature and Medicine* 23:1 (2004): 88–111. Reprinted in *Difference and Identity*, ed. Jonathan M. Metzl and Suzanne Poirier. Baltimore: Johns Hopkins University Press, 2005: 88–111.

——. "Risky Subjects: Public Health, Personal Narrative, and the Stakes of Qualitative Research." *Sexualities* 12:1 (2009): 61–78.

——. "Viral Sex and the Politics of Life." *South Atlantic Quarterly* 107:2 (2008): 265–85.

Trabelsi, Bahaa. *Une Vie à trois.* Brussels: Editions Labor, 2002 [repr. of Casablanca: Editions Eddif, 2000].

Varsava, Jerry Andrew. "Utopian Yearnings, Dystopian Thoughts: Houellebecq's *The Elementary Particles* and the Problem of Scientific Communitarianism." *College Literature* 32:4 (Fall 2005): 145–67.

Vico, Giambattista. *La Scienza nuova, e opere scelte.* Ed. Nicola Abbagnano. Torino: Unione tipografico – editrice torinese, 1952.

Vilrouge, Marc. *Reproduction non-autorisée.* Paris: Le Dilettante, 2004.

Voirenlion, Tom. *L'Ivresse des cimes.* Toulouse: Éditions Ankidoo, 2004.

Watt, Ian. *The Rise of the Novel: Studies in Defoe, Richardson, and Fielding.* Berkeley: University of California Press, 1957.

Zagdanski, Stéphane. *Jouissance du temps.* Paris: Fayard, 2005.

Filmography

Carné, Marcel. *Hôtel du nord.* 1938.

Cazeneuve, Fabrice. *A cause d'un garçon.* 2002.

Chéreau, Patrice. *L'Homme blessé.* 1983.

Collard, Cyril. *Les Nuits fauves.* 1992.

Curtiz, Michael. *Casablanca.* 1942.

Damiano, Gerard. *Deep Throat.* 1972.

Demme, Jonathan. *Philadelphia.* 1993.

Ducastel, Olivier and Jacques Martineau. *Crustacés et coquillages.* 2005.

—. *Drôle de Félix.* 2000.

—. *Jeanne et le garçon formidable.* 1998.

—. *Ma vraie vie à Rouen.* 2002.

Dmytryrk, Edward. *Walk on the Wild Side.* 1962.

Erman, John. *An Early Frost.* 1985.

Faure, Christian. *Juste une question d'amour.* 2000.

Goulding, Edmund. *Dark Victory.* 1939.

—. *Grand Hotel.* 1932.

Griffith, D. W. *Birth of a Nation.* 1915.

Hitchcock, Alfred. *The Man Who Knew Too Much.* 1956.

Kubrick, Stanley. *A Clockwork Orange.* 1971.

—. *2001: A Space Odyssey.* 1968.

Lee, Ang. *Brokeback Mountain.* 2005.

Lifshitz, Sébastien. *Presque rien.* 2000.

—. *Wild Side.* 2004.

Milestone, Lewis. *All Quiet on the Western Front.* 1930.

Molinaro, Édouard. *La Cage aux folles.* 1978.

Oswald, Richard. *Anders als die Anderen.* 1919.

Ozon, François. *Le Temps qui reste.* 2005

Sagal, Boris. *The Omega Man.* 1971.

Soukaz, Lionel. *Fist Power.* 2002.

—. *Ixe.* 1980.

—. *Notre trou de cul est révolutionnaire.* 2006.

—. *La Télévision nous encule.* 2002.

Welles, Orson. *The Lady from Shanghai.* 1947.

Wilder, Billy. *Sunset Boulevard.* 1950.

Index